First World War
and Army of Occupation
War Diary
France, Belgium and Germany

36 DIVISION
Divisional Troops
Royal Army Medical Corps
108 Field Ambulance
9 September 1915 - 28 June 1919

WO95/2499/1

The Naval & Military Press Ltd
www.nmarchive.com
Published in association with The National Archives

Published by

The Naval & Military Press Ltd

Unit 10 Ridgewood Industrial Park,

Uckfield, East Sussex,

TN22 5QE England

Tel: +44 (0) 1825 749494

www.naval-military-press.com

www.nmarchive.com

This diary has been reprinted in facsimile from the original. Any imperfections are inevitably reproduced and the quality may fall short of modern type and cartographic standards.

© Crown Copyright
Images reproduced by permission of The National Archives, London, England, 2015.

Contents

Document type	Place/Title	Date From	Date To
Heading	WO95/2499/1		
Heading	36th Division Medical 108th Field Ambulance 1915 Sep 1919 Jun		
Heading	36th Division 108th Field Ambulance Vol I Sept of Oct 15		
War Diary	Bordon Camp	09/09/1915	01/10/1915
War Diary	Southampton Docks.	02/10/1915	02/10/1915
War Diary	Havre	03/10/1915	04/10/1915
War Diary	Longueur	04/10/1915	04/10/1915
War Diary	Rubempre	04/10/1915	14/10/1915
War Diary	Forceville	14/10/1915	17/10/1915
War Diary	Rubempre	18/10/1915	19/10/1915
War Diary	Septenville	20/10/1915	21/10/1915
War Diary	Montrelet Pieppe	21/10/1915	22/10/1915
War Diary	Bernaville	22/10/1915	26/10/1915
War Diary	Hovdencourt	26/10/1915	28/10/1915
War Diary	Houden Court	29/10/1915	31/10/1915
Heading	36th Division 10th f.a. Vol 2 1915 Nov 15		
War Diary	Houden Court	01/11/1915	27/11/1915
War Diary	La Haie Earm	28/11/1915	30/11/1915
Heading	36th Div 108th f.a. Vol 3 Dec 1915		
War Diary	La Haie Farm	01/12/1915	31/12/1915
Heading	36th Div F/194/1 Jan 1916 1 Dec 1918		
War Diary	I.A. Haie Farm.	01/01/1916	09/01/1916
War Diary	Vacquerie	10/01/1916	31/01/1916
Heading	108th F.A. Vol 5		
Heading	108th Field Ambulance Feb 1916		
War Diary	Vacquerie	01/02/1916	07/02/1916
War Diary	Toutencourt	08/02/1916	08/02/1916
War Diary	Forceville	08/02/1916	29/02/1916
Heading	108 F Amb Vol 6		
Heading	March April 1916 108 F Amb.		
War Diary	Forceville	01/03/1916	31/03/1916
Map			
Miscellaneous	O.C.C. Section 105 f.g.	05/03/1916	05/03/1916
War Diary	Forceville	01/04/1916	30/04/1916
Heading	May 1916 108th F Amb.		
War Diary	Forceville	01/05/1916	31/05/1916
Heading	Jun 1916 No 108 Field Ambulance		
War Diary	Forceville	01/06/1916	30/06/1916
Heading	36th Division 108th Field Ambulance July 1916		
War Diary	Forceville	01/07/1916	05/07/1916
War Diary	Poutencourt	06/07/1916	10/07/1916
War Diary	Dezaincourt	10/07/1916	11/07/1916
War Diary	Neuvillette	11/07/1916	11/07/1916
War Diary	Frevent	12/07/1916	12/07/1916
War Diary	Campagne	12/07/1916	13/07/1916
War Diary	Eperlecques	13/07/1916	20/07/1916
War Diary	Bollezeele	21/07/1916	21/07/1916
War Diary	Watou	22/07/1916	22/07/1916

Type	Description	Start	End
War Diary	Le Ravets Burd	23/07/1916	24/07/1916
War Diary	La Ravets Burd	25/07/1916	31/07/1916
Heading	36th Division August 1916 108th Field Ambulance.		
War Diary	Le Ravels Berg	01/08/1916	31/08/1916
War Diary	36th Div Sept 1916 108th Field Ambulance.		
War Diary	Le Ravets Berg.	01/09/1916	30/09/1916
Heading	36th Div Oct 1916 108th Field Ambulance		
War Diary	Le Ravets Berg	01/10/1916	31/10/1916
War Diary	36th Div Nov 1916 108th Field Ambulance		
War Diary	Ravetsberg	01/11/1916	30/11/1916
Heading	36th Div 108th Field Ambulance.		
War Diary	Le Revets Berg	01/12/1916	31/12/1916
Heading	140/2696		
Heading	36th Div 140/1943 106th Field Ambulance Jan 1917		
War Diary	Le Ravetsberg	01/01/1917	31/01/1917
Heading	36th Div 140/1991 108th Field Ambulance Feb 1917		
War Diary	Le Ravets Berg	01/02/1917	20/02/1917
War Diary	Le Revets Burgh.	21/02/1917	28/02/1917
Heading	Mar 1917 Fa 36th Div 108th Field Ambulance		
War Diary	Le Ravets Burgh.	01/03/1917	15/03/1917
War Diary	Bailleul	16/03/1917	31/03/1917
Heading	106th F.A. April 1917		
War Diary	Bailleul	01/04/1917	30/04/1917
Heading	May 1917 108th F.A.		
War Diary	Dranoutre	01/05/1917	31/05/1917
Heading	Nov 108 F.A. June 1917		
War Diary	Dranoutre	01/06/1917	29/06/1917
War Diary	Fletre	30/06/1917	30/06/1917
Heading	No 108 F.A. July 1917		
War Diary	Fletre	01/07/1917	07/07/1917
War Diary	Liheuse	07/07/1917	10/07/1917
War Diary	Barlinghem	24/07/1917	26/07/1917
War Diary	Liheuse	21/07/1917	21/07/1917
War Diary	Barbing Hem	23/07/1917	23/07/1917
War Diary	Winnezeele	26/07/1917	31/07/1917
War Diary	L. 13. D. 3.2. Sheet 27 21/2 Miles S.s.e. & Watou	31/07/1917	31/07/1917
Miscellaneous	B.E.F. Summary Of Medical War Diaries Of 108th. F.A. 36th Div.		
Miscellaneous	B.E.F. 108th. F.A. 36th Div.	00/07/1917	00/07/1917
War Diary	B.E.F. 108th F.A. 36th Div.	00/07/1917	00/07/1917
War Diary	B.E.F. 108th F.A. 36th Div.		
Heading	Aug 1917 No 108 F.A.		
War Diary	L. 13. D. 3.2.	01/08/1917	01/08/1917
War Diary	21/2 Miles S.S.E. Of Watou	02/08/1917	06/08/1917
War Diary	L. 13. D. 3.2. 21/2 Miles	07/08/1917	07/08/1917
War Diary	S.S.E. Of Watou	08/08/1917	13/08/1917
War Diary	Red Farm 2 Miles E Of Poperinghe.	14/08/1917	20/08/1917
War Diary	Winnezeele	20/08/1917	26/08/1917
War Diary	Beaulencourt	27/08/1917	29/08/1917
War Diary	Ruyaulcourt	30/08/1917	31/08/1917
Miscellaneous	Moves Detachment.		
Miscellaneous	B.E.F. 108th F.A. 36th Div.	00/08/1917	00/08/1917
War Diary	B.E.F. 108th. F.A. 36th Div.	00/08/1917	00/08/1917
Miscellaneous	B.E.F. Summary Of Medical War Diaries Of 108th F.A. 36th Div.		
Miscellaneous	Moves Detachment.		

Heading	Sept. 1917 No.108 F.a.		
War Diary	Rovaul Court	01/09/1917	30/09/1917
Heading	C.P 1917 108th F.a.		
War Diary	Ruyaulcourt	01/10/1917	31/10/1917
Heading	Nov. 1917 No. 108 F.a.		
War Diary	Ruyaulcourt.	01/11/1917	18/11/1917
War Diary	Barastre	18/11/1917	21/11/1917
War Diary	Hermies	22/11/1917	24/11/1917
War Diary	Boursies	24/11/1917	24/11/1917
War Diary	Shag Heap (Cannal Du Nord)	25/11/1917	26/11/1917
War Diary	Barastre	27/11/1917	28/11/1917
War Diary	Simencourt	30/11/1917	30/11/1917
Heading	No.108 F.a. Dec 1917		
War Diary	Simencourt	01/12/1917	01/12/1917
War Diary	Achietle Grand	01/12/1917	01/12/1917
War Diary	Rocquigny	02/12/1917	05/12/1917
War Diary	Moislains	06/12/1917	18/12/1917
War Diary	Warluzel	19/12/1917	22/12/1917
War Diary	Couturelle	22/12/1917	28/12/1917
War Diary	Le Paraclet.	28/12/1917	06/01/1918
War Diary	Marcel Cave.	07/01/1918	09/01/1918
War Diary	Rosieres	10/01/1918	10/01/1918
War Diary	Nesle	11/01/1918	13/01/1918
War Diary	Ollezy	14/01/1918	31/01/1918
Heading	War Diary. Of 108th Field Ambulance. From 1st February 1918 To 28th February 1918 Vol XXIX		
War Diary	Ollezy	01/02/1918	28/02/1918
Heading	108th Field Ambulance Mar 1918		
Heading	War Diary Of 108th Field Ambulance From 1st March 1918 To 31st March 1918 Vol XXX		
War Diary	Ollezy	01/03/1918	14/03/1918
War Diary	Hlezy	15/03/1918	18/03/1918
War Diary	Ollezy	19/03/1918	22/03/1918
War Diary	Villers St Christopher	22/03/1918	22/03/1918
War Diary	La Feune Hrpptul (Esneby Hallon)	23/03/1918	23/03/1918
War Diary	Amy	24/03/1918	24/03/1918
War Diary	Amy To Section	25/03/1918	25/03/1918
War Diary	Enches	26/02/1918	26/03/1918
War Diary	Davenscourt.	26/03/1918	27/03/1918
War Diary	Hargicourt	27/03/1918	27/03/1918
War Diary	Aubvillers	27/03/1918	29/03/1918
War Diary	Naumps	30/03/1918	30/03/1918
War Diary	Saleux	31/03/1918	31/03/1918
Heading	108th Field Ambulance Apr 1918		
Heading	War Diary Of 108th Field Ambulance From 1st April 1918 To 30th April 1918 Volume XXXI		
War Diary	Woignarue	01/04/1918	04/04/1918
War Diary	Eu.	04/04/1918	04/04/1918
War Diary	Heezeule	05/04/1918	05/04/1918
War Diary	Du Hallou Camp	06/04/1918	13/04/1918
War Diary	Du Halles	11/04/1918	16/04/1918
War Diary	Prouille	17/04/1918	18/04/1918
War Diary	Proven	18/04/1918	30/04/1918
Heading	War Diary Of 108th Field Ambulance May 1918 Volume XXXII Nov 32		
War Diary	Proven	01/05/1918	31/05/1918

Heading	War Diary Of 108th Field Ambulance From 1st June 1918. To 30th June 1918 Volume XXXIII		
War Diary	Proven	01/06/1918	25/06/1918
War Diary	Cormette Camp Sheet 5A Hazebrouk 1/00,000 C.3)	26/06/1918	26/06/1918
War Diary	4 Miles W Of St Omer.	26/06/1918	30/06/1918
War Diary	Proven	30/06/1918	30/06/1918
Heading	July 1918 108th F.A.		
War Diary	Proven	01/07/1918	02/07/1918
War Diary	Wilkins Camp Sheet 27 (F. 25.a 2.8) 1 Miles N.W. Of St. Jan Ter Biezen)	02/07/1918	02/07/1918
War Diary	Wilkins Camp	03/07/1918	03/07/1918
War Diary	Eecke Sheet 27 On The Car Stre Steenvookde Road Q. 20	04/07/1918	05/07/1918
War Diary	Eecke	06/07/1918	08/07/1918
War Diary	Ochtezeele 27/H. 29.d. (4 Meles W Of Cassel & 1 Miles S Of Arneke)	08/07/1918	11/07/1918
War Diary	Ochtezeele	12/07/1918	31/07/1918
Heading	Aug 1918 108th F.A.		
War Diary	Ochtezeele 27/H 29.d. 1/40,000	01/08/1918	01/08/1918
War Diary	H Miles H Of Cassel 01 N.G.S. Of Arneke	02/08/1918	02/08/1918
War Diary	Ochtezeele	03/08/1918	31/08/1918
Heading	Sept 1918 108 F.A.		
War Diary	Near St. Marie Cappel Sheet 27 1/40,000 P. 26.d. 8.6. 2 Miles S.E Of Cassel)	01/09/1918	02/09/1918
War Diary	Eecke Same Of Map C122 C1.5	03/09/1918	03/09/1918
War Diary	Eecke	04/09/1918	10/09/1918
War Diary	Roch Farm Above 1 Mile South Of Berthen 27/to R. 25 B.c.	11/09/1918	11/09/1918
War Diary	Roch Farm	12/09/1918	14/09/1918
War Diary	Baillful A Sylum 28/1/40,000 S. 14 B 4.8	15/09/1918	15/09/1918
War Diary	Asylum Bailleul	16/09/1918	20/09/1918
War Diary	Roche Farm 1 mile S of Berthen.	20/09/1918	20/09/1918
War Diary	P. 30 C. 6.5 Farm 1 Mile E of S Signal Cappil on The Eecke Road.	21/09/1918	21/09/1918
War Diary	Watou Hospice D/K. 4.C. 5 Miles D Of Poperinghe	22/09/1918	22/09/1918
War Diary	Gwalia Farm 28/A. 23.c. 3.8 3 Miles N E of Poperinghe on the Elverdinghe	23/09/1918	23/09/1918
War Diary	Gwalia Farm	24/09/1918	28/09/1918
War Diary	Prison Ypres Sheet 28 1/20.000 I 7.6.22	29/09/1918	29/09/1918
War Diary	Ypres (Prison)	30/09/1918	30/09/1918
Heading	Oct 1918 108 F.A.		
War Diary	Ypres (Prison)	01/10/1918	16/10/1918
War Diary	Passchendaele E 8 D 4.8 Sheet 28 1/40,000 8 Miles N.E. Of Ypes	17/10/1918	18/10/1918
War Diary	Passchendaele Station.	19/10/1918	29/10/1918
War Diary	Les Triez Caillou 28/R. 3. B. 7.3. 1/40,000 1 Miles Sie Of Halluin.	29/10/1918	29/10/1918
Heading	Nov 1918 108th F.A.		
War Diary	Le Truez Coileux	01/11/1918	06/11/1918
War Diary	Mouscron	07/11/1918	14/11/1918
War Diary	Mouscron Near Tourcoing Sheet 09 1/40,000 S. 23.	15/11/1918	17/11/1918
War Diary	Mouscron	17/11/1918	30/11/1918
Heading	Dec 1918 No 108 F.A.		
War Diary	Mouscron	01/12/1918	15/12/1918
War Diary	Triez Cailloux	16/12/1918	25/12/1918
War Diary	Lestriez Caieloux	26/12/1918	31/12/1918

Heading	36th Box 2298 No 108 F A Jan 1917		
War Diary	Les Triez Cailloux	01/01/1919	01/01/1919
War Diary	1 Mile South Of Halluin	01/01/1919	06/01/1919
War Diary	Les Triez Cailloux	07/01/1919	31/01/1919
Heading	Feb 1919 No 108 Field Ambulance.		
War Diary	Lestriez Cailloux (Clox To Hallin)	01/02/1919	05/02/1919
War Diary	Les Triez Cailloux	06/02/1919	28/02/1919
Heading	Mar 1919 108th F.A.		
War Diary	Les Triez Cailloux	01/03/1919	01/03/1919
War Diary	Des to Halluin	01/03/1919	04/03/1919
War Diary	Mouscron Quit School	05/03/1919	10/03/1919
War Diary	Mouscron	11/03/1919	26/03/1919
War Diary	Jesenit College Mouscron	27/03/1919	31/03/1919
Heading	Apr. 1919 108th F.a.		
War Diary	Mouscron.	01/04/1919	30/04/1919
Heading	May 1916 No 108 Field Ambulance.		
War Diary	Mouscron	01/05/1919	31/05/1919
Heading	June 1919 108th F.A.		
War Diary	Mouscron	01/06/1919	28/06/1919

WO 95/2499/1

36TH DIVISION
MEDICAL

108TH FIELD AMBULANCE
JAN 1916 - DEC 1918
1915 SEP   1919 JUN

DI
7517

36th Division

108th Field Ambulance
Vol I
Sep 1 & Oct 15

Sep 1 1915
Oct

WAR DIARY 108th Field Ambulance, Army Form C.2118

Instructions regarding War Diaries and Intelligence Summaries are contained in F.S. Regs., Part II. and the Staff Manual respectively. Title pages will be prepared in manuscript.

INTELLIGENCE SUMMARY.
(Erase heading not required.)

Place	Date	Hour	Summary of Events and Information	Remarks and references to Appendices
BORDON CAMP	9-9-15	—	Blood equipment ledgers.	
"	10-9-15	—	No events to record	
"	11-9-15	—	No events to record	
"	12-9-15	—	No events to record.	
"	13-9-15	—	No events to record	
"	14-9-15	—	No events to record	
"	15-9-15	—	No events to record	
"	16-9-15	—	No events to record.	
"	17-9-15	—	No events to record	
"	18-9-15	—	No events to record	
"	19-9-15	—	No events to record	
"	20-9-15	—	No events to record	
"	21-9-15	—	Field ambulance visited by Major General NUGENT, commanding 36th Division.	
"	22-9-15	—	No events to record.	
"	23-9-15	—	No events to record	
"	24-9-15	—	No events to record.	
"	25-9-15	—	Medical and Surgical Equipment Received	
"	26-9-15	—	No events to record	
"	27-9-15	—	No events to record	
"	28-9-15	10.05 a.m.	Rehearsal Review at HANKLEY COMMON.	
"	29-9-15	—	No events to record	
"	30-9-15	11.30 a.m.	Reviewed by HIS MAJESTY the KING at HANKLEY COMMON.	
"	1-10-15	5.15 P.M.	Marched to BORDON STATION and entrained for SOUTHAMPTON DOCKS, entrained in two trains, first train left BORDON at 6.40 P.M. arriving at SOUTHAMPTON DOCKS at 8.40 P.M. Second train left BORDON

Army Form C. 2118.

108th Field Ambulance

No. 20.

WAR DIARY
or
INTELLIGENCE SUMMARY.

(Erase heading not required.)

Instructions regarding War Diaries and Intelligence Summaries are contained in F.S. Regs., Part II. and the Staff Manual respectively. Title pages will be prepared in manuscript.

Place	Date	Hour	Summary of Events and Information	Remarks and references to Appendices
BORDON CAMP	1/10/15		CAMP at 8:5 P.M. arriving at SOUTHAMPTON DOCKS at 10:30 P.M. Bivouacked on Baggage field.	
SOUTHAMPTON DOCKS	2/10/15	9 am	Party of four officers and 180 men detached from No 26 Butts to Berth 39. embarked on S.S. Connaught, which sailed at 5 P.M. Transport, Lieutenants J.C. Smith & Hunt: 9 Patrons, and Transport officers with horses and stores embarked on Transport No 201. S.S. ARCHLM EDE which sailed at 4 P.M. Officers Commanding noted to be O.C. Troops during the voyage, accompanied on Transport by 8 N.C.O's of the Field Ambulance.	
HAVRE	3/10/15	4 AM 9 am 3.10.15 12.20 P.M.	Arrived by Party which arrived in S.S. CONNAUGHT. Proceeded to No. 87. REST CAMP.	
	4/10/15	7 A.M.	Entrained at POINT No. 3.	
LONGUEAU	4/10/15 4.19 A.M. 4/10/15 1.20 P.M.		left HAVRE. Destination unknown. D.G.F. Curtis actg as O.C. Train. Arrived at LONGUEAU (3 miles S.E. of AMIENS). Detrained at once marched through AMIENS to RUBEMPRE arriving there at 8 P.M.	
RUBEMPRE	10.10.15 8 P.M. 5/10/15		Proceeded to Billets allotted to us official and men obtained. Spent the day improving sanitation of Billets, dryness fatigue and Reline. Pilot Role to MONTON VILHERS in reurd Historic hutted by A.D.M.S. Opened a DRESSING and RECEPTION STATION at the TOWN HALL.	
	6/10/15		Continued cleaning of quarters, rented Brigade Headquarters at MONTHUINS AUBOIS, also DIVISIONAL HEADQUARTERS at FLESSELLES, carried mails to A.D.M.S., also returned maps at HAZEBROUCK, arrived at BORDON.	

2353 Wt. W2511/1454 700,000 5/15 D. D. & L. A.D.S.S./Forms/C 2118.

WAR DIARY 108th Field Ambulance

Army Form C. 2118.

INTELLIGENCE SUMMARY.
(Erase heading not required.)

Instructions regarding War Diaries and Intelligence Summaries are contained in F. S. Regs., Part II and the Staff Manual respectively. Title pages will be prepared in manuscript.

Place	Date	Hour	Summary of Events and Information	Remarks and references to Appendices
RUBEMPRE	7/10/15	9 am	Weather fine. Received A.34. Visit by A.D.M.S. at 4 P.M.	
	8/10/15	8.30	No events to record with exception that 7 motor ambulance cars (No. 14 Division) joined the Unit, with three N.C.Os.	
	9/10/15		Heard intrigues; therefore developed anxiety; took off wagon orderlies to Motor Ambulances.	
			Capt. Lieut. A. Dunlop proceeded to BERTRANCOURT; returned ambulance for three days; returned with 11th Field Ambulance; with 12th Field Ambulance	
			Major Campbell to FORCEVILLE — curiosity with 12th Field Ambulance.	
	10/10/15		Visited Brigade Office at MOLLIENS AU BOIS. 600 cases of scabies in Hosp. to-D. These seeming to now again the troops have landed in the country show want of proper supervision on the part of medical officers in charge of Infantry Battalions. Shame, no Bn. Col. is Sypho or Surg. Hydneg, therefore we are so B of Gynd. for panting MacCody did Burns daily, and took advance on D. brought in Sol. Lt Lieut C. Creo, die slowly, mend improved. Represented on A.D.M.S. for by. Ciled-Sypho and Surg. Hydneg.	10.10.1915 Guest for BELLE 7/60/90
	11/10/15		Weather chilly & cloudy.	

certificate.

WAR DIARY 108th Field Ambulance Army Form C. 2118.

INTELLIGENCE SUMMARY.

(Erase heading not required.)

Instructions regarding War Diaries and Intelligence Summaries are contained in F. S. Regs., Part II. and the Staff Manual respectively. Title pages will be prepared in manuscript.

Place	Date	Hour	Summary of Events and Information	Remarks and references to Appendices
RUBEMPRE	11/10/15		Lieut. Baird C. selected outpost posts namely, A. sections on fatigues cleaning road, pursuing supplies, and attending to water carts. The new pattern water cart is extremely unsatisfactory as regards to strength; the supports to the cylinder have always before this section supporting the tool box have broken out and they have been placed to keep them in position.	
	12.10.15		No events worthy of record.	
	13.10.15		No events to record.	
	14.10.15		Sent Lt. Hogg and myself with two N.C.Os. reviewed to BERTRANCOURT and FORCEVILLE respectively for two days training with the 11th and 12th Field Ambulances. Went down to the Trenches in the afternoon, very little rifle fire; some shrapnel fire later; returned at	
FORCEVILLE		4.P.M.	Inspected Hospital at ambulance headquarters.	
	15/10/15		Spent the day reviewing notes of ambulance arrangements and obtaining information from the Lieutenants.	
	16/15		Visited Rest Station where to worked at CLAIRFAYE by No. 10. Field Ambulance. It is intended as intended at present the patients are sent and brought up into the building.	

Army Form C.2118.

WAR DIARY
or
INTELLIGENCE SUMMARY.   108th Field Ambulance

(Erase heading not required.)

Instructions regarding War Diaries and Intelligence Summaries are contained in F.S. Regs., Part II. and the Staff Manual respectively. Title pages will be prepared in manuscript.

Place	Date	Hour	Summary of Events and Information	Remarks and references to Appendices
FORCEVILLE		2.30 P.M	Returned with Sect. HODE and two N.C.Os to RUBEMPRE	Field Amb Billets ¥160.145.
	17/10/15	4.10 P.M	4 IEOts. SPARROW and G.REA took over places with two N.C.Os at FORCEVILLE and BERTRANCOURT.	
RUBEMPRÉ	18/10/15		No events worthy of record.	
	19/10/15		A.D.M.S. visited Ypres at SEPTENVILLE, where I proposed that the Ambulance should occupy. A.D.M.S. considered buildings admirable. Wanted shortly forty-four accommodations of Officers, brick & floor of one barn to extend to damp, Hotel Moeyses for sitting cases. Started building incinerator, clay bottom 3ft 6 ins deep, with cooler-closed seats. Removed in to new Posts. Finished incinerator. D.A.D.M.S. and Capt. J. DAVIS inspected field ambulance, both much pleased with arrangements made.	
SEPTENVILLE	20/10/15	12 P.M	Received order at 12 midnight to proceed immediately to MONTRELET, 13 miles N.W of present position. Ordered reveille at 5.30 a.m.	
	21/10/15	5.10 AM	SEPTENVILLE by way of VILLERS-BOCAGE	Field Amb Billets ¥64.

Army Form C. 2118.

WAR DIARY
108th Field Ambulance
INTELLIGENCE SUMMARY.
(Erase heading not required.)

Instructions regarding War Diaries and Intelligence Summaries are contained in F. S. Regs., Part II. and the Staff Manual respectively. Title pages will be prepared in manuscript.

Place	Date	Hour	Summary of Events and Information	Remarks and references to Appendices
MONTREHET PIEPPE.	21/10/15	3.30 P.M.	PLESS ELES, HAVERNAS, CANAPLES, MERRE arrived at MONTREHET at 3.30 p.m., about to return to PIEPPE, and billet for the night. Found suitable billets for all,	Paid for Billets £17
	22/10/15	10.25 A.M.	arrived at 10.25 a.m., arrived at BERNAVILLE at 12.15 P.M.	
BERNAVILLE	22/10/15	12.15 P.M.	after some difficulty succeeded in obtaining suitable billets for the men, never drag carts medical cart, tried to supply forage. obtained billets for officers in the town.	
"	23/10/15		In consequence of news from BOMB THROWING field of 109th Battalions of 109th Brigade. There were we not ordered to occupy us ordered to occupy these extreme sheds convicts keeping of Reduct Sheds.	
BERNAVILLE	10/24/15		No events to record except that the ambulance was provided billets in ACQUERIE about 2 miles E. of this town, we proceeded to clean the houses which had been left in a condition of indescribable filth by Indian Cavalry when we had spent six hours at this work we were	

Army Form C.2118.

108th Field Ambulance

WAR DIARY
or
INTELLIGENCE SUMMARY.
(Erase heading not required.)

Instructions regarding War Diaries and Intelligence Summaries are contained in F.S. Regs., Part II. and the Staff Manual respectively. Title pages will be prepared in manuscript.

Place	Date	Hour	Summary of Events and Information	Remarks and references to Appendices
BERNAVILLE	24/10/15	6 P.M.	Informed by greater of the Brigade Staff that Div. could not have this village. Spent the evening touring the country in search of a suitable place to form a reception station. It is absolutely essential to have several barns for sick and shows of sorts, not only for spaces to sleep in but for hospital accommodation. Found no suitable place in the several villages	
	25/10/15	2.30 a.m.	Started again, accompanied by Captain DUNLOP, visited HYANSU and found it not suitable, visited HOUDENCOURT and found it suitable. Telephoned the Ambulance by 'phone. Went to Div. Hd.Qrs. at DOMART and represented permission to occupy HYANSU, refused, but allowed to occupy HOUDENCOURT. Returned to BERNAVILLE.	
BERNAVILLE	25/10/15	9.20 A.M.	Transport and men marched via new ground from BERNAVILLE to have started. Transport took to new ground and did not arrive until 1 P.M. taking 3¾ hours to reach destination.	Paid for Billets 487.40

2353 Wt. W2341/1454 700,000 5/15 D.D.&L. A.D.S.S./Forms/C.2118.

Army Form C.2118.

108th Field AMBULANCE.

WAR DIARY

INTELLIGENCE SUMMARY.

(Erase heading not required.)

Instructions regarding War Diaries and Intelligence Summaries are contained in F. S. Regs., Part II. and the Staff Manual respectively. Title pages will be prepared in manuscript.

Place	Date	Hour	Summary of Events and Information	Remarks and references to Appendices
HOUDENCOURT	26/10/15	12.30 P.M.	Reported change of station to DIVISION H₂ HEAD QRs. Began to clean the sheds after dinner, pushed work in farmyard and started tricking pathway to billets through a trough of mud. Turned on fatigue parties to clean billets. A.S.C. to howitzer, their N.C.O. states they preferred to sleep outside than occupy such billets immediately. They could do so. to stay elsewhere. They must clean their Billets at once. They troops slept in these Billets. Weather is the evening chilly with some rain. Sufficient cover for horses but there all have goodcoats and it has not been evidenced necessary to neglect sept. They have a paddock the two of which afford considerable cover, and the ground is firm.	
	27/10/15	10 vist A.M.	Visited by A.D.M.S. and D.A.D.M.S. These officers appeared to be pleased with what they saw. Continued tricking pathway. Started to build howitzer, cleaned hollow in road to BDE HD QRS and A.S.C. Billets. Reported erection of Ambulance to BDE HD QRS.	
	28/10/15		Uncomplete all day, continued extension of Billets during the morning. Missed the men in for these of turn account of the weather.	

Army Form C. 2118.

WAR DIARY
of
INTELLIGENCE SUMMARY. 108th FIELD AMBULANCE
(Erase heading not required.)

Place	Date	Hour	Summary of Events and Information	Remarks and references to Appendices
HOODEN COURT	29/10/15		Began to erect Bowwood Bath House, continued to unpack kits, reclassify kit cases where kahari officers might well trek with them white.	
	30/10/15		Completed Boiler Bath House Considerable for O.R. etc.	
	31/10/15		Completed Bath House. The men appear glad to have it. Plenty of hot water and soap available, the baths consist of extra tubs.	

R F Fawcett
Major RAMC
O.C., 108th Field Ambulance

108th F.A.
Vol: 2

12/7678

36/M/Kuraun

Nov 15

Nov 1915

Army Form C. 2118

WAR DIARY
or
INTELLIGENCE SUMMARY.

(Erase heading not required.)

108th FIELD AMBULANCE

Instructions regarding War Diaries and Intelligence Summaries are contained in F. S. Regs., Part II. and the Staff Manual respectively. Title pages will be prepared in manuscript.

Place	Date	Hour	Summary of Events and Information	Remarks and references to Appendices
HOWDEN COURT.	1/4/15		Cleared two stables for use as Medical Inspection Rooms and Pack Stores, scraped the earthen floors which would otherwise be covered with chalk dust, beaten in with a sledge hammer. This material makes an excellent floor. Heavy rain will soon turn a hub and it to to seams deep exposed road into turn & hub as it to seams. Hurry and is apt to flavow the men to adventure.	
	2/4/15		Shopped.	
	3/4/15		No events worthy of records.	
	4/4/15		Nothing to record.	
	5/4/15		No events to record.	
	6/4/15		Inspection by Inspector General Nugent, accompanying the Division who states that arrangements are very good and premises with stables suitable to the Unit. Intents to recommend.	
	7/4/15		Rumours received (6 or 8) act to remove to better Billets.	
	8/4/15		Owing to which most of the men are infested with lice obtained in their Billets. Some ventured to the old old shed in A.D.S.S./Forms/C. 2118.	

2353 Wt. W2544/1454 700,000 5/15 D. D. & L.

Army Form C. 2118

WAR DIARY
or
INTELLIGENCE SUMMARY.
(Erase heading not required.)

Instructions regarding War Diaries and Intelligence Summaries are contained in F. S. Regs., Part II. and the Staff Manual respectively. Title pages will be prepared in manuscript.

Place	Date	Hour	Summary of Events and Information	Remarks and references to Appendices
NOUDEN COURT.	8/4/15		To think that they have extracted lice from their troops acquired by troops from India who usually same fulls not a disgraceful creation. Sanitary authorities are to change clothing and blankets every fortnight, except when these too full, beware. Dirty and blankets to be washed without station and the new clean blankets until clothing is fit for wear.	
	9/4/15		Accommodation for sick insufficient, therefore approached the landlady with a view to obtaining a larger part of a house. She seemed at the outset. This was unfortunately refused, as it was imperative that further accommodation be obtained for sick, as not being in my opinion quite right for patients in violent wet weather, opened the room by the back door. A future mess, made space for patients by placing the iron bedsteads there being very badly packed with straw. The dust of aged chaff of guns going, it contained. A supply of barn, appreciated as would, if had eventually been used. Some twice up-abbots from the 2nd cavalry Div. Cav. Field Ambulance. Put in more patients.	

WAR DIARY

INTELLIGENCE SUMMARY.

Army Form C. 2118

108th FIELD AMBULANCE

(Erase heading not required.)

Place	Date	Hour	Summary of Events and Information	Remarks and references to Appendices
HUMENCOURT	11/7/15		Started for this Town for supply. My went into DOMART. Visited shop & got duty stores, bought enamel "Entree" for 7.29 and home pping for 76.	
	12/7/15		Continued teaching. Brought up to DOMART to get stones unwashed. Arranged to bring three thousand bricks at once ENH.O.S. CAPTAIN DUNLOP treated upwards of acute appendicitis.	
	13/7/15		Started to extricate from 107 ENH.O.S. Continued treating sick, worked at making a drying room for clothing by screening off part of Ballroom with tarpaulin sheet. Laid ground. Ordered to lay bricks to start with temporary requirements for bathing. Started, sent to application for fifty three tonh requirements for bathing. Started, sent to application of 6.7.E.	
	14/7/15		With which implements to C.R.E. Finished Mortuary, etc. Started to move on to new mortuary (large). Continued cutting bricks for STATES, and Drying Room.	
	15/7/15		Received Latrines with Straw, washing, rebuilt, being improved for front of States, havg. appendicitis doing well.	
	16/7/15		Completed Drying Room, visited work above FRANQUEVILLE and arranged with Interp. to buy a squared amulet 2.3 metres by 8. Visited for people for Matting, went to DOMART and telegraphed to C.R.E. for authority to purchase same, got ground in rear to lift and begrass to lay bricks. Cases of appendicitis doing well. Temp. normal. Slept & drank, patient big hungry, fell of four inches of snow! Supply was in stock. He writes from base that little relieves the brigade supplies, sharp frost tonight.	

W+W—3811439 700,000 5/15 D. D. & L.   A.D.S.S./Forms/C.2118.

Army Form C. 2118

WAR DIARY
of
INTELLIGENCE SUMMARY. 108TH FIELD AMBULANCE.
(Erase heading not required.)

Place	Date	Hour	Summary of Events and Information	Remarks and references to Appendices
HOOD ENSCOURT	16/4/15	6.30 P.M.	Quincy Q.M. Recd per manis.	
	17/4/15		Put up stove in Dying Room. continued payment for Stable. Very little overhead shrapnel burst at 11 & 105th Brigade left for the work. No inches treaties on the 13th repriment.	
	18/4/15		no events to record	
	19/4/15		nothing to record	
	20/4/15		nothing to record	
	21/4/15		no events worthy of record	
	22/4/15		no events to record	
	23/4/15		nothing to record with exception that a few persons visitors in I rather annoyed by the noises of the house. This was quickly put a stop to by our man's, no events to record	
	24/4/15			
	26/4/15		received orders to move tomorrow at 7. am by way of FRANQUEVILLE and DOMART to LA HAIE Farm. applied to transport officer served as ordered. Major S. Smith D.A.D.M.S. visited no events to date.	
	27/4/15		proceed to transport (explained order to do so) no events to record	
LA HAIE FARM.	28/4/15		Unit now attached to 108th Brigade. Rode to 107th Brigade HDQTRS, no officers in. 108th Brigade HDQTRS, no officers in.	

WAR DIARY

INTELLIGENCE SUMMARY. 108th FIELD AMBULANCE.

(Erase heading not required.)

Army Form C. 2118

Place	Date	Hour	Summary of Events and Information	Remarks and references to Appendices
LA HAIE FARM	29/11/15		Visited 107th BDE HQ, QRS, saw Brigadier, went to ST ODENT, in fact site for Brigade Baths, returned to Bde: Hd Qrs Brigadier went with me to see the place from there, went to HQ CAMP to see the Regimental Battns, 10th, 11th, R. Innistilling Fus, went out to DOMQUEUR and saw house proposed as Brigade Bath House. Returned at 5.30 pm to Field Ambulance, saw divisional cortege this morning between BRYCAM Nyd main road to DOMQUEUR enquired this to be a poor place for our hospital as we are fully off for accommodation about this house is in good repair, which is pretty to clear cottage; went to FREVILLE and hoped it as there was nothing who plans for hospital received.	

B.J.Butterworth
Major
O.C. 108th Field Ambulance

10 pp. 2 a.
Vol 3

1784/151

36 MS

Dec 1915

Army Form C. 2118.

WAR DIARY

INTELLIGENCE SUMMARY. 108th FIELD AMBULANCE

(Erase heading not required.)

Instructions regarding War Diaries and Intelligence Summaries are contained in F. S. Regs., Part II. and the Staff Manual respectively. Title pages will be prepared in manuscript.

Place	Date	Hour	Summary of Events and Information	Remarks and references to Appendices
LA HAIE FARM.	1/12/15		Went to DOMQUEUR and saw G.O, 9th to 3rd Royal Irish Rifles. Furnished a Bath house. Arranged to send out our N.C.O. and small party tomorrow to assist in the work of establishing and carrying on the working of the Bath. Orders to DOMART send bought a stove. Put up a stove in the new hospital.	
	2/12/15		Went into DOMQUEUR and visited Bath House, R.E. at work.	
	3/12/15			
	4/12/15		Made map of area worked by 108th Field Ambulance, reports of my teams received. A.D.M.S. visited Field Ambulance	
	6/12/15		Completed ablution stand. C.O. of 8th Div. visited DOMQUEUR, Bath house inspected by Battalions	
	6/12/15		but are still few and come in slowly. Went to 91st Battalion, new C.o.t house, received in Headquarters house with Lanterns agreed, but Ambulance outs strictly admitted French fire which needs to be very well told to my 100 beds Now Breakfast at 700 ENFL Os, repeated that no Sookey of sick might be sent to DOMART and house to in one bed cubicle went to DOMART Ambulance Moved July...	

Army Form C. 2118.

WAR DIARY
INTELLIGENCE SUMMARY.
(Erase heading not required.)

108th FIELD AMBULANCE.

Instructions regarding War Diaries and Intelligence Summaries are contained in F. S. Regs., Part II. and the Staff Manual respectively. Title pages will be prepared in manuscript.

Place	Date	Hour	Summary of Events and Information	Remarks and references to Appendices
LA HAIE FARM	6/12/15		Continued work at BATH HOUSE. Road to DOMQUEUR and New Bath House. There it will not be completed before the end of this week. Returned by way of ETAMIES and BROUCAMPS. Capt. d.W.R.E.A. left to do duty with 16th Royal Irish Rifles at RAINECHEVAL.	
	8/12/15		Nothing to record	
	9/12/15		Nothing to record	
	10/12/15		Nothing to record	
	11/12/15		Nothing to record. CAPTAIN'S HOQ. left for temporary duty with 32nd Bn Royal Innis.	
	12/12/15		LIEUT. BOND gave us sketch & specifications for hospital at DOMVILLIERS.	
	13/12/15		Brought a small quantity of timber at DOMART. Began to build Reception tent.	
	14/12/15		Continued work on Reception tent.	
	15/12/15		Went with the officer Brigade Battle Hosp. at DOMQUEUR. No estimate allowed. Telephoned to C.R.E. asking	
	16/12/15		permission to erect a complete of tent either two of BUSSUS and the wards. A.D.M.S. once arranged	
	17/12/15			

WAR DIARY
INTELLIGENCE SUMMARY

Army Form C. 2118.

108th FIELD AMBULANCE

108 Field Ambulance

Place	Date	Hour	Summary of Events and Information	Remarks and references to Appendices
LA HAIE SAINTE	17/2/16		Recce made with a view to improved or better supplementary dugouts. Advisable to make no radical change. Suggest the construction of two shelters to take 6 cases each. The cavettes revetted with boards, to occupy a terrain exactly of old trench. Worked on one at LONGFAERS and one at DOMART. The advanced dressing station to be built immediately two feet in height in roof and is being made of corrugated iron covered with earth. Dimensions 20' x 10' with cover of 8' deep. Heights to eaves 7' 10". Endeavoured to keep space for cart in DOMART without success. Several Regimental Headquarters and an average that messes occupy the adjacent cavetto.	
	18/2/16		No events to record	
	20/2/16		Nothing to record	
	21/2/16		No events to record	
	22/2/16		Visited Brigade Headquarters and went with acting Brigadier and Major H. M. to the trenches. Selected site for Communication trench cut which to run Dug-outs	

Army Form C. 2118.

WAR DIARY
INTELLIGENCE SUMMARY. 108th FIELD AMBULANCE.
(Erase heading not required.)

Place	Date	Hour	Summary of Events and Information	Remarks and references to Appendices
LA HAIE HARIN.	22/12/15		Handed over to the DOM QUEUR to BRIGADIER to screw by O.C. 9th Bn. ROYAL INNISKILLING FUSILIERS	
	23/12/15		Reconnaissance -	
	24/12/15		Completed Recreation Hut and put in a stove. Concert in evening in Recreation Hut.	
	25/12/15		Nothing to record	
	26/12/15		Nothing worthy of record	
	27/12/15		No events to record	
	28/12/15		Nothing to record	
	29/12/15		Bought old table in DOMART to build a Hospital hut with	
	30/12/15			
	31/12/15		Work on Hospital Hut proceeding well	

487 F. Wentworth
Major. R.A.M.C.
O.C., 108th Field Ambulance

10th F.A.
Vol: 4

36 U Bo

F194/1.

Jan 1915
—
Dec 1915

Army Form C. 2118.

WAR DIARY

INTELLIGENCE SUMMARY. 108TH FIELD AMBULANCE.

(Erase heading not required.)

Instructions regarding War Diaries and Intelligence Summaries are contained in F. S. Regs., Part II. and the Staff Manual respectively. Title pages will be prepared in manuscript.

Place	Date	Hour	Summary of Events and Information	Remarks and references to Appendices
LA HAIE	1/7/16		Nothing worthy of record.	
FARM	2/7/16		Nothing to report.	
	3/7/16		Captain G.W. REA proceeded on 14 days' leave.	
	4/7/16		No events to record.	
	5/7/16		Nothing of interest to record.	
	6/7/16		Nothing worthy of record.	
	7/7/16		Visited VACQUERIE and saw O.C. 98TH FIELD AMBULANCE. Village is in a disgraceful condition of dirt and neglect.	
	8/7/16		Began to pack. Baggage wagons used removed patients from Hospital on BRUCAMPS road to RECREATION HUT at LA HAIE FARM.	
		9.7PM-9PM	Finished packing.	
VACQUERIE	9/7/16	7.30	Marched to VACQUERIE by way of DOMART.	
		A.M.	Started at once to clean the village.	

Army Form C. 2118.

WAR DIARY

INTELLIGENCE SUMMARY. 108th FIELD AMBULANCE.

(Erase heading not required.)

Place	Date	Hour	Summary of Events and Information	Remarks and references to Appendices
VACQUERIE	11/7/16		Started to floor a loft from which flooring had been removed. This is to be used as a Billet. Began to clean farmyard; removed 7 cartloads of manure and filth from yard, and numerous cartloads of weed from the village street.	
	12/7/16		Continued work as above.	
	13/7/16		Finished carting manure from yard. Began to cart stones (flints) from field begun DOMENOID. These to be used in farmyard and to make a stand for wagons. The hospital is next door and is established in a house formerly used as a Summer Home for Children brought from PARIS. It is well provided with Spring BEDS. Here, though at first the patients find very comfortable. Began to build a bathhouse.	
	14/7/16		Continued work at cleaning the road.	
	15/7/16		Built oven for heating water in Hospital ground.	
	16/7/16		Put in two stoves in Hospital wards upstairs. The Hospital	

WAR DIARY

INTELLIGENCE SUMMARY. /68th FIELD AMBULANCE.

Army Form C. 2118.

Place	Date	Hour	Summary of Events and Information	Remarks and references to Appendices
HEADQRS	16/7/16		Will accommodate 40 patients. Finished flooring loft. Put windows in loft. In the event of a large number of patients arriving, the new site 7. Amb. would be transferred to Brees at E. End of village and nearly 200 patients could be accommodated in the farm by flooring another Barn.	
	17/7/16		Began to floor above BARN. Completed Ablution Shed.	
	18/7/16			
	19/7/16		Have now removed 150 cartloads of mud from Farmyard and village street.	
	20/7/16		Built a new Cook House at end of Farm & wellow House.	
	21/7/16		Repair and completed BATH House in Farm Fifteen.	
	22/7/16		Completed flooring of second BARN.	
	23/7/16		Completed Rock Pit for slops. Crates for Hospital & Waste House.	
	24/7/16		Picked pottes to be evacuated. Both Rouse, and Bath House both Pit.	

Army Form C. 2118.

WAR DIARY
or
INTELLIGENCE SUMMARY. 108th FIELD AMBULANCE
(Erase heading not required.)

Instructions regarding War Diaries and Intelligence Summaries are contained in F. S. Regs., Part II. and the Staff Manual respectively. Title pages will be prepared in manuscript.

Place	Date	Hour	Summary of Events and Information	Remarks and references to Appendices
VACQUERIE	25/1/1916		Erected patents fences & for cleaned village streets.	
	26/1/16		Obtained a good supply of bricks (old) also a small supply of 9 bars for windows & for winter temporary huts; Col. ONEB.	
	27/1/16		Put three small windows in BARN, made a wooden trough for washing of men's clothing and placed the BATH HOUSE. Obtained an iron cistern and placed same at upper end of ablution shed for water supply of stand for washing purposes.	
	28/1/16		Repaired Farrier's House (leading to cellar). This is to be used as a forage store.	
	29/1/16		Visited A.D.M.S. at BERNAVILLE and received various instructions regarding the making of extemporised trench shelters and the building of Dugouts.	
	30/1/16		Visited 108th BRIGADE HEADQUARTERS, saw Staff Captain re making of trenches Dugouts.	
	31/1/16		Repaired road in village with transomes and broken bricks from which floor of village F.A.D.M.S.	

B.J.M. Fawcett
Lieut. Colonel
O.C. 108th

108th F.a.
vol: 5.

108th Field Ambulance

Feb 1916

Army Form C. 2118.

WAR DIARY
INTELLIGENCE SUMMARY

108th FIELD AMBULANCE.

(Erase heading not required.)

Hour, Date, Place	Summary of Events and Information	Remarks and references to Appendices
VACQUERIE. 1.2.1916.	No events to record.	
2.2.1916.	No events to record.	
3.2.1916.	No events to record.	
4.2.1916.	No events to record.	
5.2.1916.	No events to record.	
6.2.1916.	Rode to Curlus to reconnoitre roads. Advance party of Lucheux field ambulance (1 Officer, 1 N.C.O. and 2 men) arrived in	
7.2.1916.	VACQUERIE. Marched from VACQUERIE at 9 a.m., by way of CANDAS, FERME DE ROSEL, VAL DE MAISON, PUCHEVILLERS, to TOUTENCOURT, distance 16 miles. Got a man fell out although they have done so-long marches have arrived in France. Billeted for the night in TOUTENCOURT.	
TOUTENCOURT. 8.2.1916.	Marched at 10 a.m. Reinforcements on a hill between TOUTENCOURT and HARPONVILLE for Thones. Marched by way of HARPONVILLE, and VARENNES to HEDEUVILLE, via FORCEVILLE at 2 p.m., distance 5½ miles.	

WAR DIARY

INTELLIGENCE SUMMARY

(Erase heading not required.) 108th FIELD AMBULANCE

Army Form C. 2118.

Hour, Date, Place	Summary of Events and Information	Remarks and references to Appendices
HORNOY. 8.2.1916.	Capt. J.W. REA proceeded in advance to take over from 12th FIELD AMBULANCE.	* a very capable Scotch officer, knowing of advancements.
9.2.1916.	Visit from A.D.M.S. and D.A.D.M.S. *Capt. J.M. DUNLOP took over charge of hospital arrangements. Visited advanced post at MESNIL with the A.D.M.S. and D.A.D.M.S. Lieut. Capt. J.W. REA, R.M.C.O. was sworn to take over advanced post at MESNIL in relief of 110th F.A. Visited AVELUY HOSPITALS advanced post in the afternoon. Took down a party of 1 O.Off. and 3 men, at night to HAMEL advanced post, in relief of 110th F.A.	The Hospital occupies the whole of a moderately large French house, right wing used medical cases, is on left of whole, dressing station before large top of the building, severe
10.2.1916.	Escorted several necessary repairs in Billets and Hospital, put up one stove in Ward upstairs.	
11.2.1916.	Went to DOULLENS and bought two stoves.	
12.2.1916.	Put up a second stove in ward upstairs, continued repairs to Billets, cleaned Square above Cook-houses at House. Visited Advanced Dressing Station at MAILLY MAILLET.	

Army Form C. 2118.

WAR DIARY
INTELLIGENCE SUMMARY
(Erase heading not required.)

108th FIELD AMBULANCE.

Hour, Date, Place	Summary of Events and Information	Remarks and references to Appendices
FORCEVILLE.		
13.2.1916.	Visited MAILLY Collecting Post and Dud outs on Serre Road. Only one enemy shell over road while there.	
14.2.1916. 3.45 P.M.	Visited AUCHONVILLERS DRESSING STATION at 8.45 P.M. Scott went over ground towards enemy lines endeavouring to find a suitable way for bearers in case roads so heavily shelled. Found a suitable way.	
15.2.1916.	Went to DOULLENS and bought one storeman for ambulance. Covered vessels for use as water supply for DUGOUTS.	
16.2.1916.	Rode to COUIN and saw Lieut: COLONEL F.Q. FITZGERALD, O.C. 12th FIELD AMBULANCE. W arranged to be paid weekly for billets occupied by this Unit in FORCEVILLE. heavy rain all the morning followed by hail, very violent wind blowing all day. Went to AUCHONVILLERS in the evening. Visited R.A.M.C. BOMB PROOF shelters; quiet, with exception of occasional bursts of rifle fire. Scored out Fritz are empty.	

Army Form C. 2118.

WAR DIARY
INTELLIGENCE SUMMARY
(Erase heading not required.)

108th FIELD AMBULANCE.

Hour, Date, Place	Summary of Events and Information	Remarks and references to Appendices
FORCEVILLE, 16-2-1916.	cellar in which to make a third Shelter, all cellars being occupied by the R.E. Tunnelling Company. CAPTAIN S.P. REA, returned from 14 days leave.	
17-2-1916.	Capt. S.P. REA relieved CAPTAIN A REA at MESNIL. Relieved also N.C.O and 9 men stationed there. Visited Div. Hd. Qrs. and conferred with A.D.M.S. and D.A.D.M.S. re friction of D/D 6/78 in communicating re friction of D/D 6/78 in communicating freeshes. D.D.M.S. 17th Corps, visited Field Ambulances 3 - 4 P.M.	
18-2-1916.	Visited AVCHONVILLERS with A.D.M.S. and D.A.D.M.S., went round Trenches N. of AUCHONVILLERS with D.A.D.M.S., returned to village. Oct 5 p.m., owing to muddy state of trenches it took two hours to get round. Selected site for R.A.M.C. bearers in the Town rebellier Termed TENDERLOIN STREET.	
19-2-1916.	Proceeded to DOMART and LA HAYE FARM and bought timber, glass etc with which to construct hut for extra hospital accommodation.	

WAR DIARY

INTELLIGENCE SUMMARY

108th FIELD AMBULANCE

Army Form C. 2118.

Hour, Date, Place	Summary of Events and Information	Remarks and references to Appendices
FORCEVILLE, 19.2.1916. 20.2.1916.	Capt: A.W.REA proceeded with C. Section to MAILLY. Capt: A.H.R.DUNCAN proceeded to AUCHONVILLERS to charge of ADVANCED DRESSING STATION. Visited MAILLY in the morning and arranged for supply of material for R.A.M.C. Shelter in AUCHONVILLERS. (from 152nd Coy. R.E.) Went to AUCHONVILLERS at 8.15 p.m. and inspected shelters. The W. Shelter requires plenty of sandbags certainly bricks on the E. Wall and the roof needs to be covered with 2 feet of bricks. The E. Shelter requires E. end of cellar to be blocked with bricks. Told Capt. DRNCAN what was required.	
21.2.1916.	Visited MAILLY Dressing Station. Got considerable quantity of material for building of the Hut.	
22.2.1916.	Handed over to CAPT. L. DUNLOP. Proceeded on 10 days leave to England.	

R.Fawcett.
Lieut. Colonel,
O.C.

Army Form C. 2118.

108th FIELD AMBULANCE

WAR DIARY
or
INTELLIGENCE SUMMARY
(Erase heading not required.)

Hour, Date, Place	Summary of Events and Information	Remarks and references to Appendices
Foncville 22/2/16	Lieut Col Fawcett went on leave at 3 P.M. leaving me in command of the Field Ambulance. Pte Martin admitted with compound fracture & upper end of Right Femur and badly shattered left foot, in addition to numerous other superficial wounds on Right leg. At 3.30 P.M. I amputated the foot at junction of lower & middle thirds of leg, further first aid dressings in gutter splints owing to the lacerated condition of the skin. Wound thoroughly washed with EUSOL and dressed with BIPP & BEtreatment administered by Capt S.B. CAMPBELL. Pte Brown 11th R Innis Fus. admitted with gunshot wound of Knee wounds of Scalp & Neck about 3" apart; Brown Wrattle bleeding from Best wound, No loss of consciousness but pulse very slow (50). Chloroform administered by Capt. S.B. CAMPBELL. Patient shows a deep V shaped flap including both wounds. The artery beyond skin soft hardens the Skull, but the bone Cavity part of the scalp beyond was a considerable opening in the occasion which was bleeding freely. The dura was torn away from this area, the cleansing away blood clot and brain matter, the brain ceased to bleed freely. The perforated exposed bone at the edges went removed and a piece above indicated through. The wound in the full grown of the perineum arrested the opening. wound dressed and E&S.O.L. Patient stood the anaesthetic very well. Several other slightly wounded cases admitted, all also 2 rifle wounds & bruises. Pte Coates ? Irwin fus admitted. Got an opening in the floor of the orbital bone over the internal canthi Large enough to admit a stripling with a fistura and loss of Conjunctiva, unable to give up mobility & sense of lower eyelids shortly and the globe from the plane also.	

WAR DIARY or INTELLIGENCE SUMMARY

Army Form C. 2118.

7

108th FIELD AMBULANCE

Hour, Date, Place	Summary of Events and Information	Remarks and references to Appendices
FORCEVILLE 22/1/16	Arranged with Sergt. Strains to send out two men at 6 A.M. tomorrow if there is any snow on the ground to clear the road to MAILLY as requested by the Town Commandant. Sent a sketch and short description of the Detachable Headrest I have designed and used with great success for stretchers.	
23/1/16	Both cases operated on yesterday cleaned and left strong, will be sent to hospital, but have case demicated showing T. 99°. Rode over to MAILLY & visited DRESSING STATION. Visited the AUCHONVILLERS ADVANCED DRESSING STATION. Visited the DUG-OUTS and round of the TRENCHES & saw the advanced collecting posts. The men there are carrying out the work of clearing away the Defences in TENDERLOIN and cemetery showing tonight. Word of an impeded Hun trench at the REDAN. Everything very quiet on the front. No heavy cannonade today. So much snow on the ground that the horses was not able to come from MAILEY to visit Ambulance this am. Received word that FORCEVILLE Road has resisted & the ADMS who has gone on orders to proceed FORCEVILLE and proceed to BEAUSSART and open ordinary station there. The Casualties admitted today except one case of gas poisoning from an exploded miner.	

Army Form C. 2118.

108th FIELD AMBULANCE

WAR DIARY
or
INTELLIGENCE SUMMARY
(Erase heading not required.)

Hour, Date, Place	Summary of Events and Information	Remarks and references to Appendices
FORCEVILLE 24/2/16 10 a.m.	Visited A.D.M.S. re move. Lunch with D.A.D.M.S. & went with BEAUSSART and found out what accommodation we could get. Roofs known as present. A.D.M.S. informed me that move had been postponed for 3 days.	
25/2/16 11 a.m.	Visit from A.D.M.S. Move to BEAUSSART cancelled. Went to see C.R.E. about material for Ride, and for smashing bricks & insisted on accommodation. Still snowing heavily, making motor ambulances traffic very difficult, one slipping off our road on the part. Lost 1 H.T.H., 3 men & about room in Beyout. Manned with ambulance had great difficulty getting up without help on account of the snow clogging the road.	
26/2/16	CAPT WHITE P.G. Died & relieve CAPT DUNCAN AMT at entrenched & railway station AUCHONVILLERS. C.R.E. visited the hospital and promised to build the R.R. and huts, and about next ready to receive sketches from to-Colt. Snow very deep but beginning to thaw. Returned CAPT REA S.P. G.So with a convoy 2 b.r. & 9 wagons to DOMART for wound & build the huts.	
27/2/16	Heavy fall of snow during the night which made journey to DOMART impossible. Obtained a quantity of wood from C.R.E. to the Put and began the clearing of the ground for its. Pit was also begun to building of the huts in the barrel in the yard. Thawing rapidly tonight.	

Army Form C. 2118.

WAR DIARY
or
INTELLIGENCE SUMMARY.
(Erase heading not required.)

108th FIELD AMBULANCE 9

Place	Date	Hour	Summary of Events and Information	Remarks and references to Appendices
FORCEVILLE	28/2/16	7.30 AM	Capt REASP proceeded to DOMART with a party of 1 N.C.O., 4 S.S. wagons and a loading party of 4 RAMP men to obtain wagons & the Red. Made a start on the Red, cleared the ground and got some of the uprights in.	
		3 P.M.	Walked to MAILLY and inspected site of proposed DUG-OUTS which are to be built on the ADVANCED R? MAILLY and for the sister of wounded in case the A.D.S is shelled. Met A.D.M.S in MAILLY on the road forward.	
	29/2/16		No events to record.	

J. Rupert Dunlop
Capt.
O.C.

108 F Amb

Vg 6

36th Div.

March & 1918.
April

108th F. Amb.

WAR DIARY
or
INTELLIGENCE SUMMARY.

Army Form C. 2118.

108th FIELD AMBULANCE

Place	Date	Hour	Summary of Events and Information	Remarks and references to Appendices
FORCEVILLE	1/3/16	10 a.m.	Proceeded to MAILLY and held Court of Enquiry on "Accidental Burning" of Pte. M. MUISE whilst at place at MESNIL.	
		2 P.M.	Detailed Capt S.B.B. CAMPBELL to proceed to MESNIL in relief of Capt F. HOGG	
		4 P.M.	Bact:ologist from DDMS 17th Corps came to investigate an epidemic of Pyrexia resembling Influenza which is considered may be a form of TRENCH FEVER. At present the hospital is filled with cases, a form of foot ones arriving daily. J. Pyrexia, T. 101-103°. Pains all over body & headed - Previously diagnosed INFLUENZA.	
FORCEVILLE	2/3/16		Large number of cases of Trench feet admitted and a number of cases showing an exactly similar condition in the hands. Hitherto the condition of hands seems in some cases to have TRENCH FEET, but occurring of occurs in the hands only, not continuous only, not condition only, and hands. Detailed ten men for Canteen at ACHEUX.	
FORCEVILLE	3/3/16	10.0.a.m.	Received orders from A.D.M.S. to hand over Dressing Station at MAILLY and evacuated posts at AUCHONVILLERS & DUG OUTS to 109th FIELD AMBULANCE and to take on the Right Sector of trenches from 3" (HAMEL-AUTHOILLE) on Left bank of river AVERE. An advanced Dressing station to be opened at MARTINSART in this respect. Visited A.D.M.S. 49th Division at SENLIS and made arrangements about evacuation of wounded	
		2. P.M.	Visited MARTINSART and saw TOWN MAJOR about a suitable house for an advanced Dressing station. Reported progress to A.D.M.S. Small outbreak of TRENCH FEET from 14th R.I.R. of all degrees of severity. Number of patients in hospital tonight 125.	

Army Form C. 2118.

WAR DIARY
or
INTELLIGENCE SUMMARY.
(Erase heading not required.)

108th FIELD AMBULANCE

Place	Date	Hour	Summary of Events and Information	Remarks and references to Appendices
FORCEVILLE	4/2/16	12.30 a.m.	Received following Order from A.D.M.S:— The O.C. 108th Field Ambulance will arrange to take over the collecting Post at BLACK HORSE BRIDGE from 108th Sanitary Field Ambulance at 9 a.m. on the 5th inst., with the following detachment: 1 Officer, 2 N.C.O's, 18 men.	
			One motor Cycle and from wheeled stretcher will be kept at this post.	
FORCEVILLE	5/2/16	8.30 a.m.	Proceeded to MARTINSART with one N.C.O. and two men and then went on to BLACK HORSE BRIDGE. Visited DOG OUTS and Regimental aid Post, Royal Engineers on return to MARTINSART issued the orders, a copy of which is attached. Left the M.E.O. and two men at MARTINSART i.e. near the party, the position of the different posts when they went to take over the Collecting Post on the following day.	
		8.30 a.m.	Capt. G.W. REA proceeded to MARTINSART with "C" Section. Two N.C.O. advance party for BLACK HORSE BRIDGE. and reported to me at 11.30 a.m. that he had opened an advanced Dressing Station at MARTINSART. This Report was forwarded to A.D.M.S.	
		7.30 p.m.	Received notification from A.D.M.S. that Lieut. Col. R.F.M. FAWCETT O.C. 108th Field Amb., had been granted an extension of Leave for 3 days. The place, FORCEVILLE, had a few shells burst in in the afternoon, apparently intended for ACHEUX. Sent 1 N.C.O. and three men to relieve detachment in HAMEL.	
FORCEVILLE	6/2/16		Sent from A.D.M.S. who informed me that 32nd Division closes the dug out at BLACKHORSE BRIDGE, consequently he had to revisit the exists of Washrooms and the village of AUTHUILLES "C" in the detail. He also recommended that ten Cases to kept with the Advanced Dressing Station one at MARTINSART, and one at AVELUY.	
			Lieut BURROWES R.A.M.C. joined the unit during it.	
FORCEVILLE	7/2/16	11.a.m.	Lieut Col. R.F.M. FAWCETT returned from Leave and resumed command of the unit	
			J.R. [signature] Capt. R.A.M.C.	

Army Form C. 2118.

WAR DIARY

INTELLIGENCE SUMMARY.
(Erase heading not required.)

108th FIELD AMBULANCE

Instructions regarding War Diaries and Intelligence Summaries are contained in F.S. Regs., Part II and the Staff Manual respectively. Title pages will be prepared in manuscript.

3

Place	Date	Hour	Summary of Events and Information	Remarks and references to Appendices
FORCEVILLE	8.3.16	12 P.M. 30	Returned from leave, but in Recommendations for previous in Birthday Honorees to A.D.M.S. Reported arrival to A.D.M.S.	
	9.3.16	2.30 P.M.	Walked through ENGLEBELMER to MARTINSART, which during future and Butter. CAPT. A. HOGG in charge of Battn. which will be taken into accommodation for sick and wounded at MARTINSART is very limited.	
	10.3.16	10. a.m.	Proceeded to MARTINSART, from there with CAPTAIN ANDREA to AVELUY, visited Advanced Post under CAPTAIN S.T. REA, returned at 1 P.M. Walked conference with A.D.M.S. at DM ADRE at ACHEUX at 3.30 P.M.	
	11.3.16	10 a.m.	Heavy shelling from 11 P.M. to 4 a.m. AUTHUILLE shelled; 4.2 casualties. D.D.M.S. VI Corps visited FIELD AMBULANCE and advanced Posts, accompanied by A.D.M.S.	
	12.3.16	10 a.m.	D.D.M.S. and D.A.D.M.S. 36th DIVISION. Visited MAILLY MAILLET in an endeavour to obtain wood with which to complete hospital hut, could obtain none; while there aeroplanes dropped Bomb, wounding no one, but injuring no one. Sent 8 men to reinforce MARTINSART Advanced U.P.O.S.T.	
		6 P.M.	Visited C.R.E. at ACHEUX regarding wood for hospital hut; expect to obtain it tomorrow.	
	13.3.16	10.15 a.m.	Rode to MARTINSART; walked from there to AUTHUILLE; went into fire trenches 665, 615 D.G.A. A.D.S. & M.D.S.; very muddy; visited CAPTAIN S.T. REA.	

Army Form C. 2118.

WAR DIARY

INTELLIGENCE SUMMARY. 108th FIELD AMBULANCE.

(Erase heading not required.)

Place	Date	Hour	Summary of Events and Information	Remarks and references to Appendices
FORCEVILLE	13.3.16.		at his Post; village shelled from 2/15 to 2.45 p.m.; with light calibres & percussion ("Whiz-Bangs") No casualties. Telephone; our return to be given worth Stueyhaven.	
	14.3.16.	10.30 AM	MARTINSART. Saw O.C. 121 H. Coy. R.E. who promised to begin work Stueyhaven Post at AUTHUILLE tomorrow morning.	
	15.3.16.	10.30 AM	Rode to BOUZINCOURT to try and find alternate route for evacuation of sick from AUTHUILLE Tournebouts at N.E. end of BOUZINCOURT closed, as by day it is under direct observation from the German lines. Rode to MARTINSART, from there walked to MESNIL and saw Lieut. BURROWES in charge of DRESSING STATION. arranged to believe him tomorrow. Visited MARTINSART DRESSING STATION. Visited FORCEVILLE CEMETERY to note graves for records. Building of Hut No. 1 progressing fast, half completed and roof is being painted. Surface of ground where Horses are kept is unable transport waggons to reach there.	
	16.3.16.	9.30 a.m.	Rode to ACHEUX and drew 76000 for pay of men.	
	17.3.16.	10.30 am	Rode to MARTINSART and paid Detachment. Returned thro' village Shelled slightly with shrapnel from 12 noon to 12.30 p.m. C.S. Major 121 H. Coy. R.E. threw sleigh by Wood, his head just behind Dressing Station. (slightly wounded) arrived at Headquarters at 6 p.m. in New Hut	

Wt. W.5111/1454 700,000 5/15 D.D.& L. A.D.S.S/Forms/C.2118.

Army Form C. 2118.

WAR DIARY
INTELLIGENCE SUMMARY.
(Erase heading not required.)

108th FIELD AMBULANCE. 5.

Place	Date	Hour	Summary of Events and Information	Remarks and references to Appendices
FORCEVILLE	17.3.16	6 p.m.	the plan of which is now completed.	
	19.3.16	10 a.m.	Took out ROAD WORKING PARTY near MARTINSART, work proceeding well.	
	19.3.16	9 a.m.	Picked 6 Marques immediately north of the church. This has been painted with a mixture of deep green and yellow paints to make the canvas less conspicuous.	
	20.3.16	11 a.m.	Inspection by D.M.S. 4th Army. (Surgeon General O'Keefe) he considers out building the Hospital & Hut ourselves to be very creditable, and it appears to me to be a useful piece of work and of solid construction and will accommodate 45 patients lying down. The Surgeon General also expressed himself as very pleased with our Transport, and Horses which we pride ourselves, and he considered our Billets to be in very good order. Proceeded to MARTINSART and inspected ADVANCED POST there. D.M.S. left FORCEVILLE at 12.40 p.m. after return from MARTINSART.	
	21.3.16	9.30 a.m.	Rode to MARTINSART. Walked from there through AVELUY WOOD to AUTHUILLE and visited Advanced Post there; all correct. Doorway will soon require additional strengthening above by (1) use three (2) Steel Rails. (3) Corrugated Iron (4) Sandbags. Walked back to MARTINSART and rode fourth across country after

2353 Wt. W.3544/1454 750,000 5/15 D.D.&L. A.D.S.S./Forms/C. 2118.

WAR DIARY
INTELLIGENCE SUMMARY

108th FIELD AMBULANCE.

Army Form C. 2118.

Instructions regarding War Diaries and Intelligence Summaries are contained in F.S. Regs., Part II. and the Staff Manual respectively. Title pages will be prepared in manuscript.

(Erase heading not required.)

Place	Date	Hour	Summary of Events and Information	Remarks and references to Appendices
PUCHEVILLEES		Evening	ENGLEBELMER relieves the distance to PUCHEVILLE by road.	
	22.8.16.	10 am	Rode to MARTINSART and AVELUY WOOD with D.A.D.M.S, walked to HAMEL ADVANCED POST, back to AVELUY WOOD and across mill (ANCRE) to AOTHUILLE, walked up to A.D. POST in "PAISLEY AVENUE", returned through AOTHUILLE and rode back to MARTINSART. Quiet. Left D.A.D.M.S. at MARTINSART. Rode across country to HEDAUVILLE and fenced there bush to PUCHEVILLE by road. Saw Officers Lieuts MATTHIAS and RIVERS.	
	23.8.16	6.30 pm	75th FIELD AMBULANCE at present lying at LIERCOURT, 6 miles E of ABBEVILLE arrived after three days motor journey. Lieut 1 Officer and 1 N.C.O. to MESNIL, 10 officers and 1 N.C.O. to AOTHUILLE, returned 1 N.C.O. at HEADQUARTERS. One June Bennoist MESNIL injured by falling sandbags in dug-out. The first casualty in the FIELD AMBULANCE.	
	23.8.16		Occupied new Hospital Hut.	
	24.8.16		Rode to MARTINSART; nothing of importance occurred.	
	25.8.16		Rode to MESNIL and visited Captain Scott A.D.M.S. and D.A.D.M.S.	

WAR DIARY

INTELLIGENCE SUMMARY.
(Erase heading not required.)

108th FIELD AMBULANCE

Army Form C. 2118.

Place	Date	Hour	Summary of Events and Information	Remarks and references to Appendices
FORCEVILLE	25/3/16	3.15 P.M.	Visited FIELD AMBULANCE Received orders then to VARENNES on Billeting scheme, returned at 4.45 P.M.	
	26/3/16 10 a.m.		Proceeded to MARTINSART, and we then from there by way of AVELUY WOOD to AOTHUILLE. Bearers Tent Subsection over MARSH in foot paths for Bearers without addition of stores whilst only one tent opened to receive cases. There are a few shell holes in the Authuille scheme to be filled up. Strengthening of DRESSING STATION at AOTHUILLE is now nearly completed.	
	27/2/16 11 a.m.		Rode by way of CHAIRFAYE to ACHEUX, Saw A.D.M.S. was D.A.D.M.S. I am probably a journal of Hut at our headquarters, this retofore my objecting tent for patients to bed in. Today relieving Officers at HAMEL, MESNIL, and AOTHUILLE. Capt. D. Hedd and Lieut. HERD, BURROWS to AOTHUILLE in relief of Capt. A.W. REA and Capt. R.M. WHITE. Capt. S. P. REA to MESNIL in relief of Capt. J. SCOTT, attended Conference Divisional Headquarters with A.D.M.S., D.A.D.M.S., acting O.C. 109th in Field Ambulance, acting O.C. 110th Field Ambulance.	

WAR DIARY

INTELLIGENCE SUMMARY.
(Erase heading not required.)

Army Form C. 2118.

108TH FIELD AMBULANCE.

Place	Date	Hour	Summary of Events and Information	Remarks and references to Appendices
FORCEVILLE	28.3.1916.	2 p.m.	Bail crew returned from out stations. Visit by D.D.M.S. and D.A.D.M.S. 10th Corps. Began to build additions to Hospital Hut. Recalled LIEUT. BURROWS from AUTHUILLE.	
	29.3.1916.	9.30 a.m.	LIEUT. BURROWS proceeded to CHAIRPAYE to join 110TH FIELD AMBULANCE. Visited MESNIL, HAMEL and AUTHUILLE with A.D.M.S. and D.A.D.M.S.	
	30.3.16.	9.30. a.m.	Proceeded to DOMART and bought 220 placards (tree names and nos.) for use in construction of Hut. Bought also 4 Lanterns and 2 galvanized iron vessels for water for use at Advanced Posts.	
	31.3.16.		No events worthy of record.	

John Fawcett
Lieut; Colonel,
O.C. 108th Field Ambulance

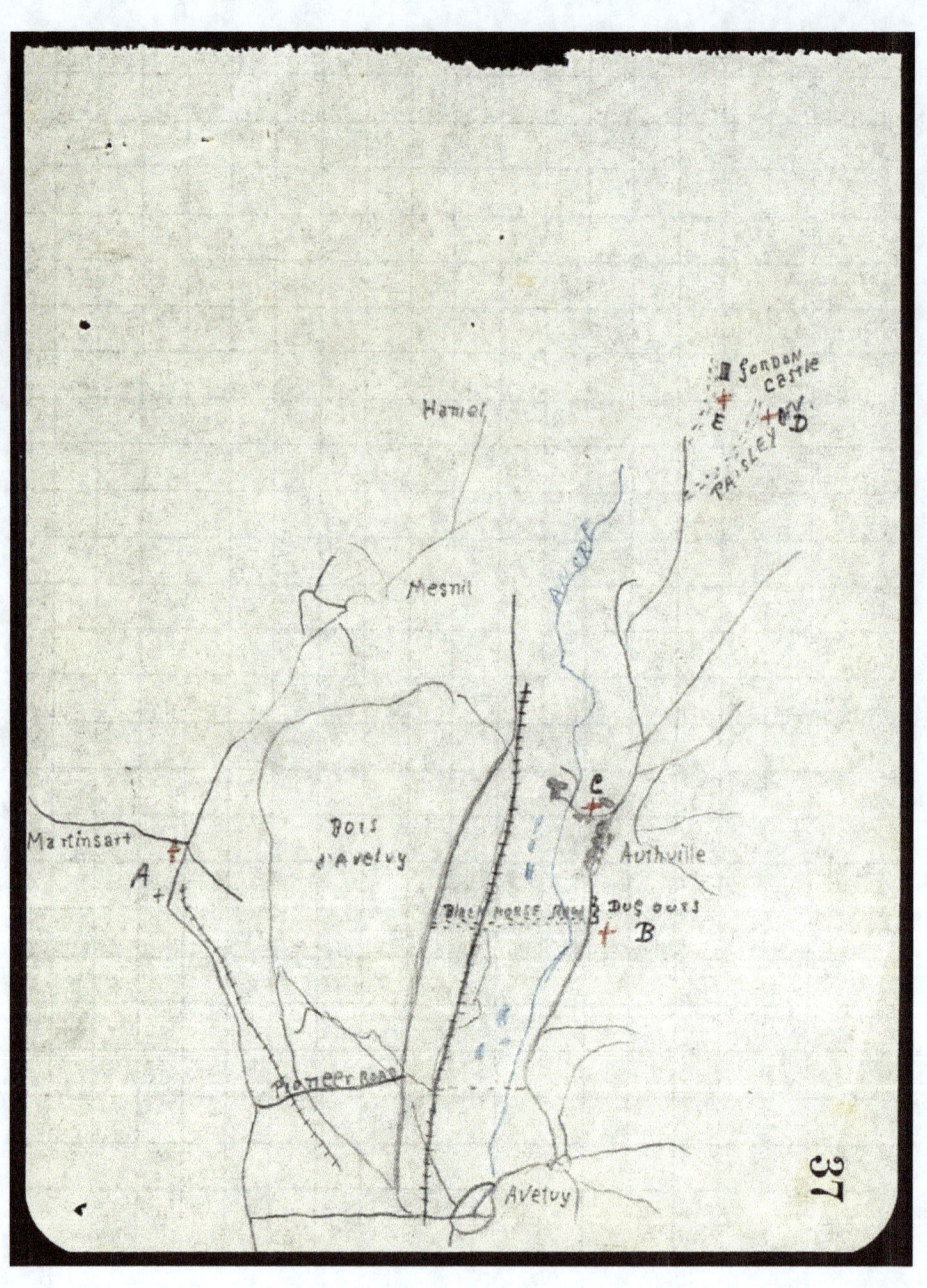

O.C. C Section 108 F.A.

Ref Enclosed Sketch

You will open an advanced Dressing Station at MARTINSART on the morning of the 5/2/16.

You will detail CAPT. S.P. REA with two N.C.O's and 18 men including a motor bicycle orderly to proceed from MARTINSART to BLACK HORSE BRIDGE at 8 a.m. 5/2/16. He will take over the advanced collecting post there and distribute his men as follows.

1. Two men will be sent to R.A.P. PAISLEY AVENUE, and two to R.A.P. GORDON CASTLE. They will be relieved every 24 hours and will remain there with Regtl. S.B's.
2. Four men to the Advanced post "C" in the village of AUTHUILLE
3. Two men to the baths
4. One man who will always stay at the Signal Office in AUTHUILLE to carry messages to the bearers when notified of a casualty.
5. The remaining men will stay at the DUG OUTS at "B".

He should bring with him three stretcher carriers and one motor bicycle.

2.

You will follow this scheme for evacuation of sick and wounded.

1. The casualty is brought into Gordon Castle or Peasley avenue. One of the bearers goes to the signal office which is quite close & sends a message to office at AUTHUILLE. The N.A.M.T. orderly brings the message to the man at B. Message should state whether serious or walking case & whether stretcher cases is brought up if required. Two men from C proceed up to the end of Peasley av., take over the casualty and bring him down to B. If it is not an urgent case he remains there till six have been collected, if serious the motor cycle orderly takes a message to MARTINSART where the cars remain. The cars can then go to BLACK HORSE BRIDGE. At night it is safe for the cars to go through AVELUY right up to AUTHUILLE

Army Form C. 2118.

Vol 7

WAR DIARY
or
INTELLIGENCE SUMMARY
(Erase heading not required.)

108th FIELD AMBULANCE

Instructions regarding War Diaries and Intelligence Summaries are contained in F.S. Regs., Part II. and the Staff Manual respectively. Title pages will be prepared in manuscript.

Place	Date	Hour	Summary of Events and Information	Remarks and references to Appendices
FORCEVILLE	1.4.1916	grand*	Sent motor lorry (Daimler 3 tons) to DOMART for wood purchased from 80th ——— R.E.	
	2.4.16		Rode to AUTHUILLE and examined shelters in AVELUY WOOD where our men are at work, found a good site across river and immediately to front of staff N. of AUTHUILLE	
	3.4.16	8.30 am	Proceeded to DOMART and bought 190 planks (blue stained and almost bought a large galvanised iron covered kennel in DOUILLEN'S for patients' station hut. D.M.S. and D.A.D.M.S. 4th army. and D.D.M.S. and D.A.D.M.S. 10th B.Corps, with A.D.M.S. and D.A.D.M.S. 36th Division visited Field Ambulance at 5 p.m. to look at retreat huts.	
	4.4.1916		Put up part of framework of Irwant hut between Church and — rectory; rode to MARTINSART and saw O.C. 121st Coy, R.E., re site of wood where saplings can be obtained.	
	5.4.16	10.30	Rode to HARPONVILLE and as C.R.E and Adjutant were out, wrote letter asking for sparing timber and fuel for huts with which to build eight huts. Rode to HEDAUVILLE at 3½ pm in search of wood. Obtained none.	

No. 2353. Wt. W3141454 700,000 5/15 D. D. & L.   A.D.S.S./Form/C. 2118.

WAR DIARY

INTELLIGENCE SUMMARY. 108th FIELD AMBULANCE.

Army Form C. 2118.

Place	Date	Hour	Summary of Events and Information	Remarks and references to Appendices
FORCEVILLE	6.4.16	9.30 A.M.	Rode to AVELUY WOOD to inspect progress of work on shelters. There are completed and two are progressing well; one completely evacuated. The other partially.	
	7.4.16		Spent the morning superintending the construction of HUTS. Rode to WARPONVILLE in the afternoon and returned orders from O.B.E. for tents and 5 x 3 trailers. MESNIL and HAMEL field last night by 9 shells chiefly casualties 4.3 wounded through the field ambulance one of whom we have. Rode to HEDAUVILLE in limber, arranged to see wood tomorrow.	
	8.4.16	10.0 a.m.	Rode to HEDAUVILLE and saw Lieutn. Col. Inwood, Enginrs arranged to cut wood required. Only one casualty last night. Lyt! P.W. WHITE relieved Captain J. WILSON in orderly charge of 12th R.I. RIFLES, sick.	
	9.4.16		Continued work on Huts.	
	10.4.16	9 a.m.	Took out a party and two G.S. Wagons to HEDAUVILLE WOOD and started to cut Sapling & fascines of dead Het, began carting loads of them in the afternoon. Rode to VARENNES in the afternoon and attended Conference with D.A.D.M.S., and O.O. 107th & 110th Field Ambulances. Relieved AUTHUILLE and MESNIL and HAMEL. No casualties treated.	
	11.4.16		Sent Q/M near Epluiz, loose green reed in Reserve near Orderly Room. Saw O.C. 107th Field Ambulance as relief of parties of this Unit at AUTHUILLE and MARTINSART.	

WAR DIARY
INTELLIGENCE SUMMARY
(Erase heading not required.)

Army Form C. 2118.

108th FIELD AMBULANCE

Place	Date	Hour	Summary of Events and Information	Remarks and references to Appendices
HERBEVAL	12/4/16	9.30 am	Walked AVELUY WOOD, walked down HAMEL ROAD TRENCH, walked over to FROMAGE. Enlarged width of TRENCH HEDGE to within its path, on being relieved today by party from 107th Field Ambulance walked to MARTINSART and received with CAPTAIN D.W. REA to WILLENCOURT his party on being relieved by party from 109 the Field Ambulance. Captain D.W. REA and party returned to HERBEVAL at 8 pm.	
	13/4/16	9.30 am	Walked to HEDAUVILLE. I am and CAPTAIN MOORE R.E. telephoned to 10 pm there we brought to HERBEVILLE where a party is at work cutting & fixing torses hospital huts. All buses stopped, telegraphed arrival of peas and men on leave.	
	14/4/16	9.30	Proceeded to AMIENS and bought materials for hospital and then went to DOMART and brought turpentine for new hut. Capt A.H.R. DUNCAN returned from leave.	CAPT. DUNCAN relieved CAPT S. PREA at MESNIL.
	15/4/16		Work as usual.	
	16/4/16	9 am	Regains work and received Hospital Hut. Hut is to be constructed of framework of scantling, fitted and with roof, sapling pieces and mud walls and wooden floor. It is to be 100 feet in length. 27 feet in width. 7 feet perpendicular height with a low pitched roofs one 20 in width. The DALLENCO, D.D.M.S. X Corps visited Ambulances.	

Army Form C. 2118.

WAR DIARY
or
INTELLIGENCE SUMMARY.   108th FIELD AMBULANCE   W/
(Erase heading not required.)

Place	Date	Hour	Summary of Events and Information	Remarks and references to Appendices
HEDAUVILLE	17.4.1916		Weather cold, damp and stormy. Sent Fatigue Party to cut saplings for HUT walls, in HEDAUVILLE WOOD. Lieut CAPTN in S.R. R.F.A. to DOMART to pay for timber used by R.A.M.C. to obtain an additional 100 planks. Capt: REA returned at 3:30 p.m. having obtained 150 additional planks, he brought back with him 380 planks, 300 these for roofing with felt faced so leaving 80 ples. The balance will have to be sent for probably by horse transport. Tested water for poisons in the afternoon/required. Patient admitted to hospital this afternoon with a temperature of 106.6°, mental condition clear, no skin eruptions, face covered with boils, possibly representing vertebra. Temperature reduced to 104.6° by sponging with cold water and ½ to Vini grette. No wounded admitted here today. Tarrant Hut completed and white washed, walls distempered.	
			Weather continues cold, wind's went with heavy rain. Walked to HEDAUVILLE WOOD to see amount of small wood that has been cut. D.A.D.M.S. called	
	18.4.16.	10.am	Again sent in to Lony to DOMART for planks, obtained 200, 200 purchased, still three separately demanded. Another cold, windy and rainy day. No casualties since Sunday. Capt S.J. SCOTT Litnant Fevers leave at 2.am.	
	20.4.1916		Work progressing well on second Hut, Heavy rain squalls rendering it difficult to cut turves' interact. A.B.S.S./Form C. 2118. A.B.S.S./Form Storey W. air chilly.	

Distempered whole of one top walls of Tarrant H.S.

Army Form C. 2118.

WAR DIARY
INTELLIGENCE SUMMARY
(Erase heading not required.)

108th FIELD AMBULANCE

61

Place	Date	Hour	Summary of Events and Information	Remarks and references to Appendices
MORCEVILLE	21.4.1916		Continued work on second Hut, baled out to HEDAUVILLE WOOD with Capt. S.P. BEA. a considerable amount of pine firewood is obtained there.	
	22.4.1916		Continued work on Hut.	
	23.4.1916		Work as usual. No casualties with the exception of one Officer, slightly wounded by shrapnel.	
	24.4.1916	8.30 a.m.	Proceeded to DOMART and hung out 24 bivvies for use in continuing of 2nd Hut. Called at BEAVAL on return journey to see about wound.	
	25.4.1916		Work as usual. No casualties. attended conference at A.D.M.S. Office at HEDAUVILLE at 8.30. p.m.	
	26.4.1916		Went to Captain S.P. BEA to BEAVAL and ABBEVILLE to canvas. Went to VARENNES - HARPONVILLE Road re chalk for floor of 2nd Hut. Captain A. HOOD relieved Captain A.H.B. DUNCAN at MESNIL. Weather warm and bright with a light westerly breeze.	
	27.4.1916	9 a.m.	Proceeded to AVELUY WOOD with Staff Sergt. Dixon. Steered him just on AVELUY - HAMEL ROAD at which to begin digging trench, returned at 10'30" a.m. 11 a.m. a fire broke out among the bombs stored in a hangar 70 yards E of Field Ambulance buildings, continuous and violent explosions took place until 12.30 p.m. when they became less frequent, but very violent. Took out a party of new guns at 12.30 p.m. and reported in ambulance over hills beneath the ground. One of our bullets	

WAR DIARY
INTELLIGENCE SUMMARY
(Erase heading not required.)

108th FIELD AMBULANCE

Army Form C. 2118.

Place	Date	Hour	Summary of Events and Information	Remarks and references to Appendices
MORCEVILLE	27.4.1916		Together with the history of the Unit &c, our division has cancelled during the week. Three casualties (slight) among infantry and artillery. Hospital bearing used their stretchers very frequently by bombs, two loads of the hutting being received every hour. Explosions continued until 3.30 p.m. CAPTAIN J. WILSON, R.A.M.C. founded in bottle pierced by shrapnel at HAMEL.	28.4.1916. Sent to AVELUY WOOD at 7 p.m. where later work on AVELUY WOOD-HAMEL communicating trench.
	28.4.1916	10 a.m.	Sent party with motor lorry to DOMART for balance of planks bought there (200). That not mentioned before wholly drunk). Went to TOUTENCOURT and drew 72000 to pay men going on leave and some office men at advanced posts on leave. Paying.	
		2 p.m.	Began to fill inside of postcastle to footdoth, fleet completed yesterday. Rein men going on leave and two others.	CAPT. BOYD CAMPBELL proceeded on leave.
		5.30 p.m.	Captain W. WHITE proceeded to HAMEL to form 12th Bn. Royal Irish Rifles.	
	29.4.1916	10 a.m.	Rode to CHAIR PAYE. No repairs have yet been made to the road between VARENNES and CHAIR PAYE which is in a very bad state for conveyance of wounded. Sent 6 stretchers to MESNIL for men in case of heavy casualties.	
	30.4.1916		Took wound cart to Cemetery to make note of new Church. Heavy thunder shower 3-4 p.m. Considerable account of heavy gun fire on our side all day.	

R. M. Fawcett
Lieut. Colonel,
O.C. 108th Field Ambulance.

May 1916.

108 = F. Amb.

COMMITTEE FOR THE
MEDICAL HISTORY OF THE WAR
Date   26 JUN 1915

Army Form C. 2118.

VH 8/1

WAR DIARY

INTELLIGENCE SUMMARY
(Erase heading not required.)

108th FIELD AMBULANCE

Instructions regarding War Diaries and Intelligence Summaries are contained in F. S. Regs., Part II. and the Staff Manual respectively. Title pages will be prepared in manuscript.

Place	Date	Hour	Summary of Events and Information	Remarks and references to Appendices
MORCEUILLE	1.5.1916	10 am	Rode to MARTINSART and arranged for working Party tomorrow morning in HAMEL VILLAGE. Arranged also for 1000 sandbags and 20 log pits to be sent to MESNIL. This evening for excavation of Shelters.	
	2.5.1916		Work as usual. Busy with houses & intervals.	
	3.5.1916		Went with A.D.M.S. to HAMEL by way of MESNIL to look at shelters for Regimental Aid Posts. Returned by way of AVELUY WOOD.	
	4.5.1916		Went to Cemetery and buried MAJOR EMERY up to date, 46 British soldiers buried there up to the present date.	
	5.8.16		Rode to MARLY and saw Hospital there.	
	6.5.16		Went to AVELUY WOOD. Walked from there to HAMEL VILLAGE, a few German shells passing over the village, went over trenches entering from narrow trench at rear village into the Fire trench. Looked at Regimental Aid Post. Inspected R.A.M.C. Post at HAMEL ROAD. Work in Hut as usual. CAPT. Q.W.REA reported from 13th Br. R.T. Rifles.	
	7.5.1916		Over fifty casualties brought in to ambulance between 11 am & 2 am & died of wounds on the German trenches not	
	8.5.1916		THIEPVAL WOOD. Went to ASHED and bought huts for use in construction of Huts. CAPT. Q.W.REA proceeded on leave.	
	9.5.16	8.30	Went to DOMART and bought timber from contractors of Huts & also nails, bolts and screws. CAPT. BOYD CAMPBELL returned from leave.	

2353 Wt. W3114/1454 700,000 5/15 D. D. & L.   A.D.S.S./Form/C. 2118.

Army Form C. 2118.

WAR DIARY
INTELLIGENCE SUMMARY
(Erase heading not required.)

108th FIELD AMBULANCE

Instructions regarding War Diaries and Intelligence Summaries are contained in F. S. Regs., Part II. and the Staff Manual respectively. Title pages will be prepared in manuscript.

Place	Date	Hour	Summary of Events and Information	Remarks and references to Appendices
FORCEVILLE	10·5·1916.	9.30 a.m.	Visited A.D.M.S. A/C Left for H.Q. by French Medical Board to CHAPPAYE at 3 P.M. and saw Lieut. Colonel DUNBAR, in command MRC.	
	11·5·1916.	10.30 a.m.	Rode to TOTENCOURT and drew Frs 6500 with which to pay the men used to pay for materials for the huts etc. Captain J.S. SCOTT joined of the ROYAL IRISH FUSILIERS on relief of CAPTAIN BERRY proceeding on 10 days leave to IRELAND. Paid the men.	Received consignment of timber from DOMART.
	12·5·1916.	8.30 a.m.	Work as usual. Began to lay church foundations for Reception Hut on hospital yard.	
		11.45 a.m.	Inspection by G.O.C. The Division. At the close of his inspection the G.O.C. informed me that he considered our arrangements to be very good, and that our Horse Transport was a pattern.	Received consignment of Timbers from DOMART
			Heavy rain and wind which made things wet 20 bags for MESNIL Shelter to clean, and sent INCO and 4 men in MOTOR AMBULANCE to MARTINSART to clean these stores and remove them to MESNIL went on to AVELUY WOOD and walked into HAMEL VILLAGE. Meet over all trenches which we have to deploy with Lieut. LYTTLE and visited them carefully.	
	12·6·1916.	9 a.m.	Proceeded to Regtl Aid Post. LIEUT JONES 12th R. I. Rifles informed me that the THORSDAD left 11th instant. CAPT P. WHITE R.A.M.C. went to the STONE BRIDGE by daylight, crawling 200 yards in the open in a very exposed position to attend a wounded rifleman who could not be removed until dusk. Inspected R.A.M.C. Post at AMBULANCE at 12.30 P.M.	

Army Form C. 2118.

WAR DIARY
or
INTELLIGENCE SUMMARY.
(Erase heading not required.)

108th FIELD AMBULANCE.

Instructions regarding War Diaries and Intelligence Summaries are contained in F. S. Regs., Part II. and the Staff Manual respectively. Title pages will be prepared in manuscript.

Place	Date	Hour	Summary of Events and Information	Remarks and references to Appendices
PERCEVILLE	14.5. 1916.	9 am	Took summary of evidence in case of Corpl. Williams re Cob. drunk on 12th instant. Visited MESNIL and saw the 76 in course of construction. Have officers commanding 121st Coy R.E. re strengthening of cellar roofs in HAM & VILLAGE. Visited A.D.M.S. re case of Corpl. Re Cobb acc'd offered leave to dispense with trial by court martial.	
	15.5. 1916.		Took evidence. Disposed of case of Corpl. Oprce Cobb by severely reprimanding him. Attended conference at A.D.M.S. office at 3.30 p.m. Nothing of importance discussed. Heavy cannonade round AUCHONVILLERS farm 12.20 am till 1.45 am. No casualties.	
	16.5. 1916.	10.20 am	Rode to AVELUY WOOD and saw some shelter which we have to evacuate. Only one casualty. Sent to ABBEVILLE and bought asbestos cured sheets for huts to remove dampness from hospital. Building to Aveluy wood.	
	17.5. 1916.		Continued work on huts. Rode to HEDAUVILLE at 3 p.m.	
	18.5. 1916.	9 am	Went to DOMART and purchased wood with which to complete second hut. Wagonload also needed. Lowered acc'd Potts. Knee. Resulted.	
	19.5. 1916.		Sent a fatigue party with G.S. Wagon to HEDAUVILLE WOOD. Rode there later, project is general of hospital, also one kind. Tel. Gothic Farm. By Lieut Col Frederick A.M.S. acc'd D.D.M.S. X Corps, at 3.45 p.m. Capt: A.W. REA returned off leave.	
	20.5. 1916.	9 am	Went pretty to HEDAUVILLE WOOD, rode there at 10 am, am attempting sending Kitchen. No casualties last night.	Received instructions to send Lt Tyndale from DOMART

Army Form C. 2118.

WAR DIARY
INTELLIGENCE SUMMARY.

of 108th FIELD AMBULANCE.

(Erase heading not required.)

Instructions regarding War Diaries and Intelligence Summaries are contained in F. S. Regs., Part II. and the Staff Manual respectively. Title pages will be prepared in manuscript.

Place	Date	Hour	Summary of Events and Information	Remarks and references to Appendices
MORCEVILLE	21.5.16. 1916.		Sent usual wood party to HEDAUVILLE WOOD. Rode there at 10 o'clock. No casualties. Last night. 1 LEO. & DUNDEE joined at 6.30 p.m. M.O.R.	21-5-1916. Capt. D'WREA proceeded to SCHOOL, NOYELLES ANTI-GAS
	22.5. 1916.	9.30. a.m.	Rode to AVELUY WOOD and inspected work on trench to HAMEL and shelter in AVELUY WOOD at present being excavated by our men. LIEUT. C. DUNDEE joined at 6.30. p.m. No casualties. Relieved HAMEL and B. MESNIL.	
	23.6. 1916		Evacuated two sitting cases. Officers covered in Lieut L.S. Wagon and party to MARTINSART. Saw 2000 ft planks. Work on hut as usual.	
	24.5. 1916.		Drew balance of 2000 ft planks from MARTINSART. Rode to HEDAUVILLE. Employment for logs obtained. Heavy rain in evening. CAPT. TREA returned. CAPT. L. HOLL. at MESNIL. CAPT. BOYD CAMPBELL returned from MARTINSART.	
	25.5. 1916		Completed flooring of second hut, begun shelter N. of Chulchtower, to provide for the being looted.	
	26.5. 1916.		Went to AVELUY WOOD with CAPT. DUNLOP; walked to HAMEL VILLAGE, inspected the trench being dug by men of this AMBULANCE. This communicates from the road (where it is intended to underground trench leading to foot of village and Reg. AID POST) with a cellar at present occupied by Rouen Company but to be used as an AID POST in case of heavy fighting. From the lone of this below an opening leads into an old ordnance French trench. This will be deepened and widened and will then form a good means of communication to a trench 40 yards E. running at right angles to which be succeeded by way of the trench will be altered.	

2353 W. W5H/1154. 700,000. 5/15 D. D. & L.
A.D.S.S./Form/C. 2118.

Army Form C. 2118.

WAR DIARY
or
INTELLIGENCE SUMMARY.
(Erase heading not required.)

108th Field Ambulance

Instructions regarding War Diaries and Intelligence Summaries are contained in F. S. Regs., Part II. and the Staff Manual respectively. Title pages will be prepared in manuscript.

Place	Date	Hour	Summary of Events and Information	Remarks and references to Appendices
ROBECOURT	26.5. 1916		Named JOHNSE AVENUE. Inspected ADVANCED POST at HANEL. Bomb shell fell wood inspecting field across the road on the way back to AVELUY WOOD. Inspected work it shelter in AVELUY WOOD. Cricket and DRUM and Flute contest in evening in Reception Hut on Foot-paths.	Began to
	27.5. 1916	10 a.m.	New Hut now completed except for west windows. Captain R. DUNCAN proceeded to 12 th R.I. Rifles in relief of Capt. P. WHITE proceeding on leave, and Capt. A. HOGG proceeded to 10th R.I. Rifles in relief of Capt. GRAHAM, proceeding on leave. Finished Cook's Shelter. Rode to MARTINSART and walked to MESNIL. Inspected shelter in course of construction. Went to DOULLENS in the afternoon and bought equipment for advanced Posts. It is difficult to obtain water except from a distance, so that it is necessary to keep a supply in covered hot water kettles at advanced posts. Also water to conveyed daily from F. A. Hdqrs. by ambulance wagon.	Begin new Cook's shelter. MARCEVILLE MAILLES UX. Picked from trench head (Capper's) licking.
	28.5. 1916		Work as usual. Rode to CHAIRFAYE, returning through ACHEUX. Completed oven in Cook's Shelter. Completed Frame of Reception Hut.	
	29.5. 1916	10 a.m.	Rode to AVELUY WOOD. Inspected shelter there. Excavation will be completed today. Stopped at MARTINSART and on the way back had seen MAJOR CRAIG, R.E. and MAJOR HARDY, R.E. arranged for furnishing of materials with vehicle to complete shelter in AVELUY WOOD. attended conference at VARENNES at 2.30 p.m. with D.A.D.M.S. and O.C. 108th & 109th Field Ambulances. Subject of above report. Loads of ammunition.	MARCEVILLE and ACHEUX Shells Picked from Trench head some fuse and no casualties. but two men with hip Jan Offs. etc.

Army Form C. 2118.

WAR DIARY
or
INTELLIGENCE SUMMARY.
(Erase heading not required.)   108th FIELD AMBULANCE.

Instructions regarding War Diaries and Intelligence Summaries are contained in F. S. Regs., Part II. and the Staff Manual respectively. Title pages will be prepared in manuscript.

Place	Date	Hour	Summary of Events and Information	Remarks and references to Appendices
POREEVILLE	29.5. 1916	2.30. P.m.	Sent to DOULLENS for Putty and Screws, also wire gauze to put at foot in billets from flies.	
	30.5. 1916		Heavy rain during the night. Drill and chilly. Work as usual. Begun to make truck in order to be able to remove more rapidly the dressings, clothing etc to Incinerator. Hut to used to counter occupied by A.S.C. Wagons and horses in order to make room for Divisional Train. Placed A.S.C. and horses together in two marquees about 50 6 inch shells fell between POREEVILLE and SUCRERIE, ACHEUX, between 1 P.m. and 4 P.m.	
	31.5. 1916	3.15 P.m.	Work as usual. Weather hot with no wind. Inspection by Surgeon general MACPHERSON. Fourteen wounded from MESNIL.	

R F M Fawcett
Lieut. Colonel,
O.C. 108th Field Ambulance.

No 108 Field Ambulance

June 1916

51

COMMITTEE FOR THE
MEDICAL HISTORY OF THE WAR
Date 31 AUG 1916

WAR DIARY

INTELLIGENCE SUMMARY

Army Form C. 2118.

108th FIELD AMBULANCE

June Vol 9

Place	Date	Hour	Summary of Events and Information	Remarks and references to Appendices
FORCEVILLE	1.6.1916	10 a.m.	Evacuation of yesterday's casualties. Work on improvements and usual. Some considerable improvements in Hospital Building arrangements suggested by Capt R. DUNLOP. Some of these can be carried out at once, the rest will be effected as soon as I can obtain more building material. Visit by A.D.M.S., 49th Division. Capt 4. W. REA and LIEUT. C. DUNDEE proceeded to MESNIL; Capt. S.P. REA returned from MESNIL.	
	2.6.1916.		Work as usual. Nothing worthy of record.	
	3.6.1916.	9 a.m.	Proceeded to DOMART and bought a bulk lot of timber, planks and lathes, for use in the lining of main hospital building and for Head tents in Huts; went also to FRANSU and FRANQUEVILLE in search of small logs for piecing scheme by Torow means of FORCEVILLE, was unable to obtain any. Returned at 4.45 p.m.	
	4.6.1916		Visit to Field Ambulance by A.D.M.S. at noon. Visited A.D.M.S. Gazetted Companion of the DISTINGUISHED SERVICE ORDER by command of His Gracious Majesty, to whom God Send	

Army Form C. 2118.

WAR DIARY
or
INTELLIGENCE SUMMARY.   108TH FIELD AMBULANCE.
(Erase heading not required.)

Instructions regarding War Diaries and Intelligence Summaries are contained in F. S. Regs., Part II. and the Staff Manual respectively. Title pages will be prepared in manuscript.

Place	Date	Hour	Summary of Events and Information	Remarks and references to Appendices
FORCEVILLE	4.6. 1916.		Long life and many years of peace after this permanent aid for men crocked. Rode to WARLOY. Weathercock just so visited. Breezes and blowing up for rain.	
	5.6. 1916.		Work as usual. Heavy rain during the night and early morning. MART IN SAFT. Last admitted party of 8 men to be billeted in "H" hut who work in HAMEL. Sent in recommendations for military medal. Recommended Pte Arthur Grinfield and Holmes for gallantry during the bombardment of AUTHUILLE during the night of March 10th 1916.	
	6.6. 10 am 1916.		Visited A.D.M.S. was still very unwell so decided not to visit the trenches in HAMEL. MAJOR BOYHAN SMITH, D.A.D.M.S. left to join VIII Corps and the sun is expected. Am at present putting a large glass window into west end of No 2 hut. It looks well and will give plenty of light.	
	7.6. 1916.		Heavy rain and hail during the morning. Sent to HEDAUVILLE for a load of clinkers to improve floor of Reception hut with.	

1577 Wt.W10791/1773 500,000 1/15 D. D. & L.   A.D.S.S./Forms/C. 2118.

Army Form C. 2118.

WAR DIARY

~~INTELLIGENCE SUMMARY.~~
(Erase heading not required.)

108th FIELD AMBULANCE. 3.

Place	Date	Hour	Summary of Events and Information	Remarks and references to Appendices
PERCEVIMRE	4/6/1916.	10 a.m.	Rode to TOUTENCOURT and drew 76000 with which to pay the Unit: 1000 Told by Paymaster that LORD KITCHENER had gone down in H.M.S. HAMPSHIRE, and send it is nature but I greatly fear that it is	Complete window in No 2, Hut.
	5/6/1916.	2.p.m. 5.p.m.	Paid the men Visit by A.D.M.S. and new D.A.D.M.S. at 3.P.M. News of Lord Kitchener's death confirmed. Heavy rain at night. CAPTAIN HODD unable to go on leave owing to fall from horse. Lieut SEROTT LOWE instead.	
	8/6/1916.	9 a.m.	Sent to MARTINSART for 1000 Sandbags with which to strengthen roofs of shelters in HAMEL. Road cut at MESNIL. CAPTAIN R. DUNLOP proceeded on visit to No 26. Gen. Hospital: ÉTAPLES. Brought Impt Cemetery up to date. Obtained Sandbags and despatched 500 of them to HAMEL.	
	9/6/1916.	9.30. a.m.	Went to HAMEL and MESNIL with A.D.M.S. and D.A.D.M.S. Rearyanis in the afternoon. No casualties.	
	10/6/1916.		CAPT HOG seconded to Officers Hospital d'ESAINCOURT, worked as aerial. Rode to SENLIS. Anyhow rain and breeze in the morning: Somewhat in the afternoon. Visit by D.D.M.S. at 5.11. a.m.	
	11/6/1916.		Thirty casualties last night from HAMEL and THIEPVAL WOOD. Evacuated 20 at 5.10 a.m. Visited A.D.M.S. who wrote of consignment of 3 sightly wounded to PUCHEVILLERS.	Capt'n L DUNLOP returned from ÉTAPLES.

1577 Wt. W10791/1773 500,000 1/15 D. D. & L. A.D.S.S./Forms/C. 2118.

Army. Form C. 2118.

WAR DIARY
INTELLIGENCE SUMMARY.
(Erase heading not required.)

108th FIELD AMBULANCE

Instructions regarding War Diaries and Intelligence Summaries are contained in F. S. Regs., Part II. and the Staff Manual respectively. Title pages will be prepared in manuscript.

Place	Date	Hour	Summary of Events and Information	Remarks and references to Appendices
PUCHEVILLERS	12.6.1916.		Work as usual. Weather cold with slight snow. 3.30 p.m. Nothing of importance occurred.	
	13.6.1916.		Weather continued wet and cold. Continued work as settled in AVELUY WOOD.	
	14.6.1916.	2.30 a.m.	Proceeded to DONART and brought timber and material for use in construction of doors for Reception Hut and seats for M.S. Wagons. Completed ANTI-GAS curtains at MESNIL. Visited CRAIRFAYE; visited A.D.M.S.	CAPT. S.P. REA returned from leave.
	15.6.1916.		Received Ton of Straw and filled 180 Pillows, put a second Stove in Reception Hut, put in arrangements for Table, Store in Reception Hut; Furniture Officers' Mess and Quarters etc.; there is improvement specifically due to the exertions Continual running up Teather; energy and ingenuity of CAPT. J. M. DUNHOE, a good number of fairly heavy shells fell in the neighbourhood at midnight (French battery here crew HOSSOX), there is with one enemy plane and the house over which they landed. No	CAPT. A. WREA relieved by LIEUT. C. DUNBER at MESNIL

Casualties. CAPT. L. HOGG returned from leave. Officer 4 SAINEDOTT

LIEUT. T. TEWKESBURY returned from leave. Weather chilly but fine.

1577 Wt.W10791/1773 500,000 1/15 D.D. & L. A.D.S.S./Forms/C. 2118.

Army Form C. 2118.

WAR DIARY
INTELLIGENCE SUMMARY.
(Erase heading not required.)

108th FIELD AMBULANCE.

Instructions regarding War Diaries and Intelligence Summaries are contained in F.S. Regs., Part II. and the Staff Manual respectively. Title pages will be prepared in manuscript.

Place	Date	Hour	Summary of Events and Information	Remarks and references to Appendices
PORCEVILLE	16.6.1916.	9 am	Sent carpenter to AVELUY WOOD to erect ANTI-GAS curtains in Shelter No.2. Removed one stone from Reception Hut and placed it in the cricolo. Sent for another Ton of stones for pillaroes. This arrived at 6 pm.	
	17.6.1916.	9 am and	Went to AVELUY WOOD with Capt. D.W. REA and Capt. S.P. REA; walked from there to HAMEL and went round trenches throughout the village by new Communication trenches. R.A.M.C. party working near AVELUY WOOD acted inspected Shelters. have made good progress for the purpose of evacuating wounded, returned to AVELUY WOOD and inspected ANTI-GAS curtains. Sent up stores and water to AVELUY WOOD in the afternoon. Proceeded to MESNIL and inspected shelters there, sent up kerosene oil and shell dumps in the afternoon. Gave Capt. D.W. REA his instructions as to duties in AVELUY WOOD.	
	18.6.1916.	9.30 am	Proceeded to MESNIL and met the D.D.M.S. X Corps with Capt. BERRY, R.A.M.C. Walked to HAMEL by way of "JACOB'S LADDER" and went round the trenches. Returned to MESNIL and so back to PORCEVILLE. Sent up sixteen Lantern, 25 Stretchers and 25 Blankets to MESNIL.	

1577 Wt. W10791/1773 500,000 1/15 D.D. & L. A.D.S.S./Forms/C. 2118.

WAR DIARY
INTELLIGENCE SUMMARY.
(Erase heading not required.)

108th FIELD AMBULANCE.

Army Form C. 2118.

G.1

Place	Date	Hour	Summary of Events and Information	Remarks and references to Appendices
FORCEVILLE	19.6.1916.	9 a.m.	Paid small party (6) for AVELUY WOOD. Capt d.W. REA and party of 24 men with T.N.C.O. and MOTOR CYCLIST (Two A.S. WAGONS with Stores) proceeded to AVELUY WOOD. Took out and inspected road for outward journey of motor AMBULANCES. (see attached sketch map). Also C to O/C the journey through HEDAUVILLE sent cars from the S. end of FORCEVILLE to a point 600 yards below branching of road to ENGLEBELMER. It is very rough and will probably cause enemy punctures to AMBULANCE Tyres. Began shelter trench for men in farmyard; one also for A.S.C. in Chateau grounds. Attended Conference at A.D.M.S.s office at 3'80' p. obs.	
	20.6.1916.	10 a.m.	Continued digging shelter trenches in yard and in front wood. Rode by way of BOUZINCOURT and MARTINSART WOOD to AVELUY WOOD. Many new guns of various caliber and the Germans stopping shells into AUTHUILLE. The 5 inch Trench Howitzers have Capt. d.W. REA, R.E. party has not got rast or alters in The wood to mind our men leave to be worried. When returning saw enemy heavy light and shells bursting just S. of ENGLEBELMER,	

Army Form C. 2118.

WAR DIARY
INTELLIGENCE SUMMARY
(Erase heading not required.)

108th FIELD AMBULANCE

Place	Date	Hour	Summary of Events and Information	Remarks and references to Appendices
PERCEVILLERS	20.6.1916	2 p.m.	Sent a Solaley MOTOR AMBULANCE to MARTINSART to report to D.D.M.S. R.A.M.C. But there in accordance with instructions from A.D.M.S.	
	21.6.1916		So little worthy of record.	
	22.6.1916	6.30 a.m.	Rode to CHATRFAYE and saw Col. DUNBAR.	
			re Army.	
	23.6.1915	7.30 a.m.	Rode to AVELUY WOOD and saw arrangements made by Capt D.W. BEA to receive wounded; he has accommodation in shelters for 40 lying down cases. Heavy rain in The afternoon. Bombardment of Thiepval line started at 4 p.m. Inspection by Brigadier Genl Jetts Pte Corps.	
	24.6.1916		Nothing worthy of record except that bombardment continued.	
	25.6.1916	10.30 a.m.	Rode over to CHATRFAYE and saw Col. DUNBAR. Bombardment heavy all day and night. Capt D. HOGG, 1 N.C.O. and 9 men left for temporary duty at GEZAINCOURT.	
	26.6.1916		Stayed up all night but there were only 5 casualties. Bombardment very heavy in morning; less heavy from 1 p.m. till 4 p.m.	

Army Form C. 2118.

WAR DIARY
INTELLIGENCE SUMMARY.
(Erase heading not required.)

108th FIELD AMBULANCE.

Place	Date	Hour	Summary of Events and Information	Remarks and references to Appendices
FORCEVILLE	27/6/1916.		Busy all day; casualties coming in at intervals; about 82 admissions of wounded to this Ambulance; sent in addition 50 slightly wounded to 110th FIELD AMBULANCE at CLAIRFAYE. Bombardment continued all day.	
	28/6/1916.		Staged up all night. Bombardment heavy during most of the night; shells passed over FORCEVILLE at 2 a.m. and fell in ACHEUX. Admitted 50 wounded. Heavy rain all day until 4 P.M., weather mild with leg. at. Desultory breeze; heavy shelling by ourselves throughout the day.	
	29/6/1916.		Bombardment not so heavy during the night. Bernalles arrived throughout the night; 8 of whom died before 8 am. Weather mild, fields wettedly breeze; slight showers during the morning.	
	30/6/1916.		Bombardment continued all day; fair number of casualties arriving. Weather n.f.	

B Hutewett
Lieut. Colonel.
O.C., 108th Field Ambulance

36th Division

108th Field Ambulance

July 1916

36 July
Army Form C. 2118.

WAR DIARY

INTELLIGENCE SUMMARY. 108TH FIELD AMBULANCE

VR 10

(Erase heading not required.)

Place	Date	Hour	Summary of Events and Information	Remarks and references to Appendices
FOREEVILLE	1/7/916		S and wounded from THIEPVAL began to arrive, walking cases with wounded, admitted all cases able to walk to TARRANT HUT and church. Cases were fed in the hut and church and dispatched in the church and used their section to CHATEAUVE.	
	2/7/916		Continued there all day. D.M.S. & the army stopped our evacuation for this base. This filling us up almost to our full capacity with stretcher cases. During first 12 hours we admitted 600 stretcher cases. Work of admission and evacuation continued all through the night of 1st – 2nd and onwards for anybody, all arrangements to evacuate worked perfectly.	
	3/7/916		Work killed for two hours and then became as heavy as before, but we were well able to cope with all cases by borrowing two M.O's from 127 and West Riding Field Ambulance. Two gave our officers a little rest.	
	4/7/916		Worked through last night and all through day. North of enemy guns were silenced.	

1577 Wt. W10791/1773 500,000 1/15 D. D. & L. A.D.S.S./Forms/C. 2118.

WAR DIARY
INTELLIGENCE SUMMARY

Army Form C. 2118.

108th FIELD AMBULANCE

Place	Date	Hour	Summary of Events and Information	Remarks and references to Appendices
POTENCOURT	4/7/16	—	Advance party of 2 Officers and 30 N.C.O's & men 1st/3rd West Riding Field Ambulance arrived at 8 p.m.	TOTAL Personnel Through PIELD AMB 1725 from 1·7·1916 to 5·7·1916
	5/7/16		Worked till 12 noon by which time we had cleared all best there was, leaving over all buildings and surplus equipment to 1st/2nd West Riding Field Ambulance. Marched from POTENCOURT to TOTTENCOURT and reached HUTS.	
		8.30 p.m	arrived at TOTTENCOURT and occupied HUTS	
POTENCOURT	6/7/16		have rested in Quarters	
	7/7/16		Heavy rain throughout the day, no remarks	
	8/7/16			
	9/7/16		Received orders to march at 7.15 a.m. for GEZAINCOURT	
	10/7/16	7.15am	marched at 7.15 a.m. arrived at GEZAINCOURT at 10.30 a.m.	
GEZAINCOURT		3.30 p.m	marched at 6 a.m. arrived at NEUVILETTE at 10.30 a.m.	
	11/7/16		Rested in BILLETS	
NEUVILETTE	11/7/16	11.30 P.M	marched from NEUVILETTE, arrived at PREVENT at 2.30 am.	

Army Form C. 2118.

WAR DIARY
INTELLIGENCE SUMMARY. 108TH FIELD AMBULANCE
(Erase heading not required.)

Instructions regarding War Diaries and Intelligence Summaries are contained in F. S. Regs., Part II. and the Staff Manual respectively. Title pages will be prepared in manuscript.

Place	Date	Hour	Summary of Events and Information	Remarks and references to Appendices
FRÉVENT	12/7/16	2.30 a.m.	Entrained, left by train at 5.30 a.m.	
	12/7/16	8.30 a.m.	Arrived at STEENBECQUE. Marched to CAMPAGNE, halting en route for breakfast.	
CAMPAGNE	12/7/16	5 p.m.	Arrived at 5 p.m. Put up in BILLETS. Village very clean.	
	13/7/16	1.30 p.m.	Marched from CAMPAGNE, through ARQUES and ST OMER, arrived at EPERLEQUES at 6 p.m., went into Billets at Chateau	
EPERLEQUES			The CHATEAU la VERGETRY. 110 other ranks placed in Billets. Put up 2 marquees for men who could not be accommodated in Billets.	
	14/7/16	11 a.m.	Visit by A.D.M.S. Began to take in sick from 107TH and 108TH Brigades.	
	15/7/16		Proceeded to ST OMER to obtain performance motor-lorries, returned to ST OMER at 5 p.m. and applied for 75100 to be drawn on 17TH instant.	
	16/7/16	2.30 p.m.	Visit by D.M.S. 2nd Army (Surgeon General PORTER). Drizzling rain falling from 2 to 5 p.m.	
	17/7/16	9 a.m.	Proceeded to ST OMER and drew ₣7,5100, paid men at 2 p.m. Finished construction of urinals and ablution stand.	

Army Form C. 2118.

WAR DIARY
INTELLIGENCE SUMMARY. 108th FIELD AMBULANCE.

(Erase heading not required.)

Instructions regarding War Diaries and Intelligence Summaries are contained in F.S. Regs., Part II. and the Staff Manual respectively. Title pages will be prepared in manuscript.

Place	Date	Hour	Summary of Events and Information	Remarks and references to Appendices
EPERLEQUES.			Rain in the morning but fine weather from noon. Visit by	
	18.7. 16.	6.p.m.	Sanitary Officer 2nd Army (Lieut. Colonel B. Brown) at 5 p.m. Received orders to move at 10 am tomorrow to BOLLEZEELE AREA	
	19.7. 16.	7.30 am	for WATOU. Began to pack wagons and transport with of patients to Divisional Rest Station.	
	20.7. 1916.	10 am	marched from CHATEAU de VERDETRY, through EPERLEQUES to WATTEN – halted at summit of hill – admiring interested ABBEY (12th Century) – halted 3/4 mile S.E. of BOLLEZEELE.	
BOLLEZEELE.	21.7. 1916.	9 am	marched from BOLLEZEELE through MERKELHEM ESQUELBECQ, NORDHOUDT, HERZEELE, to WATOU, arrived at WATOU at 4 p.m. very fine BILLETS for officers and men.	
WATOU.	22.7. 1916.	10 am	marched from WATOU through ABEELE, BOESCHEPE, BERTHEN, ST JANS CAPPEL, BAILLEUL, to LA RAVETSBURG (1 mile E.J of BAILLEUL) This is an encampment of huts used as a Divml Rest Station. 60th Fd. Field Ambulance in occupation. Arranged accommodations with them. Reported arrival to A.D.M.S. Took over Buildings stores and equipment from 60th Fd Field AMB.	Arrived RAVETSBURG at 1.15 p.m.

Army Form C. 2118.

WAR DIARY
INTELLIGENCE SUMMARY 108TH FIELD AMBULANCE.
(Erase heading not required.)

Place	Date	Hour	Summary of Events and Information	Remarks and references to Appendices
KEMMEL DURG.	23/7 1916.	9 am.	Sent LIEUT. C. DUNDEE to join 12th R.I. RIFLES as M.O. Proceeded to ADVANCED POSTS, school 101. POST, 1 Mile S.W. of NEUVE EGLISE by CAPT HODG. 1 M.O. and 4 men, not post, 1 Mile N.E. of NEUVE EGLISE by CAPT S.P. REA 2 N.C.O.S and 4 men. 3 men with 1 N.C.O. to be posted at Regimental AID POST at LA DOUVE FARM. Regarded base furnished to LA Regimental AID POST (for 2 BATTALIONS) Patrol 1 MOTOR AMBULANCE at No. 1. POST and 1 car at No. 2 POST. We have to to report up daily with Rations. Passed orders to act as Divisional Rest Station from Tournai. This unit is collecting casualties from 108th and 109th BRIGADES.	
	24/7	10.30 am	Visited to take in patients. Visit by A.D.M.S. at 2.30 p.m. Visit Colonel Downing Matron and Regimental AID POST with M.A.D.M.S. Picked two additional marquees to extra additional accommodation. To for patients for patients from 60 th Field ambulance. This unit marked packet 9.8 and.	

Army Form C. 2118.

WAR DIARY

INTELLIGENCE SUMMARY. 108th FIELD AMBULANCE.

(Erase heading not required.)

Place	Date	Hour	Summary of Events and Information	Remarks and references to Appendices
LA THIEVETOBOIS	25/7/1916.		Picked loaded wagons immediately W. of camp. Nothing of importance occurred.	
	26/7/1916.		No remarks	
	27/7/1916.		No remarks	
	28/7/1916.		Loaded collected sick from 109th Brigade.	
	29/7/1916. 2.47 P.M.		Visited Advanced Posts. Sent up additional stores to both Posts. Evacuated Capt. H. DUNCAN to HAZEBROUCK. Lieut. Sowerby joined for duty.	
	30/7/1916.		Destroyed obsoleted and useless correspondence. Wrote to C.R.E. re supply of materials with which to strengthen advanced dummy stations. Capt. P.W. WHITE joined for duty.	
	31/7/1916. 10.30 a.m.		Inspection of camp by A.D.M.S. Weather extremely hot, dry and dusty.	

31/7/1916.

Lieut. George F. Sillar Ambulance
O.C. 108th Field Ambulance

36th Div (Ulster)

108th Field Ambulance

August 1916

Army Form C. 2118.

WAR DIARY

INTELLIGENCE SUMMARY.
(Erase heading not required.) 108TH FIELD AMBULANCE

Instructions regarding War Diaries and Intelligence Summaries are contained in F. S. Regs., Part II. and the Staff Manual respectively. Title pages will be prepared in manuscript.

Place	Date	Hour	Summary of Events and Information	Remarks and references to Appendices
LE TRAMBLE, BERG.	1.8.1916	10 am	Rode to LE SEUTHE (NEUVE EGLISE ROAD) ang it to obtain wires of timber, sandbags, and nails. Tomorrow also looked wire. Visited Dummy Station at TROIS ROIS returned by way of NEUVE EGLISE VILLAGE. Inspection of Points - Tyne Helmets. Capt. L. DUNLOP rejoined.	
	2.8.1916		No remarks.	
	3.8.1916		Laid up with influenza. Visit by D.D.M.S.	
	4.8.1916		No remarks.	
	5.8.1916		Visit by A.D.M.S.	
	6.8.1916		Lt. Col. amn. Crofts. BOYD CAMPBELL relieved Capt. S. TOBEA at Advanced Post, KHANDAHAR FARM.	
	7.8.1916		Arranged to hint points of field as extra accommodation for Field Ambulances at Trones Querelle.	

Army Form C. 2118.

WAR DIARY

INTELLIGENCE SUMMARY. 108th FIELD AMBULANCE

(Erase heading not required.)

Instructions regarding War Diaries and Intelligence Summaries are contained in F. S. Regs., Part II and the Staff Manual respectively. Title pages will be prepared in manuscript.

Place	Date	Hour	Summary of Events and Information	Remarks and references to Appendices
LE RAVENS BERG	8.8. 1916.		Nomovements.	
	9.8. 1916.	2.p.m.	Paid men. Drew from FIELD CASHIER 75600 for this purpose	
	10.8. 1916.	11.20 a.m.	Proceeded to ST OMER and drew Indian C Street.	
	11.8. 1916.	9 a.m.	Proceeded to TROIS ROIS and paid Indian detachment stationed there.	
	12.8. 1916.	10.15 a.m.	Visit by D.D.M.S.	
	13.8. 1916.	11 a.m.	Visit by A.A. & Q.M.G.	
	14.8.1916.		Heavy showers during the day.	
	15.8. 1916.	9.30 a.m.	Sifted advanced Post at TROIS ROIS and KHANDAHAR FARM, good progress is being made at Sand bagging the building W. of the NEUVE EGLISE — WULVERGHEM ROAD. Withdrew two men from TROIS ROIS	

Army Form C. 2118.

WAR DIARY
INTELLIGENCE SUMMARY.
(Erase heading not required.)

108th FIELD AMBULANCE

Place	Date	Hour	Summary of Events and Information	Remarks and references to Appendices
LE RAVEN BERG	15.8.1916		Tractor Mercey Autoplio at Mained Quarry Patrols, Heavy rain from 11.20 am to 4 p.m.	
	16.8.1916	10 am	Proceeded to BAILLEUL and bought Bricks and piping for Drying Room. Sent for 500 Bricks for use in constructing drains.	
	17.8.1916		Half of field occupied by one Transport taken over by 4 & 5th MOBILE VETERINARY SECTION (Capt CHOWNE.) Visit by A.D.M.S. at 10.30 am. Heavy rain from 2 p.m. till 3.30 7.M.D. this to O.R.E. re manure for roads and seed bricks for horse standings. Work continued on Drying Room.	
	18.8.1916			
	19.8.1916		Obtained wooden boarding for front of mens' marquees.	
	20.8.1916		Obtained additional bricks and began new incinerator.	
	21.8.1916		Visit by G.O.C. 36th Division at noon, finished Drying Room with exceptions of Stove piping.	
	22.8.1916		Proceeded to BAILLEUL and arranged to send for Stove piping. Bought food books to be used in having away felt roofs for Flannel Stove piping. Began shelter for washing place & field platform.	

WAR DIARY
INTELLIGENCE SUMMARY

(Erase heading not required.) 108th FIELD AMBULANCE

Army Form C. 2118.

Place	Date	Hour	Summary of Events and Information	Remarks and references to Appendices
LE TRAHET. BERG.	23.8.1916.	9.30. a.m.	Proceeded to BAILLEUL and bought two trowels for pickaxes. Continued work on shelter for watering platform. Finished new incinerator. Began road in Transport Lines, having obtained 100 fascines from R.E. Parks de SEULE. Old hutr is not yet forthcoming though I have already sent lorries to NIEPPE for it.	
	24.8.1916.	9.30. a.m.	Proceeded to BAILLEUL and saw O.C. No 2. Casualty clearing station re days for admissions of casualties. Obtained two men handled for pic hooks. Continued making of road and wagon stand in Transport Lines. The road is being constructed of fascines, earth and broken bricks. Inspection of gas helmets. Obtained one load old brick.	
	25.9.1916.		Work as usual. Sent Capt S.F. REA to relieve Lieut. C. DUNDEE (12 R.IRIFLES). Sent Capt P.W. WHITE to relieve Capt S.F. REA (TROIS ROIS).	
	26.8.1916.	9.15. a.m.	Visited KHANDAR FARM and TROIS ROIS with Lieut. TEWKESBURY, visited A.D.M.S. at 12.15. p.m. Heavy showers during M.O. morning.	
		2.30. p.m.	Rode to MONT NOIR re gravel for cement work. Visited by D.D.M.S., 9th Corps.	

Army Form C. 2118.

WAR DIARY
INTELLIGENCE SUMMARY
(Erase heading not required.) 108TH FIELD AMBULANCE.

Instructions regarding War Diaries and Intelligence Summaries are contained in F. S. Regs., Part II. and the Staff Manual respectively. Title pages will be prepared in manuscript.

Place	Date	Hour	Summary of Events and Information	Remarks and references to Appendices
4E RAVETSBERG	27.8.1916		Heavy rain at intervals during the morning. Nothing to record.	27.8.1916. One of our Bearers wounded by Shrapnel.
	28.8.1916		Continued work at Wagon Lines.	
	29.8.1916		Heavy rain all day and most of the night.	
	30.8.1916		Heavy rain with strong S.W. wind. Cool.	
	31.8.1916		Obtained 2 trucks and 2 tons of stones for repairing Horse Standings etc. Weather fine with light W. breeze. LIEUT. SOWERBY proceeded to CASSEL for instruction in Gas Defence.	

R H Fawcett
Lieut. Colonel.
O.C. 108th Field Ambulance.

31/8/1916.

140/1734

36th Divn

108th Field Ambulance.

Oct. 1916

COMMITTEE FOR THE
MEDICAL HISTORY OF THE WAR
Date 30 OCT. 1916

Army Form C. 2118.

SEPTEMBER

WAR DIARY
INTELLIGENCE SUMMARY
(Erase heading not required.) 108th FIELD AMBULANCE.

Instructions regarding War Diaries and Intelligence Summaries are contained in F.S. Regs., Part II. and the Staff Manual respectively. Title pages will be prepared in manuscript.

Place	Date	Hour	Summary of Events and Information	Remarks and references to Appendices
LERAVETS BERG	1/9/16		Began forming of Horse Lines. Paid men at P. nes. hut galvanised iron huts when extra northern hut to contain water from vino case of pits. 31 cases of gas poisoning brought in. 3 steps from 11th R.J. Rifles, as result of our gas attack at 1.30 a.m. today. Balance of 145 cases sent direct from KHANDAR FARM to BAILLEUL. None died here in transit to BAILLEUL.	
	2/9/16 9:15am		Proceeded to KHANDAHAR FARM. Ques detachment two/ Paid men at TROIS ROIS also. Paid for hire of field in which our men had been encamped (month of August).	
	3/9/16		Rode to head of KEMMEL HILL and through LOCRE. CAPTN. DUNLOP and CAPTN. J. SCOTT proceeded to CANDAHAR FARM. Relieved heavy Field. LIEUT. E.S. SOWERBY returned from anti-gas school, CASSEL.	
	4/9/16		Took over huts of medical cases previously held by CAPT. SCOTT, CAPT. E.H.TRAP (previous from POUEN) and KHANDAHAR FARM on Aug 4/9/16. Received orders to evacuate TROIS ROIS and KHANDAHAR FARM on Aug 4/9/16. CAPT. J.W. REA joined 15th Bn. R.I. RIFLES on temporary duty.
	5/9/16 11 am		relieved by pieces from 110th FIELD AMBULANCE. Went to BAILLEUL and from O.C. 110th Field Ambulance re instrs. LIEUT. E.S. SOWERBY Proceeded to ACHEUX with 9th LABOUR Bn. R.E.	

1577 Wt. W10791/1773 500,000 1/15 D. D. & L. A.D.S.S./Forms/C. 2118.

Army Form C. 2118.

WAR DIARY
INTELLIGENCE SUMMARY
(Erase heading not required.) 108th FIELD AMBULANCE.

Instructions regarding War Diaries and Intelligence Summaries are contained in F. S. Regs., Part II. and the Staff Manual respectively. Title pages will be prepared in manuscript.

Place	Date	Hour	Summary of Events and Information	Remarks and references to Appendices
LERAVETS BERQ.	6/9/16		TROIS ROIS and KHANDAHAR FARM relieved by parties from 1110 TO field ambulance. CAPT. R.W. WHITE reported from TROIS ROIS. CAPT. L. DUNLOP and J.S. SCOTT reported from KHANDAHAR FARM.	
	7/9/16		Continued work on Wagon Lines. Fenced in water supply for horses. Refreshment used by Water Cart, in farm yard W. of Camp.	
	8/9/16	1.30 p.m.	LIEUT. C. DUNDEE returned from BOULOGNE, he proceeded to 12TH R. RIFLES at B.P.W. in relief of CAPT. S.P. REA. Obtained 300 foot run of planks, and 5 rolls of felt. I am using these materials for roofing ablution stands and putting shelves in our wards. Sunburst Weather fine with temp. about 76° in shade. Numbers of patients in hospital, 139, chiefly from an undulating type with violent headache and pains in the back and limbs.	
	9/9/16	10.30 am	Rode to S. JAN'S CAPPEL and visited DIV H. Q. R.S. No supply of timber, wrote to C.R.E. W. Downe.	
	10/9/16	10.30	Rode to R.E. PARK, BAILLEUL and obtained permission to have 6"x 3" Timber from some heavy thing. Obtained reply from R.E. Stating that no timber will be available for two weeks.	

1577 Wt. W10791/1773 500,000 1/15 D.D.&L. A.D.S.S./Forms/C. 2118.

Army Form C. 2118.

WAR DIARY
INTELLIGENCE SUMMARY
(Erase heading not required.) 108th FIELD AMBULANCE.

Instructions regarding War Diaries and Intelligence Summaries are contained in F. S. Regs., Part II. and the Staff Manual respectively. Title pages will be prepared in manuscript.

Place	Date	Hour	Summary of Events and Information	Remarks and references to Appendices
LE RAVETS FERM.	12.9.1916.	10.30 a.m.	Saw A.A. & D.M.S., 36th Divisionre supply of trecks. Went to MERVILLE at 2 p.m. and arranged to buy some logs for building purposes.	
	12.9.16.		Wrote to A.D.M.S. for authority to construct a hut for use of Two Field Ambulances. Capt BOYD CAMPBELL proceeded on temporary duty with Corps Cavalry.	
	13.9.1916. 11.30 a.m.		Visit by A.D.M.S. Heavy rain during the morning: rode to S. JANS CAPELLE in the afternoon, my horse fell on me by backing into a ditch and attempting to rise fibow one again, got severely injured but much bruised and shaken. Returned by way of country roads.	
	14.9.1916.		Heavy rains which had filled up to tanks of artificial appliances cleared. hut completed. Obtained two loads of cuddies for horse lines. Obtained also two pricks for same purpose. began shelter outside each store.	
	15.9.1916.		Went to MERVILLE for 30 poles with which to construct horse coverings.	
	16.9.1916.		Began construction of woodwork of stables by digging hole for supports. Continued buying of straw. A.D.S.S./Forms/C.2118. Completed shelter outside each store	

Army Form C. 2118.

WAR DIARY
INTELLIGENCE SUMMARY.

(Erase heading not required.) 108th FIELD AMBULANCE.

Instructions regarding War Diaries and Intelligence Summaries are contained in F. S. Regs., Part II. and the Staff Manual respectively. Title pages will be prepared in manuscript.

Place	Date	Hour	Summary of Events and Information	Remarks and references to Appendices
LE RAVETSBERG.	16.9.1916		Brought 2 stoves used 100 feet of piping for woods extension copes or the temperatures. Captain J.L. DUNLOP proceeded on 10 days leave.	
	17.9.1916	7.30 am	LIEUT. J TEWKESBURY proceeded on 10 days' leave. Unable to continue work on horse lines today as so many men have this week been taken for work at KHADAHAR FARM and with the Hutting Company. Weather fine, cold last night. Began to put up Stove in B Hut (Ward)	
	18.9.1916	7.30 am	No. C. BARKER, C.F., C.E., proceeded on 15 days' leave, after which Revd returns to our Infantry Battalions. Revd. C. MANNING to return to this Unit. Weather warm stormy. Men preparing work on horse lines.	
	19.9.1916		Continued work on horse lines. Weather stormy with frequent heavy showers, distinctly chilly, got one stove to working order.	
		4.0 pm	Held Courtesy Inquiry on accident to Civilian Francis Octavius on BAILLEUL – ARMENTIERES ROAD on August 13th 1916. Heavy rain most of the day. Visit by A.D.M.S. at noon.	
	20.9.1916			

Army Form C. 2118.

WAR DIARY
INTELLIGENCE SUMMARY.
(Erase heading not required.)

108th Field Ambulance.

Place	Date	Hour	Summary of Events and Information	Remarks and references to Appendices
LE RAVETSBERG	21.9.1916	10 a.m.	Went to MERVILLE; paid for logs and ordered 50 planks for roof of stable. Obtained order for 600 foot run of planks and something to send for same at once and obtained half.	
	22.9.1916		Sent a man of Sanit: Para: to Isolation Hospital. Lacked putting up 16 windows and uprights of stables, obtained there G.S. Wagon loads of gravel for stable floor from MONT NOIR. Finished tresserrs for one half of stables, and began rafters.	
	23.9.1916		Finished supply of rafters; started to plank roof	
	24.9.1916			
	25.9.1916		Sent to MERVILLE and obtained planks; rode to ESTAIRES and obtained a small quantity of 9" x 3" planking, or heavy wood. Continued work at Wash House and stable.	
	26.9.1916		Arranged to send a fire logs to Saw Mills, BAILLEUL, to be sawn into two and three thus making more available timber for uprights.	

Army Form C. 2118.

WAR DIARY
INTELLIGENCE SUMMARY.
(Erase heading not required.)

108th FIELD AMBULANCE.

No. of Appendices: 6

Place	Date	Hour	Summary of Events and Information	Remarks and references to Appendices
LE RAVETS BERG.	27.9.1916		No reconnoissance that A.D.M.S. proceeded on 10 days leave.	
	28.9.1916		Regular visit of Staff; visit by A.D.M.A.D.C., R.E. attended to A.D.M.S's office to hear necessary documents.	
	29.9.1916	10.30 a.m.	Went to LINDENHOEK with D.A.D.M.S. and inspected R.A.M.C. POST there; deeper dug-out or small M.D. dugout to any of three semi-efficient "Shell proof" Shelters. Already at A.D.M.S's office at 2 P.M., Capt. BOYD CAMPBELL returned from duty with Cavalry. Capt. H.E.H. TRACY relieved Capt. G.W. REA who proceeds on 15 days leave tomorrow. Lieut. GRANT proceeded for duty.	
	30.9.1916		Visited A.D.M.S's office at 2.p.m., Capt S.P. REA relieved Capt. H.E.H. TRACY. (with 13 Br.T.TR.HRS) Capt H.E.H. TRACY proceeded to ETAPLES, for duty there.	

W.T.M. Powitt
Lieut. Colonel.
O.C., 108th Field Ambulance

160/215

36th Div

Oct 1916

108th Field Ambulance.

COMMITTEE FOR THE
MEDICAL HISTORY OF THE WAR
Date −9 DEC. 1916

VOL 13

Army Form C. 2118.

WAR DIARY
INTELLIGENCE SUMMARY.
(Erase heading not required.)

108th FIELD AMBULANCE.

Place	Date	Hour	Summary of Events and Information	Remarks and references to Appendices
LE RAVETS BERG.	1.10.1916.	7 a.m.	Capt. BOYD CAMPBELL proceeded on 10 days' leave.	Number of patients
	2.10.1916.	10.30 a.m.	Proceeded to BAILLEUL and drew 76000 watts which to Prov. men. Rain all day. Section of Field amb. Workers 32.	
		2 p.m.	Heavy rain throughout the afternoon. Section of Field amb. men employed in making improvements to huts. Very bad weather.	
	3.10.1916.	11 a.m.	Proceeded to BAILLEUL and paid account for same piping & wire. Received Pte. C. BARKER and looks. Received throughout morning fine from H.Q. re our arrivals, returns for men of detachment A.S.C., Tram, by car to draw materials in return for two huts for detachment A.S.C., Tram.	
	4.10.1916.		Heavy rain from 9 a.m. Paid 710 frs field occupied by H.Q. and men of Units. Heavy rain during the night and early morning. Continue work at Hats. Further clearing material for A.D.S. Huts.	
	5.10.1916.			
	6.10.1916.	10 a.m.	Party from KHANDAHAR FARM. fetched and supplied with R.E. Respirators, wrote to O.C. Hutting Company re fitting of Boo Respirators for men of this Unit attached to their company. Wrote to C.R.E. for timber for Zbogar Linio. Sent to DE SEULE for timber. Wind fresh. W.S.W. overcast.	Obtained 400 yards canvas for stretcher.

Army Form C. 2118.

WAR DIARY
INTELLIGENCE SUMMARY.
(Erase heading not required.)

108th FIELD AMBULANCE

Place	Date	Hour	Summary of Events and Information	Remarks and references to Appendices
LE RAVETSBERG	7.10.16.		Newmarkets. LIEUT: GRANT relieved CAPT S.P. REA (with 15th too R.I. Rifles). A.F.	
	8.10.16.		Newmarkets.	
	9.10.16.		Began to erect Huts for A.S.C. in field near Horse Lines, continued work at stables, A.D.M.S. returned from leave, reported to him at 2.15 p.m. He visited Rest Station at 3.15 p.m.	
	10.10.16. 10 a.m.		Continued work at stables & Huts for A.S.C. Visit by A.D.M.S. Capt. Green G.S.O. and M. BEAMISH. ETAT MAJOR. FRENCH MISSION, re railway which will pass through this Rest Station asked then for Notes. General S. of camp, also for matters on which to build Huts reserved on account of encroachment by railway line.	Capt: S.P. REA
	11.10. 12 noon 1916.		Inspection by Army Commander (General Sir HERBERT PLUMER) accompanied by D.M.S. 2nd Army. Received orders from Army command that no cases whatever are to remain in the present Divisional Rest Station longer than 7 days. All cases must obey through return to duty or proceed to Hospital at Convalescent Stations, leave. R.E. began to move Huts to the new site for Railway Triangle camp.	R.E.A.

Army Form C. 2118.

WAR DIARY
INTELLIGENCE SUMMARY.

108th FIELD AMBULANCE, 3.

(Erase heading not required.)

Instructions regarding War Diaries and Intelligence Summaries are contained in F. S. Regs., Part II. and the Staff Manual respectively. Title pages will be prepared in manuscript.

Place	Date	Hour	Summary of Events and Information	Remarks and references to Appendices
LERAVETSBERG.	12.10.1916	11.30 a.m.	An ambulance army commanders orders concerning 88 Casualty Clearing Stations. Both of moving hrs to contained. Visit by D.D.M.S. and D.A.D.M.S. IX Corps, to S720 progressing with our search. Half of Staff progressing well. dull but no rain. Completed huts for details A.S.C. Quartermasters Stores moved today to new site. Huts to C.R.E. for more Timber and nails for Staple.	CAPT. BOYD CAMPBELL to S720 progressing journey
	13.10.16.			
	14.10.16	10 am	CAPT BOYD CAMPBELL proceeded on Temporary duty with 17th August to R.T.O.; New C.R.E. to water supply for horse lines. Waynes Harness Room. Granted 10 days leave to ENGLAND. Handed over to CAPT. LEEPER DUNLOP.	

A.P. Pritzcroft
Lieut; Colonel,
O.C., 108th Field Ambulance)
14/10/16

Army Form C. 2118.

WAR DIARY
~~INTELLIGENCE~~ SUMMARY
(Erase heading not required.)

108th FIELD AMBULANCE

Place	Date	Hour	Summary of Events and Information	Remarks and references to Appendices
LA REVETSIDE	15/10/16		Continued work on stables. Sgt "A" hut ready for reception of patients and presented "B" hut. The Divisional Interpreter, M. Bernard visited us and made arrangements with the owner of the field in which the personnel of the ambulance are camped, that we pay possession of the whole tract of the field for the purpose of building huts to be used instead of the present marquees. Pte C.C. MANNING C.7. returned off leave.	
	16/10/16		"B" hut totally denuded canvas by the R.E. without any attempt except of taking off the floor. Several personnel without an extra blanket on last night were very cold. Three 4 boards of stove chippings from R.E. dump, also 12 walls of jute, and 5 carrels for the stoves in the wards. Pte Lockey sent to the base, being claimed for munition work at home.	
	17/10/16		Continued work on new huts made necessary by railway. Put stove in O.M. store and in recreation room. Lieut W.E. FRASER reported for duty. Establishment of F.A. temporary increased to 8 officers.	
	18/10/16		Obtained 1000 bricks, 3 Stevens FLA Tanks, 20 feet of stove piping from R.E. which was obtained today. Lieut GRANT returned to duty today on Capt REA's return off leave.	

1577 Wt.W10791/1773 500,000 1/15 D. D. & L. A.D.S.S./Forms/C. 2118.

Army Form C. 2118.

WAR DIARY
or
INTELLIGENCE SUMMARY.
(Erase heading not required.)

105th FIELD AMBULANCE

Place	Date	Hour	Summary of Events and Information	Remarks and references to Appendices
LA REVETSDERE	19/10/16		No remarks	
	20/10/16	11.30am	Visit by A.D.M.S. and Lt. Conyers G.S.O. Battery told bit slow & pretty worgette. Received 200 duck boards, 100 poles and wire for new paths necessitated by construction of camp on account of the Railway. Purchased 2 mules & wire staples for same purpose.	
	21/10/16		Completed work on stables. Sergt J LOWE and Pte HEXNOR awarded the military medal.	
	22/10/16	2.P.M.	Inspection by Commander 9 IX Corps (Lieut Gen. HAMILTON GORDON) accompanied by A.D.M.S. IX Corps.	
	23/10/16	12 noon	A.D.M.S. presented ribbons to Sergt LOWE and Pte FLEXNER. Capt S.P. REA. returned from leave.	
	24/10/16		Detailed LIEUT W.E. FRASER to temporary duty for 10 days with Divi Train. Heavy fall of rain all day and last night.	
	26/10/16		Detailed Capt R.E.A. S.P. to temporary duty with 12th R.I.R. to 10 days.	
	27/10/16		Lieut Col Fawcett returned from leave & resumed command.	

27/10/16
J.C. Dunlop
Capt n.a.m.c

Army Form C. 2118.

WAR DIARY
or
INTELLIGENCE SUMMARY. 168th FIELD AMBULANCE.
(Erase heading not required.)

Place	Date	Hour	Summary of Events and Information	Remarks and references to Appendices
4E RAVETSBERG	27.10.1916	1.30 A.M.	Returned from leave, took over from CAPT J.W.DUNLOP. Work as usual. Visit by A.D.M.S.	
	28.10.1916		No remarks.	
	29.10.1916		No remarks.	
	30.10.1916		Work as usual. Retired portion of Forge via Houtkerke.	
	31.10.1916		Visit by D.M.S. 2nd Army and D.D.M.S. IX Corps. Spoke to both of them re want of stores for wards, and stated that we required a Recreation Room.	

R.F.Titsworth
Lieut. Colonel,
O.C., 108th Field Ambulance

31/10/1916

36th Div

108th Field Ambulance

Nov 9th

140/1862

COMMITTEE FOR THE
MEDICAL HISTORY OF THE WAR
Date −3 JAN. 1917

Army Form C. 2118.

Vol 1

WAR DIARY
or
INTELLIGENCE SUMMARY

(Erase heading not required.) 108th FIELD AMBULANCE.

Hour, Date, Place	Summary of Events and Information	Remarks and references to Appendices

1.11.1916. LE RAVETSBERG
Proceeded to BAILLEUL and drew 76300 from Field Cashier IX. Corps.

2 p.m. Recd. orders (76225).

2.11.1916. Obtained some logs from R.E. Park, IX Corps. BAILLEUL, also obtained 100 yards canvas.

3.11.1916. Visit of D.D.M.S. and D.A.D.M.S., IX Corps. Began to erect Huts for particular transport & obtain one truck load of clay. Began to make a new stand for Motor Cars loading stays.

4.11.1916. Immediately below many entrances to camp. This site was suggested by Colonel BOYD CAMPBELL.

5.11.1916. Very violent S.W. wind all day. Continued works. Improving roads. Heavy violent night.

6.11.1916. Heavy rain throughout the day. Continued work on new road east of road. The road to cross the ditch at the S. side thereof. The efforts being five heavy logs 20 feet in length, these will cross the ditch and supermposed on these will be 7 foot split pit props, 6 to 7 inches. The stand for the cars entrance to apply we Poilus deep in begins mud and materials for repairing the road are not obtainable.

Army Form C. 2118.

WAR DIARY
of
INTELLIGENCE SUMMARY

(Erase heading not required.) 108th FIELD AMBULANCE.

Instructions regarding War Diaries and Intelligence Summaries are contained in F.S. Regs., Part II. and the Staff Manual respectively. Title pages will be prepared in manuscript.

Hour, Date, Place	Summary of Events and Information	Remarks and references to Appendices

LE RAYETSBERG.

7.11.1916. Very wet and violent wind (S.W.) Throughout the day. Obtained one new pattern Hut (NISSEN BOW) from DESERLE. Continued work so far as weather permitted on Water Cart Stand.

8.11.1916. Wind introducing morning; Much lower evening and began erection of NISSEN BOW Hut. Continued work on Water Cart Platform. During the evening enemy began to bombard.

9.11.1916. 8.30 a.m. Sent for two more Huts for the men; continued work on NISSEN BOW Hut and on Water Cart Stand; weather fine; spent last night. Began to dig a lair down Facing of field in which Hut to are situated.

10.11.1916. Weather fine; planes frequent last night; several German aeroplanes overhead at 10.20 am. the fragments of Shells from our anti aircraft guns falling over the Number of patients near. Pushed on with Latrine digging well. Red to Stakes.
Levelling of Huts and Stands. 112.

11.11.1916. Weather dull but fine; continued work on Huts. Stands; and Water Cart Stand, completed NISSEN BOW Hut.

12.11.1916. Begun work on Hut 2y of the new improved pattern Hut completed Huts by end of day.

Capt. S.B. CAMPBELL proceeds on temporary duty with 178th Brigade R.F.A. and
LIEUT. FRAM SBORNAM with 109 E FRAMB

1247 W 3209 200,000 (E) 8/14 J.R.C.&A. Form C.2118/11.

Army Form C. 2118.

WAR DIARY or INTELLIGENCE SUMMARY

(Erase heading not required.) 108th FIELD AMBULANCE

Hour, Date, Place	Summary of Events and Information	Remarks and references to Appendices
4.E. RAVENSBERG, 13.11.1916.	Continued work on Huts, had to discontinue work on Water Cart Stand temporarily for want of wood. Weather mild with heavy rain.	
14.11.1916.	Work as usual. Weather fine.	
15.11.1916.	Completed work on three huts. Continued writing side of gutter, went to advanced dressing station DE SEULE, no stone piping available; proceeded to BAILLEUL and obtained 10 toise with 30 feet 8 in piping and three elbows, also 10 feet 6 in piping and 6 elbows. Very heavy frost last night, died this morning.	Patients suffering from coldness of hands began to get up. Three men "A" Hut
16.11.1916.	Weather clear, wind bitter N.E., freezing all day, proceeded to BAILLEUL and bought one stove and sixteen feet of piping, began to put up stove with platform in ward Hut 5, the patients being feverish cold. Continued work on water cart stand, completed, change no more snows wrote to C.R.E. for nails, bolts, died timber.	

WAR DIARY or INTELLIGENCE SUMMARY

Army Form C. 2118.

108 2/0 FIELD AMBULANCE

Hour, Date, Place	Summary of Events and Information	Remarks and references to Appendices
RAVETSBERG 17.11.1916	Freezing hard. Battle last turned & got stoves up in all huts. The huts slowly purchasing stoves and ordering our own/responsibility as no one would sanction purchase and in my opinion it is not only cruel but bad economy to put patients in huts and keep them freezing. It was even suggested [?] by A.D.M.S. that stoves should not be ordered important but much increased because our pair old slippers and one of the beds found in corner of room also because there was to be not Notched D. Regret to be told General Hut.	
18.11.1916.	Continued work at Irmaul Hut. Battle N.E. wind and freezing hard, much trench board immediately outside hut & need to see to reduce amount of mud taken into huts.	
19.11.1916.	Went to BAILLEUL and bought a stove and infantry there to be placed in one officers' hut and the infirmary hut. They & Willow Stove purchased heat them, at any rate to [?] it to the best advantage and I are cheap and I shall probably be at last to pay for this stove.	Heavy raining the night, wind veered from N.E. to S.W. warmer. Completed damage of transport lines.

Army Form C. 2118.

5

WAR DIARY
or
INTELLIGENCE SUMMARY

(Erase heading not required.) 108th Field Ambulance

Hour, Date, Place	Summary of Events and Information	Remarks and references to Appendices
LE RAVETSBERG. 20.11.1916.	Wind S.W, but cold; showers during morning; organised inspect: Guard House; continued drainage of camp.	10 officers to no Port Nation.
21.11.1916.	Wind a.s.w. extremely foggy. LIEUT: A. GRANT proceeded to 110th Field Ambulance for temporary duty.	
22.11.1916.	Completed rotos but tents. Engaged on reconstruction of foundation of Recreation building: the kettle and 20 feet in length, these formed are covered trenches by 8 ft it long, used these again by furnace May ft to 26 feet by 20 feet and roofed cabin mudde to the Wales water Cells. Began to build Reception Hut immediately S. of Guard Hut: ground not allowing completion got frames of trenches that newly completed, it will be a great improvement on the present arrangement as regards admission and evacuation. Dimensions :- 30' x 15"; Heights 7'. Floor: tent boards; saw C.R.E. who stated that he would give me another Hut for the men.	

WAR DIARY
INTELLIGENCE SUMMARY.
(Erase heading not required.)

108th Field Ambulance

Army Form C. 2118.

Place	Date	Hour	Summary of Events and Information	Remarks and references to Appendices
H.E. RAVENSBERG.	24/11/1916.		Continued work at GUARD HUT and Reception Hut, Weird S.W. fourth. 27 cases of Scabies in this Rest Station.	
	25/11/1916.		Capt'n S.T.B. REA detailed for temporary duty with the Divisional Ammunition Column. Weird S.W. mid/Ravensland.	
	26/11/1916.		Finished work on Guard Hut by covering outside wall Tarred canvas and lining with wood obtained from huts being.	
	27/11/1916.		Lieut. Col. Tanett proceeded on leave and handed over command of the unit to me (Capt J.L. Dunlop).	
	28.11.16.		This week announced the Military Medal to gallantry in the field awarded to bombardment J. AUTHUILLE on 10th MARCH 1916 — Pt. ARTHURS, GREENFIELD and HOLMES. Capt S.T.D. CAMPBELL was detailed as temporary M.O. to 172 Bde R.F.A. Detailed 6 men for temporary duty with 111th HEIDAMBOLANCE & turn a special Scabies hospital to the IX Corps.	
	29.11.16.		No remarks	
	30.11.16.		LIEUT. RAMSBOTTOM was detailed for temporary duty at 4th Corps Scabies hospital	

Army Form C. 2118.

108th FIELD AMBULANCE

WAR DIARY
or
INTELLIGENCE SUMMARY.
(Erase heading not required.)

Place	Date	Hour	Summary of Events and Information	Remarks and references to Appendices
LE REVEL BURG	30.11.16		Commenced work on stand to note ambulance which I propose to make of sleepers with a bricked approach. Continued work on Reception hut. Bitterly cold, frost & foggy weather.	

J Robert Dundas
Capt. R.A.M.C.
108th Field Ambulance

30/11/16

140/1903

108th Auto Ambulance

COMMITTEE FOR THE
MEDICAL HISTORY OF THE WAR
Date 31 JAN. 1917

WAR DIARY
or
INTELLIGENCE SUMMARY.

(Erase heading not required.)

Army Form C. 2118.

Vol 15
108th FIELD AMBULANCE

Instructions regarding War Diaries and Intelligence Summaries are contained in F.S. Regs., Part II. and the Staff Manual respectively. Title pages will be prepared in manuscript.

Place	Date	Hour	Summary of Events and Information	Remarks and references to Appendices
LE REVEN BOIS	1/12/16		Bitterly cold day. Proceeded to BAIZIEUL and drew 8,000 francs to pay the men of the unit.	
	2/12/16		Continued work on Mobile ambulance standing and on Reception hut. Continued work on M.T. Standing. Altered 28 Rowley sleepers and one truck of clayton Rowley sleepers to make a track for the cars to run in. Got two loads of sand from MONT NOIR in which to set the bricks to stand on. Continued work on Reception hut.	
	3/12/16		Capt G.W. REA suffering from influenza and went to Officers Rest station MONT NOIR. Detailed Capt E.S. SOWERBY to act temporarily on M.O.E D.A.C. vice Capt S.P. REA who is on sick furlough. Proceeded to BAIZIEUL to interview A.D.M.S as an order to detail an officer temporary duty with 12th R.I.R. No officer available but myself.	
	4/12/16		Continued work on Reception hut and M.T. Standing. To afford increased accommodation for patients during winter, proposed to make hut tables and forms movable by taking any iron board in the breadth of hut. This will give good accommodation for at least 15 men at each meal.	
	5/12/16		Continued work on Reception hut and M.T. Standing. Arranged to a fatigue party to be drawn from employed men at 9 a.m daily to clean rifles and equipment from the front store daily.	
	6/12/16		Continued work on Reception hut and M.T. Standing.	
	7/12/16	10 a.m	Visit from A.D.M.S who inspected the whole camp. Continued work on Reception hut, and M.T. Standing to visit. 9 feet 2 feet 6 in with and 5-0 feet high from C.R.E. and R.C Clayton from Rly Coy R.E.	Capt E.S. Sowerby returned from duty with D.A.C.

Army Form C. 2118.

WAR DIARY
or
INTELLIGENCE SUMMARY.
(Erase heading not required.)

108" FIELD AMBULANCE

Place	Date	Hour	Summary of Events and Information	Remarks and references to Appendices
LE TREPORT BURG	8.12.16		Heavy downpour of rain, so put the men to caulking the crevices in the floors of their huts with tarred twine. Continued work on M.T. Standing.	
"	9.12.16		Lieut Col Trevor D.S.O. returned from leave and resumed command of the unit.	
			J. F. Patrick Capt RAMC	
	9.12.16 8 am		Owen returned from special leave 9.12.16	
	10.12.16		Overhauled all admission & discharge books. 7.7.Trevor Lt Col O.C. Lieut Colonel Rowe O.C. Lines. Sinclair Brooks went to G.H.Q. Office at S. JANS CAPPEL and applied for timber or for authority to purchase same for the purpose of erecting a Drying Room. Have the ability to erect will need it platoted as Recreations Room for the men. Continued work as usual. Heavy rain at night. Rest to Room is nearing completion.	
	11.12. 9.16		Turned to sect at 8.15 am and snow at 9.30 am unable to obtain materials and not the wood in war messing, drying, and Recreation Rooms nor can I obtain authority to purchase the same although to know what further may be need at a reasonable price. Meanwhile I have asked that a Dry Room kept from Dining Room is necessary for patients; know there is to to be done without recreation of Lieut Glover. The horses are in good health the horse has pumper suffer partly by buying materials maintaining sanitation of horses to get rid of flies, built partly by buying materials maintaining sanitation of horses	
	12.12 13.16			

WAR DIARY
or
INTELLIGENCE SUMMARY.
(Erase heading not required.)

Army Form C. 2118.

108th Field Ambulance

Place	Date	Hour	Summary of Events and Information	Remarks and references to Appendices
AF RAVETSBERG	12.12.1916	2 P.M.	Proceeded to MERVILLE and bought 4 beams 18"x8"x3". Made the same trip into town for reception Hut. Bought also 83 flanks of timber slats to support the felt roof.	
	13.12.1916		Obtained over the NISSEN BOW HUT and started to erect same. Completed Reception Hut, which is now expected today, sent to MERVILLE for timber bought on 12th inst. and next to	
	14.12.1916	8.30 am	DE SEULE for Welsh Boards, nails and screws. Continued work at NISSEN BOW HUT.	
	15.12.1916		Weather cold, wet, muddy, reviewing the night. Roads deep in mud. Began work on Reception Hut. Cement no B. the day members of the 6th Wells Church Company. This was very much enjoyed by everyone. Rain at night.	
	16.12.1916		Weather fine with no wind, frosty, continued work outside. Sent forces Riche from NIETRE Road. Work as usual.	
	17.12.1916		No remarks.	
	18.12.1916		Began to erect 3rd NISSEN BOW HUT. This is to be used as a Recreation Rooms for Patients. Visit by A.D.M.S.	
	19.12.1916		Captain J. DUNLOP, Captain BOYD CAMPBELL, and Lieut. TEWKESBURY proceeded on leave to IRELAND.	
	20.12.1916	2 P.M.	Visit by A.D.M.S. 2. P.M. Arrivals of N.C.M. personnel at BAILLEUL - Artillas Electricity Road.	

WAR DIARY
or
INTELLIGENCE SUMMARY

Army Form C. 2118.

(Erase heading not required.)

108th FIELD AMBULANCE

Instructions regarding War Diaries and Intelligence Summaries are contained in F.S. Regs., Part II. and the Staff Manual respectively. Title pages will be prepared in manuscript.

Place	Date	Hour	Summary of Events and Information	Remarks and references to Appendices
LE TRANSLOY	21.12.1916		Work much impeded by heavy rain.	4
	22.12.1916		Wet weather. Hampered.	
	23.12.1916		No remarks.	
	24.12.1916		No remarks.	
	25.12.1916		Lieut Col Heugs to Divisional Headquarters at 4.45 p.m. Supplies received. Capt. J.P. REA rejoined from Temporary duty with 13th R.I. Rifles.	
			Wet weather. Concert in B. Hut at 5.30 p.m. very successful.	
	26.12.1916		Completed last NISSEN BOW Hut. Completed roof, sides, and floor of Recreation Hut.	
	27.12.1916		Started to improve and widen Kerb, trail path ways & layout the convenience. Considerable quantity to this convenience of Aidstate bearers.	
	28.12.1916		Frosty hard, white front covering the ground. Began to fence ground, providing entrance to camp with fence. Wagon has become much trampled by horse traffic. Applied to O.R.E. for wooden slats with which to frontpave, walk of Recreation Hut.	

Army Form C. 2118.

WAR DIARY
or
INTELLIGENCE SUMMARY.
(Erase heading not required.) 108th Field Ambulances

Place	Date	Hour	Summary of Events and Information	Remarks and references to Appendices
FRANCE	29/12/1916		Battln. wet tired Stormy but mild. Bought glass and putty for windows of Recreation Hut.	
	30/12/1916		Heavy rain all night and till noon. Sports 2 p.m till 3.45 p.m.	
	31/12/1916	8.28	LIEUT J. TEWKESBURY returned from leave. Dark and stormy every day but not cold. Continued widening boundary walls deep centered room on Recreation Hut. Began to widen water course through so as to give room for foot bath.	

31/12/1916

B.F. Fawcett
Lieut. Colonel
O.C. 108th Field ambulances

140/19+3

36

36 F.A.

101st Field Ambulance.

COMMITTEE FOR THE
MEDICAL HISTORY OF THE WAR
Date 13 MAR. 1917

Vol 6. 1.

Army Form C. 2118.

WAR DIARY
or
INTELLIGENCE SUMMARY.   108th FIELD AMBULANCE.
(Erase heading not required.)

Instructions regarding War Diaries and Intelligence Summaries are contained in F. S. Regs., Part II. and the Staff Manual respectively. Title pages will be prepared in manuscript.

Place	Date	Hour	Summary of Events and Information	Remarks and references to Appendices
LE RAVETSBERG.	1.1.1917.		Finished Sports.	
	2.1.1917.	2 p.m.	Paid men.	
	3.1.1917.	2 p.m.	Lieut. I.A. GRANT and 6 N.C.O's and men proceeded on leave.	
	4.1.1917.		Hear that Capt. J.A. DUNLOP has been awarded the Military Cross, most well deserved for fine service rendered while coming to France, but especially by excellent work at MORSEVILLE, July 10th to July 8th 1916.	
	5.1.1917.		Hear that Sergt. E. TUFFL, 1771.E has been awarded the Distinguished Conduct Medal for gallant conduct, superintending the digging of trenches through HAMEL VILLAGE for a period of seven weeks during the early summer of 1916. Two work and the following day carrying to Sandbags was carried out under constant machine gun fire, sniping, and shell fire.	
	6.1.1917.		5 men proceeded on leave; new Field train NCO vacancy completed.	
	7.1.1917.		No remarks.	
	8.1.1917.		No remarks.	
	9.1.1917.		Medical Board was the between Officers 'Mess' Mess and Mr. Hut's, Capt. STREA proceeded on leave.	

(a 2353) Wt. W5441/1531 200,000 5/16 D D & L A.P.S.S./Forms/C. 2118.

Army Form C. 2118.   2.

WAR DIARY

INTELLIGENCE SUMMARY. 108th FIELD AMBULANCE.

(Erase heading not required.)

Instructions regarding War Diaries and Intelligence Summaries are contained in F. S. Regs., Part II. and the Staff Manual respectively. Title pages will be prepared in manuscript.

Place	Date	Hour	Summary of Events and Information	Remarks and references to Appendices
LE RANDESBERG	10.1.1917		Very cold and thick, wind fresh N.N.E. Started to build Barbed Wire depot.	
	11.1.1917		Freezing slightly and snowing at intervals, continued work on Reception Hut and Barber's shop.	
	12.1.1917		Heavy rain during the morning. Continued work as usual. Number of patients in Rest Station — 86.	
	13.1.1917		Runs and etc turning to snow in the afternoon. Proceeded to A.D.M.S. Office in afternoon; examined 38 men at S.J.A.S. CAPELLE, seventeen men by time to the bone as unfit. These men are seldom so the result of insufficient examination where medically examined adherents most of them being quite unfit for the duties of soldiers.	
	14.1.1917		Sharp frost, half made to see on the ground.	
	15.1.1917		Sharp frost last night and snow flurries, LIEUT J.A. GRANT returned from leave. Completed Barber's shop, an excellent piece of works.	
	16.1.1917		Slight fall of snow last night; freezing sharply, very cold. LIEUT F.A. GRANT returned yesterday afternoon for support. Temporary duty with 9th Bn. R.I. Rifles. Gas mens proceeded on leave yesterday.	
	19.1.1917.		Snowed the whole day, but not heavily and there is very little again. Attached (at A.D.M.S. Office) Capt. Rose, 2 n.p.t. no.	

(353. Wt.W15448 354. 700,000 5/15 D.D.&L. A.D.S.S/Paris./C.2118.)

Army Form C. 2118.

WAR DIARY
or
INTELLIGENCE SUMMARY.
(Erase heading not required.)

108th FIELD AMBULANCE.

Place	Date	Hour	Summary of Events and Information	Remarks and references to Appendices
LE TRANSLOY	17/1/1916		Weather very mild, hampered outdoor improvements.	
	18/1/17		No hard frost, kept men, Captain G.W. REA and 5 men	
	19/1/17		proceeded on leave. Began to widen sweep for Motor Cars at upper entrance by helping the drain, made a good foundation of the trench.	
	20/1/17		Emergency kept moved for Motor Cars. Platform for Motor Cars	
	21/1/17		Continued hard frost, drill, but no more snow. Capt. F.S. SOWERBY returned from duty with 10th R.I. Rifles.	
	22/1/17		Sent party of 1 Staff Sergeant and 5 men for weeks training in Gas Sanitation at No 4 Sanitary Section, BAILLEUL. This necessitated the closing of "D" bearer lorry to vicinity of mess. Began to make entrance from road immediately opposite the passage way leading from "A" Hut. This is to be used for evacuation of cases in the event of heavy casualties. Weather overcast, snowing lightly. Freezing sharply. Erected a small canteen for men of the Field Ambulance in the Recreation Hut.	

Army Form C. 2118.

WAR DIARY
or
INTELLIGENCE SUMMARY.

(Erase heading not required.) 108th FIELD AMBULANCE.

Instructions regarding War Diaries and Intelligence Summaries are contained in F. S. Regs., Part II. and the Staff Manual respectively. Title pages will be prepared in manuscript.

Place	Date	Hour	Summary of Events and Information	Remarks and references to Appendices
L.E RAVETSBERG	23/1/1917		Continued to fit with Brousiul Instants with interpretation; weather bitter cold impossible to get Burroux. Heavy frost day and night.	
	24/1/1917		No remarks.	
	25/1/1917		Wind continues in N.E. Bottles and bottles of medicine frozen, rated no way but to get up for the afternoon. Wind N.N.E. fresh. Frost harder than yesterday. Fire Buckets burst by this frost. Found fozzee, wet men shaking on it. Got up no the morning.	
	27/1/1917		Wind N.N.E. Fresh. Hard frost. Duty of 5 men proceeding on leave stopped owing to congestion on Railways. Returned to duty. Weather very cold. Wind N.E. Violent.	
	28/1/1917		Wind N.E. Frost about same as yesterday. Completed interchange Capt S.P. REA with 111th Field Ambulance. Capt S.P. REA proceeded temporarily in lieu of Capt S.P. REA for new arrangements.	REA returned for new arrangements
	29/1/1917		Wind N.E. Slight snow flurries at intervals.	
	30/1/1917			
	31/1/1917		Wind N.E. Frost continues hard. 6 inches of snow reported. Slight snow flurries during the morning. G.O.C. Division visited Port Ethin yesterday morning at 11 am and expressed himself pleased with our arrangements.	

2353 Wt. W2411/1454 700,000 5/15 D.D.&L. A.D.S.S./Forms/C. 2118.

Army Form C. 2118.
No. 57

WAR DIARY
or
INTELLIGENCE SUMMARY
(Erase heading not required.) 108th FIELD AMBULANCE.

Instructions regarding War Diaries and Intelligence Summaries are contained in F. S. Regs., Part II. and the Staff Manual respectively. Title pages will be prepared in manuscript.

Place	Date	Hour	Summary of Events and Information	Remarks and references to Appendices
LE RAVETSBERG.	31.1. 1917.		Completed Stove in R.A.M.C. Recreation Hut. Heavy and continuous artillery fire which appear to be just S.E. of KEMMEL. Boarded walls of C. of E. Chaplains Hut with felt as the canvas were gaping and the cold desperate.	

B.F.Fawcett
Lieut. Colonel,
O.C., 108th Field Ambulance.

31/1/17

140/991.

36th Div.

106th Field Ambulance.

Feb. 1917

COMMITTEE FOR THE
MEDICAL HISTORY OF THE WAR
Date 4 APR. 1917

Vol 1

WAR DIARY

INTELLIGENCE-SUMMARY. 108th FIELD AMBULANCE.

Army Form C. 2118.

(Erase heading not required.)

Instructions regarding War Diaries and Intelligence Summaries are contained in F.S. Regs., Part II. and the Staff Manual respectively. Title pages will be prepared in manuscript.

Place	Date	Hour	Summary of Events and Information	Remarks and references to Appendices
LERANSBERG.	1.2.1917.		Forwarded to BAILLEUL cash cheque for £300.0.0, with which to pay the men. Wind N.E. Light; sharp frost but less severe. Snow kind cold	
		10 am.	weather began; weather clear. Considerable artillery fire from	
			S. was noticed.	
	2.2.1917.	2 p.m.	Captain G.W. REA returned from leave.	
			Wind N.E. Light; hard frost; visit by A.D.M.S. 36th Division and Colonel Burke, Indian Army; brought 16 buckets for use at the	
			Baths, to replace R.E.G. two formerly in use, for that purpose	
			and burnt by the recent heat shell of frost.	
	3.2.1917. 12 noon		Visit by A.D.M.S. Wind very light, N.N.E. Frost gave. Began 13° R.I.	
			to paint the buckets obtained yesterday. 2nd Lieut. Nicholas Co. Rifles and Corporal BRAHAM, W. & R. LEWIS, R. Eng., Bombing School, two men were	
			killed at the Bombing School this morning	
			as a result of an explosion of rifle grenades while	
			at drill. Five men wounded.	
	4.2.1917.		Wind light, slight tendency to veer S.E. cold. Capt. G.W.REA	
			proceeded on temporary duty with the Heavy Artillery, Headquarters	
			at DRANOUTRE.	
	5.2.1917.		Wind E. Light. Did not till noon, then clear; freezing sharply.	
			Improved, boarded, walk attendance to Mess, Capt. E.S. SOWERBY	
			13th R. of Rifles. Ceased, with 13th R. of Rifles.	

Army Form C. 2118.

WAR DIARY
or
INTELLIGENCE SUMMARY.
(Erase heading not required.)

108th Field AMBULANCE.

Instructions regarding War Diaries and Intelligence Summaries are contained in F. S. Regs., Part II. and the Staff Manual respectively. Title pages will be prepared in manuscript.

Place	Date	Hour	Summary of Events and Information	Remarks and references to Appendices
LERAVETSBERG	6.2.1917.		Wind N.E. Fresh, Increasing. Genl D.D.M.S. IX Corps reconnoitred Hut accommodation in case this camp may be used as Main Dressing Station. He was not in favour of the scheme.	
	7.2.1917.		Wind N.N.E. Weather the same as yesterday, sent D.D.M.S. IX Corps detailed statement of twelve injured to constitute a hut 50' x 30' x 7' for fly tent wounded cases.	
	8.2.1917.		No change in the weather. Wired E. and Jerks. Class. Nothing of importance occurred. 106 patients in Rest Station.	
	9.2.1917.		No change in the weather, strong E. Wind and piercing keen. Recommended Capt; LYTTLE, SERGT; KERR, and Corp: WHEELHOUSE for internment to substantive ranks. Put up tents and wire at edge of barrel walk in front of Imp. and Officers' Mess. 101 Patients in Rest Station.	Party returned from KHARJDAHAR FARM.
	10.2.1917.		No change in weather. Began to widen N. side of tramp entrance to Camp to as to improve access for traffic, cutdown ahead tree to assist in this project. Drew £2,070 proceded to pay men. 2nd m. paid men. LIEUT: RAMSBOTHAM returned from leave.	Party visiting Military Company.
	11.2.1917.		Wind still E. but not as much milder, but piercing, no rent, granted Party visiting to go on leave. Wheelwright and had a funeral at the Barrels continued work on traffic sweep.	

Army Form C. 2118.

WAR DIARY
or
INTELLIGENCE SUMMARY

(Erase heading not required.)

108th Field Ambulance

Instructions regarding War Diaries and Intelligence Summaries are contained in F. S. Regs., Part II. and the Staff Manual respectively. Title pages will be prepared in manuscript.

Hour, Date, Place	Summary of Events and Information	Remarks and references to Appendices
LERAVETSBERG	Arrested leave of absence, handed over to Capt. Jh. Dunhop M.C.	B.F. Moncrieff Lieut. Colonel O.C. 108th Field Ambulance 12/2/19M
12.2.1917	Continued work on tunnels and repaired roof of officers mess. Weather very mild and bright sun.	
13.2.1917	Hard frost again last night. Drew 100 yards of canvas from O.E. and 100 ft of wood 4 x 3 to repair & trough for watering horses. The archway being thrown in. The camp is to be developed consequently will have to remove water cart stand. Recontinued it to tent addition stand. Began this work today.	
14.2.1917	Detailed tent RAMSBOTTOM to look after a party of the 10" R.Z.N. contacts & another special meningitis who are isolated in a farm beside WATERLOO CAMP. Visit by adjutant E.C.D.E.	
15.2.1917	Visit by A.D.M.S. who made a very detailed inspection of camp and found times. Still freezing rather hard.	

Army Form C. 2118.

WAR DIARY or INTELLIGENCE SUMMARY
(Erase heading not required.)

108th FIELD AMBULANCE

Place	Date	Hour	Summary of Events and Information	Remarks and references to Appendices
LE RAKETSBURG	16.2.17		Sent to STIENWERCK for wood and canvas to build the shelter for wounded at DRANOUTRE. Received an order from A.D.M.S. that all dogs in the camp are to be destroyed in given away on account of a case of rabies. Capt. G. Mc REA returned from duty with 41st H.A.G. Sergt BEDDOES and Pte McCULLAGH - A.S.C. M.T. left to take temporary commission.	
	17.2.17		Weather mild and wet. "Three Traffic Rotations" came into force today, but I did not receive warning until wagons had gone out.	
	18.2.17		LIEUT RAMSBOTTOM returned from duty with 36th D.A.C. O 36th DIV TRAIN. Continued work on water cart stand and began renovation of Hospital Bantleaux. Had all drains of the camp cleaned out as the ice in weather very wet and foggy. the bottom had not melted and was blocking them up. Received 7.55 from D.D.M.S. for use of Aux R Station. Received 7.55 from Capt GAVIN who proceeds to Detailed Capt G. McREA to duty with 14th R.I.R. in relief of Capt GAVIN who proceeds to HAZEBROUCK for one weeks Sanitary Course. Detailed Sergt TURNER and 5 men for one weeks sanitary course.	
	19.2.17		Continued work on water cart stand. Had evacuation room disinfected green. Parcheed from panes 2 hours. From people of Caestre, and sent them put in the windows of potatoe room when room until was covered with oiled canvas.	
	20.2.17		Heavy rain all day. Made partition in orderly room so that a man can always sleep within sound of telephone. Have all the drains of the camp cleaned out as the hard crumbled after the frost.	

Army Form C. 2118.

WAR DIARY
or
INTELLIGENCE SUMMARY
(Erase heading not required.)

108th FIELD AMBULANCE

Place	Date	Hour	Summary of Events and Information	Remarks and references to Appendices
LE REVETS BURGH	21.2.17	9.45 a.m	Had interview with A.D.M.S. in BAILLEUL who visited & knew of we could take over the building occupied by No 8 C.C.S and that it till it would be taken over by another C.C.S. Supported partly Capt. CAMPBELL's one section of the ambulance is at work about 50 Convalescent patients. Proceeded to the building and interviewed the C.O. and Q.M.	
LE REVETS BURGH	22.2.17		Received 6 weeks clothes to patients evacuation per man from D.R.C.S. also some clothing to the wards. Completed work on water cart standing.	
"	23.2.17		Nothing of importance to note.	
"	24.2.17		Capt G.W. REA returned from duty with 10th R.I.R.	
"	25.2.17		Attached Capt G W REA to duty with 11th R.I.R. Lieut A GRANT returned from duty with the 9th R.I.R.	
"	25		Visit from A.D.M.S. & S.S.O.I. inspected & discussed scheme for growing vegetables in waste ground around the Camp. On measuring up, I find I can put in 1½ acres potatoes, ½ acre of Cabbage, ½ acre of Peas, ½ acre onions, ½ acre Carrots. 7th Division is to supply the seeds.	
"	26.2.17	9.30 a.m	Lieut E. CRAWLEY 10th R Irwin Fus brought in dead by a M.T. Sergeant who found him lying in the road. He was then dead	
"		10.30 a.m	Lieut A GRANT did a Post mortem on the body of LIEUT CRAWLEY. Cause of death. Asphyxia	

WAR DIARY
or
INTELLIGENCE SUMMARY

(Erase heading not required.)

Army Form C. 2118.

108th FIELD AMBULANCE

Place	Date	Hour	Summary of Events and Information	Remarks and references to Appendices
LE REVERT DUNEM	26/2/17	a.m.	Began work of Collection and preparation of the Land for road by forming rammers. Borrowed a plough to the field at the transport.	
		2.30 p.m.	Sent report C.A.D.M.S. re LIEUT CRAWLEY.	
	27/2/17		Began to plough. Also started men to dig pits across the Lake. Detailed Capt S.B.B. CAMPBELL to proceed to BAILLEUL with B. Section - 30 strong and take over the building lately occupied by 8. C.C.S. Detailed Lieut. & Qmr J. TEWKSBURY to proceed to BAILLEUL and take over the Red Cross and Ordnance stores on inventory, kept behind by 8. C.C.S.	
	28/2/17		Attended Court of Inquiry into death of 2 LIEUT CRAWLEY from 10 a.m. till 12.30 p.m. Continued work on preparation of ground.	

J Lefort Dunolp
Capt. R.A.M.C.

28/2/17.

140/2042.

To 36th Div.

108th Field Ambulance

COMMITTEE FOR THE
MEDICAL HISTORY OF THE WAR
Date 11 MAY 1917

May 1917

Army Form C. 2118.

Vol 18

108th FIELD AMBULANCE

WAR DIARY
or
INTELLIGENCE SUMMARY
(Erase heading not required.)

Place	Date	Hour	Summary of Events and Information	Remarks and references to Appendices
LE RAVETS BURGH	1/3/17		Proceeded to BAILLEUL and drew 77,600 Z for the men. Gave Capt CAMPBELL 7,870 out of this. Z for his detachment at Queensbury Rest Station. Continued farming operations. Completed work in hospital and horse lines, having new mounds on ovens built over East tent to counteract German Princess working on the new railway line. Felt of the Iron and fractured the clavicle.	
	2/3/17		Obtained two of the horses which were pulled in the camp along the railway lines. Purchased 2 cox. Them to replace the sustained & the Transport line. Detailed LIEUT RAMSBOTTOM for temporary duty with 9th R.E. Fm. Drew 220 will from Supt from Cholmon at his experimental purposes in connexion with stretches carrier. In my opinion they are much too heavy and unwieldy and contain much extemporarily with the JAMES MILLAR pattern of portable carrier.	
	3/3/17	10.30 a.m.	Went and met visitation by A.D.M.S. duty to town. Arranged with O.C. 118th M.S. not to send Transport for three days to get me an opportunity to repair buttons of horse lines. Capt F. W. REA returned from duty with 117 R.I.R. and Capt SOWERBY from duty with 13th R.I.R. Continued work on East.	
	4/3/17		Nothing of importance to report.	
	5/3/17		Started work on entrance to Transport lines. Continued agricultural operations.	
	6/3/17		Proceeded to 36th Div. Supply Column and arranged to do inoculations with T.A.B. at rate of 3.35 every 2 days till they are completed. Obtained 4 barrels of cement to make a cement floor to the latrines.	

WAR DIARY or INTELLIGENCE SUMMARY

Army Form C. 2118.

108th FIELD AMBULANCE

Place	Date	Hour	Summary of Events and Information	Remarks and references to Appendices
LE RAVETSBERG	7/3/17		As gravel for the cement is impossible to obtain, I started filling form which had been pressed through the incubator with clay, and laying a foundation of them in the floor of the latrine. Also plant of profiles by laying the cement floor, sloping it so cleaned in the centre, so that they can be washed down. Also began new trenches of the latrines so that the buckets could be removed from the back. Completed work on entrance to Head Horse lines for an instant pass.	
	8/3/17		Put water and a team of horses to duty, will Dismissal Supervisor School at METEREN, also a return for two men, and the team on duty with Dismissal School of Instruction at ST MARTIN CAPELLE. Have now completed the macadamy and plunging to the site of Transport lines. Bathing and Boot washed setting. Went through and M accompanied by Serjeant Robson of Count which held up all work instant. Completed Anti-emphsyma of unreserving escale. Lut is charge to commence Lewis handcarts. N.S.R. the shelter, is being from Spirit Springs attached to 4 standards at each end. B. platoon the shuttles is supported on two transverse handbrace strings at each end of the carriage. Detailed LIEUT FRANT to Temporary duty with 111th R.I. R.	
	9/3/17		Wind suddenly changed due South, but stille cold and snow drops falling. Sent 6 MONT NOIR to to tendo of gravel to the report into Horse lines, and one load of sand for latrines. Team work at Ravetsbeel carrying in weather.	
	10/3/17		Visited by A.D.M.S. who inspected the camp. Continued work on latrines.	
	11/3/17		Wired off the vegetable garden around the mess tent. Finished ploughing of field at Horse lines. Weather very mild and damp. Wood due S. Completed work on latrines to horse lines.	
	12/3/17		Forwarded the Sanitation of the latrine floors and continued the making of the new seats. Completed the wiring of of the camp.	
	13/3/17		Turned the Compostel most and sinks of addition hands, and took of hospital tent tenant. Met A.D.M.S. at Ambulance Rest Station BAILLET, who informed me that I am assigned on the change in the	

Army Form C. 2118.

WAR DIARY
or
INTELLIGENCE SUMMARY

(Erase heading not required.)

168th FIELD AMBULANCE

Place	Date	Hour	Summary of Events and Information	Remarks and references to Appendices
LE REVEILLON	13/3/17	cont	The present D.D.S wanted to instruct the area, and that consequently we should be compelled to give up the camp & the outgoing corps and open a D.R.S Temporarily in BAILLEUL. Saw D.D.M. S.IX Corps relative to obtaining a quantity of wood for building a suitable hut.	
	14/3/17		Transported ————— a quantity of Equipment & Accessories not otherwise appropriated to our present Camp and to O.C. 2 N.Z. F. Amb. to take over the hut been held by him in RUE DE MUSEE, BAILLEUL.	
	15/3/17	3.30 P.M	Handed over camp and Transport lines to 1st N.ZEALAND Field Ambulance, and marched to BAILLEUL, putting all patients and personnel in the building at present occupied as Amiens Rest Station.	
BAILLEUL	16/3/17		Handed over to Lieut Col R.F.M. FAWCETT. D.S.O on his return from Leave.	

J. Shepherdship
Capt. R. Amr.

16/3/17

WAR DIARY or INTELLIGENCE SUMMARY

Army Form C. 2118.

Place	Date	Hour	Summary of Events and Information	Remarks and references to Appendices
BAILLEUL	16.3.1917	11 a.m.	Took over from Capt. J.H. DUNLOP, M.C., R.A.M.C., Cellar at A.D.M.S's Office at 6 p.m.	4
	17.3.1917	10 a.m.	Called on A.D.M.S. Took over Bookshop in RUE du MUSÉE from 1st ANZAC Corps.	
	18.3.1917	10 a.m.	Surveying. Rain fell 11 a.m. Snowshowers at intervals then ceased.	
	19.3.1917		Cold, wet and snow at intervals during the day.	
	20.3.1917		Rain at intervals during the day, cold.	
	21.3.1917		Cold. Snowed. Went to intervals. "Gas" drill at 10 a.m.	
	22.3.1917		Snow at intervals during the day.	
	23.3.1917	10.15 a.m.	Visited DRANOUTRE with A.D.M.S. Went N.E. Front Visited NEUVE EGLISE at 3 p.m.	
	24.3.1917		Wind strong N.E., frost. "Gas" drill at 10 a.m.	
	25.3.1917		No movement.	

Army Form C. 2118.

WAR DIARY
or
INTELLIGENCE SUMMARY
(Erase heading not required.)

Place	Date	Hour	Summary of Events and Information	Remarks and references to Appendices
BAILLEUL	26.3. 1917	9.30 a.m	Took out a party of 1 N.C.O. and 10 men to DRANOUTRE to complete work on NISSEN BOW HUTS being erected as a Dressing Station. Strong wind and heavy rain, milder than yesterday.	
	27.3. 1917		Wind N.N.E. Strong, cold. Snow flurries throughout the day. Visited DRANOUTRE and inspected progress of work (2 p.m.). Spells of men's work very cold.	
	28.3. 1917	10 a.m	Went with French Interprète (M. ST IVES) in search of a field for transport. Found one half way between BAILLEUL and DRANOUTRE, negotiations at present being made with the notary in BAILLEUL to obtain it. Food prices here are rising in the wholesalers on the whole, cafés are lent with stores which there month the sign cept 71, marked up A 72. Heavy fires to the cheating.	
	29.3. 1917		Chilly: wind W. with driving rain. arranged to take no cases today from 107th and 110th Field Ambulances as it is necessary to reduce number of patients on account of our having to leave the house in the RUE DE MUSÉE.	
	30.3. 1917		No casualties	
	31.3. 1917		Group Proceeded to h. INDERHOEK accompanied by Capt. J.H. DUNLOP M.C. & LIEUT TEWKESBURY. was returned	

Army Form C. 2118.

WAR DIARY
or
INTELLIGENCE SUMMARY
(Erase heading not required.)

Instructions regarding War Diaries and Intelligence Summaries are contained in F. S. Regs., Part II. and the Staff Manual respectively. Title Pages will be prepared in manuscript.

Places	Date	Hour	Summary of Events and Information	Remarks and references to Appendices
BAILLEUL	31/3/1917	4 p.m.	(Cont.) Three aid Posts which we are taking over tomorrow. Visited KEMMEL village. Returned at 2.30 p.m.; 2nd Army. Transport partments from visit by D.M.S. Bore de Mercis to this Brigade. (SCORE S. JOSEPH).	

B J Whitworth
Lieut. Colonel.
O.C. 109 Field Ambulance

31/3/1917

140/2086

10x4 7.a.

COMMITTEE FOR THE
MEDICAL HISTORY OF THE WAR
Date −6 JUN. 1917

Vol II

Army Form C. 2118.

WAR DIARY
or
INTELLIGENCE SUMMARY 108th FIELD AMBULANCE
(Erase heading not required.)

Instructions regarding War Diaries and Intelligence Summaries are contained in F.S. Regs., Part II. and the Staff Manual respectively. Title Pages will be prepared in manuscript.

Place	Date	Hour	Summary of Events and Information	Remarks and references to Appendices
BAILLEUL	1.4.1917	9.30 a.m.	Capt. BOYD CAMPBELL and party of 15 men proceeded to DRANOUTRE, in relief of 107th Field Ambulance. LIEUT. A CRAMP proceeded to LINDENHOEK with party of 25 men in relief of same unit. Weather uncertain; short snow flurry at 9.45 a.m.	Handed over beds in hut E 6 to NUMBER 5 & 7th Field Ambulance
	2.4.1917		Slight fall of snow during the night which all disappeared during the morning. 10th Sept. JOHNSTONE, A.S.C. up to see fields allotted for our transport. He covered all and found apparently solid. There is however a pond of fairly good water. Heavy snow storm from 4.15 p.m.	
	3.4.1917		Heavy snow storm; weather fairly mild; about 2 inches of snow on the ground. Managed to put some of our horses & their kharki hospital used as our station Room.	
	4.4.1917		Heavy rain in the night. Sergt. and Murphy being at interviewing the morning. Trekked out beyond 107th Field Ambulance and found an old horse standing where huts can be obtained. Went to MONT NOIR and then to 6040 with the vehicle to pay the men, his new Headquarters at 2 p.m.	
		5 p.m.	Rest men at DRANOUTRE; good progress is being made with the huts. Evening fine but chilly. Roofs of huts require painting without delay as I think their roofs are unable from MESSINES, no beds.	

Army Form C. 2118.

WAR DIARY
INTELLIGENCE SUMMARY

(Erase heading not required.) 108th FIELD AMBULANCE.

Place	Date	Hour	Summary of Events and Information	Remarks and references to Appendices
BAILLEUL	5.4.1917		Fine weather. Walked up to new Transport lines with Capt. G.W.REA. Visit by A.D.M.S. Troops/horses to field over DRANOUTRE road.	G.W.REA.
	6.4.1917	3.45 p.m.	Fine weather till 1 p.m. no where pleasant afterwards. Bought waterwalks wheels to clean up ground (?) Horses have been restal — lebred this building. Left ourage at French Inspector. Bullet arguments the ground of replings for review in front of hutts at DRANOUTRE. Heavy showers afterwards during the afternoon.	
	7.4.1917	6 p.m.	Fine and clear throughout the day. Rode out through OUTERSTEENE. There are several mounted farm horses in this district they date from the middle of the 17th Century; they are very picturesque but I think that enlargements for (?) representation coming the review or when conveniented in the review of Cavalry, C.E. N14. Play written by Capt. J.H.DUNHOP and Capt. SOMERBY performed by casts of 1st A.D.Pn., Lieut. Colonel DUNBAR, CAP.DEMIER and their attendants, a very great success and gave dinner. Not to be made before from billets and followed.	
	8.4.1917	9.30 a.m.	Weather up to transport lines near three came to DRANOUTRE.	

Army Form C. 2118.

WAR DIARY
or
INTELLIGENCE SUMMARY
(Erase heading not required.)

108TH FIELD AMBULANCE

3.

Place	Date	Hour	Summary of Events and Information	Remarks and references to Appendices
BAILLEUL	8.4. 1917.		Heavy rain storm at night. LIEUT. GRANT relieved by LIEUT. RAMSBOTHAM at KIRSDENHOEK. LIEUT. DRANOUTRE buried about noon by LIEUT. DRANOUTRE.	
	9.4. 1917.		Stormy wet morning, showed improvement later in the day. Went to Dic Town Co. and have a case to see in field whilst waiting for the A.D.M.S. to visit Transport lines and DRANOUTRE, he did not however arrive; no arrangement to go to to two places myself, very good progress is being made in construction of Wes Hut, the outer shell of which should be completed Wed. present work, all being well. Obtained 60 yds canvas and 3 doors & fittings for me in Transport lines. Very good work being done by Cpl. G. W. REA in laying out two lines and constructing shelters for bearers near Forge. Current at 2 p.m., and storm with hail, wind began at 2.30 a.m. blew wind and stopped again at 3.15 p.m., but snowing heavily again before 4 p.m., and continued at intervals till dark. Stormy night, wild wind with flurries of snow squalls at intervals.	
	10.4. 1917.	2.30 p.m.	Visited Transport lines and DRANOUTRE with A.D.M.S. Heavy snow squall in afternoon between showers.	

WAR DIARY / INTELLIGENCE SUMMARY

Army Form C. 2118.

INTELLIGENCE SUMMARY 108TH FIELD AMBULANCE

Place	Date	Hour	Summary of Events and Information	Remarks and references to Appendices
BAILLEUL	11.4.1917		Wind S.E. Strong, very cold. Hole cut by R.E. in WHITE HOUSE happened by enemy preventing cars at our effort. Grocery with motor lorry, W.O.O. and called for the 3rd to bury the dead, which throughout the day, owing to the heads, went to CROIX DU BAC	4
		2 p.m.	BAILLEUL and arranged to choose plot for Military for cemetery N. of Street for ambulance cars at DRANOUTRE. Went to LINDENHOEK and another through tunnel to REGENT STREET shelter. Inspected two bunkers to be used as our advanced and everything being done. Snow began at 3 p.m. and continued till 6 p.m. on night. Food G.M. Bogers to please.	
	12.4.1917	8.30 a.m.	Went back to BAILLEUL. Material cold, with snow flurries. Snowing this morning. Went to DRANOUTRE at 3 p.m., and met D.M.S., 2nd Army who visited site for Main Dressing Station. He appeared to be pleased with what he saw.	
	13.4.1917	4.30 a.m.	Continued snowing. Went by car for just to Ambulance Travel, and to Pop for 3 Barns for horses and three on to DRANOUTRE. Sanitary jeep began manned arranging nothing but ambulance stand, which not worth better Thank. Built out of same Blanket authority from C.R.E. to purchase timber(s).	
	14.4.1917		Went to MONT NOIR and decor 7000 for payment cleared. Cold, strong wind. Intensely cold, ground flying.	

Army Form C. 2118.

WAR DIARY
—or—
INTELLIGENCE SUMMARY
(Erase heading not required.)

108th FIELD AMBULANCE

Place	Date	Hour	Summary of Events and Information	Remarks and references to Appendices
BAILLEUL	14.4.1917		Unfortunately forced to MERVILLE at 2 p.m and bought some squared timber and planks.	
	15.4.1917		Heavy snow during the day. Capt: S. P. REA relieved LIEUT: RAMSBOTHAM at MINDEN HOEK	
	16.4.1917		Thick & local wind N fresh, 10 noon. Part to DRANOUTRE and started party at organising a place for motor ambulances. Bought 20 tons 6cwt coal in BAILLEUL for use in & about thaw period. Thaw beginning to break.	
	17.4.1917		Violent night wind with rain and sleet. Began to send timber & moveables stuff up to DRANOUTRE, heavy from 1.30 p.m till 2.30 p.m and from C. B. in again on arrival.	
	18.4.17 9.30 a.m		Toiled up to LINDEN HOEK and visited up to the Trenches; came back by motor ambulance, collecting at DRANOUTRE on the way back. Snow nearly to arm. Three new cars C.B. 3 p.m. Finished cutting timber for men's huts to DRANOUTRE, Lieut a.g.S. Bogars.	
	19.4.17 9 a.m 1.15		Timber purchased on Saturday last, sold to DRANOUTRE and rejected rough & high, no programming intensely cold. Weather wind S.E. light. Foggy, little spring showers.	

Army Form C. 2118.

WAR DIARY
or
INTELLIGENCE SUMMARY

(Erase heading not required.)   108th FIELD AMBULANCE

Instructions regarding War Diaries and Intelligence Summaries are contained in F. S. Regs., Part II. and the Staff Manual respectively. Title Pages will be prepared in manuscript.

Place	Date	Hour	Summary of Events and Information	Remarks and references to Appendices
BAILLEUL	22/4/1917	9.30 a.m.	Rode to DRANOUTRE. Great progress is being made with the new MOTOR CAR STAND. Digging pits for cars but are down in position.	
	23/4/1917		Weather fine but cold. Rode to DRANOUTRE in afternoon. Good work being done at new HAIN DRESSING STATION near	
	24/4/1917		Rode to DRANOUTRE. Weather fine but wind N. fresh and cold. Enemy put heavy shell near dressing station. Aeroplanes dropped 2 bombs in the RUE de MOSEE, BAILLEUL at 8-3 p.m. killing four civilians, wounding others, and damaging houses nearby (one civilian New Zealander).	Capt. SOWERBY relieves Capt. G.T. REA at LINDENHOEK
			Rode to DRANOUTRE. Still cold weather though June has begun. Cloudy. Frame for trolley huts now completed. Began to install & carry walls of huts. To be erected as overflow for convalescents.	
	24/4/1917	11 a.m.	Rode to DRANOUTRE. Stands for motor ambulances should be completed in three days. Weather clear, wind North, cold.	
	25/4/1917		Dull, with thin drizzly rain. Something gone fired at 7.30 a.m. sent 9.S. wagons — load of stores to DRANOUTRE, sent 9.S. wagons at 8.30 and to HA CHYTTE to draw 50 Trench Boards for use at new Brewin Dressing Station. No Trench Boards to be obtained at HA CHYTTE	

DRANOUTRE.
Railhead Supplies still to hand from HARM.

WAR DIARY or INTELLIGENCE SUMMARY

Army Form C. 2118.

108 FIELD AMBULANCE.

Place	Date	Hour	Summary of Events and Information	Remarks and references to Appendices
BAILLEUL	26.4.1917	10 am	Rode to DRANOUTRE. Work progressing well. Reed K. Whitby.	Completed Motor Car Stand.
	27.4.1917	10 am	Rode to DRANOUTRE. Capt. S.R. REMneken and Capt. E.S. SOTHERBY & LIEUT. MENHOEK at 3.p.m. went to LINDENHOEK with Capt. REA and marched to REGENT STREET shelter. Reed rented shelter & being no one except Lino no one except Lino in the ambulance to LINDENHOEK with A.D.M.S. then they to the ambulance to LINDENHOEK with A.D.M.S. Marched to Regent Street shelter, very quiet, a few germans trench mortar shells bursting on front line.	
	29.4.1917	9.45 am	Rode to DRANOUTRE. Both going out in very fine style. Wind W.N.W. aeroplanes active, a very fine day, our guns firing steady, very little reply from the germans.	
	30.4.1917	10.30 am	Moved to DRANOUTRE. Capt. J.H. DUNLOP, M.O. marched up with the men. Went round premises, EcoLE S. JOSEPH to be party of I.M.C.O. and it was to keep the place in good order. & Methods with sheets & mine. rode up to DRANOUTRE. Weather fine with a strong breeze.	

T.J.H. McTavisgff

O.C., 108 FA.

308

1/4/1917. Full ambulances Lieut. Colonel.

140/216

COMMITTEE FOR THE
MEDICAL HISTORY OF THE WAR
Date 10 JUL. 1917

103 9 a.

WAR DIARY
INTELLIGENCE SUMMARY

Army Form C. 2118.

108th FIELD AMBULANCE

Vol 20

Place	Date	Hour	Summary of Events and Information	Remarks and references to Appendices
DRANOUTRE	1.5. 1917		Suffered various Bomb Hits for concentration of wounded for sinks. Two minor Bomb Hits without preparation in Receiving and Dressing Rooms. The Receiving Room being separated from the Dressing Room by a wooden screen and door. Another felice wounded died dirty.	
	2.5. 1917		Continued sheathing wire walls of Huts, also temporary of wire walls of those completed. Weather hot and dusty. Went to/with W. Hut to BOESCHEPE and saw plans of proposed Camp at XV Corps Sanitary School.	
	3.5. 1917		Went to MONT NOIR and saw 28,600. Rest moved R.A.M.C. Weather fine, hot with light W. wind.	
	4.5. 1917		Weather fine and warm. Moved from Billets into village & opened Hut built by the men.	
	5.6. 1917		Weather fine, warmer wind W. but at 3 p.m. veered to N.E. causing temperature to fall until by 8.30 p.m. it was distinctly cold. Rain is now needed for the crops and to lay the dust which is very bad. The Boche NORTH-WEST. from the light of the DUNHOP probably the site of KEMMEL HILL.	

WAR DIARY or INTELLIGENCE SUMMARY

Army Form C. 2118.

108th FIELD AMBULANCE

Place	Date	Hour	Summary of Events and Information	Remarks and references to Appendices
DRANOUTRE	6.5.1917 (cont)		The record part of the men available for wounded at RADENHOEK is now nearly complete. Scout morning kept out for stretcher cases being got in. Noon still E, cool, cold, bright. Heavy British wind. Germans retaliating feebly throughout the night.	
	7.5.1917		The MG fired and highly unemies. Heavy British gunfire at night scattering our defenses of enemy wire from YPRES to LAVENTIE probably. Left Stephy train from J. Motestry throughout the night. A few German shells (5".9") fell in the fields to night of our camp. They did no damage & enoprt to 2/Apps. I began to think state on Dry letter of weapp. Bullets. Nearly rain till 10 a.m., after that a dirale repaired.	
	8.5.1917		floor of staffs. Continued the putting down of Bonds in front of the Huts. LIEUT. J. TEWKESBURY left to join Second Army School of Cookery for a short course of Instruction. Improved floor of staff behind convent.	
	9.15 & 3 p.m. 1917		Wrote to MONT NOIR and drew 7600 in order to be able to pay Officers under for Turkco Allowance and anthority of few small prices of glen.	

WAR DIARY or INTELLIGENCE SUMMARY

Army Form C. 2118.

(Erase heading not required.) 1/0 8TH FIELD AMBULANCE

Place	Date	Hour	Summary of Events and Information	Remarks and references to Appendices
DRANOUTRE	9/8/1917	(cont)	Heavy hostile gunfire from KEMMEL at 11h at night. Began to make a stretcher for Horse Ambulances and water cart at the Convent in the village.	3
	10/8/1917		Weather fine, men very little to do, busy over graves. Lines, Latrines, Brushed up Ambulances, Hand used also at tents to walk from round to huts. Finished temporary cellar of Village Billets and began to clear the floor of the accumulated filth of a century, went to BAILLEUL in the afternoon. "Noted ECOLE S. JOSEPH" in which arrived a new party, and which is to be handed over to an Australian Casualty Clearing Station tomorrow morning. Bought 10 panes of glass, 20" x 13" for use in E. Hospital Hut — making Room bright also 64 yards water cable for CAMPBELL. The hand over equipment at ECOLE S. JOSEPH tomorrow at 11" am. CAPT J.L. DUNLOP M.C. proceeded to LINDENHOEK for temporary duty. LIEUT. A GRANT has been laid up for two past Mondays with what appears to be Malarial Fever.	

Army Form C. 2118.

WAR DIARY
or
INTELLIGENCE SUMMARY

(Erase heading not required.) 108th FIELD AMBULANCE.

Place	Date	Hour	Summary of Events and Information	Remarks and references to Appendices
DRANOUTRE.	11.5. 1917.	6.30 a.m.	Some German shells fell unfortunately near camp. Two wounded near tree with litter not used. Considerable shelling of British aeroplanes. Completed cleaning of ellis in village billets. Tents tarpaulin occupied, splendid. To be about two hundred years old and is well built with some fire rooms in it. Entrances worked and stands for horse ambulances prepared waiting in front of hospital huts. Began to puree in. The two ponds and to build platforms across which to place water. Any carpentery a perk-carpentery was kept into two spent packs for use as an officers mess (coin) attached privately from England. Men were now ready for any emergency. Completed the laying of Decoville train way in front of H.Q. Repairs to huts Partag and Intex House.	
	13.5. 1917.		Remainder of tent platforms completed ready for use during evening attack. Platforms for same felt being laid at T. Crests also felt of all morning but bottom windy. LIEUT A. GRANT who has been ill for 4 days transferred to No 2. C. C. Mathews cape of Keluk Fuse.	

B 2449 W. W 14957/M00 £750,000 1/16 J.B.C. &A. Forms/C.2118/12.

Army Form C. 2118.

WAR DIARY
or
INTELLIGENCE SUMMARY

(Erase heading not required.)

108th FIELD AMB. 9th Army

Place	Date	Hour	Summary of Events and Information	Remarks and references to Appendices
DRANOUTRE.	13.6. 1917.		Capt. S.P. REA returned from LINDENHOEK and Capt. E.S. SOWERBY from 12th Bn. R.I. Rifles (KEMMEL HILL). Weather fine and warm and the bus coming beautifully into leaf. KEMMEL Hill and its neighbourhood took a extremely beautiful. Some thunder and lightning at night with heavy rain.	
	14.5. 1917.		Completed partitions so as to form an Officers' Ward. This ward holds 16 Queen beds. Cement ground further ventilated pantry wall, whitewashed caves, two pantry "N" for two purposes, having reduced butter and tinned provision containers ready for wounded. The Bodies for waterlupply with a fluid, kitchen hand sieved, and pantry pans at tin cove oil on fruits and on water no two FVO trucks to check the feeding of incorrectly completed concrete floors	
	15.5. 1917. 10. a.m.		on all latrines. Capt. SOWERBY proceeded to LINDENHOEK. Walked by way of KEMMEL VILLAGE to new and well being built near Reserve Trench about midway between truck known as VIA GELLIA and eventually known as SPUD ROAD. Came back by motor ambulance road between Irening Farm and to LINDENHOEK across road repaired by shell fire and is being repaired.	

2449 Wt. W14957/M90 750,000 1/16 J.B.C. & A. Forms/C2118/12.

WAR DIARY or INTELLIGENCE SUMMARY

Army Form C. 2118.

108th FIELD AMBULANCE

Place	Date	Hour	Summary of Events and Information	Remarks and references to Appendices
DRANOUTRE	15.6. 1917	(cont)	Enemy artillery fairly active East of Pantry, bursting fine, chilly at night.	
	16.6. 1917	10 a.m.	Attended conference convened by Head Quarters & continued of the name "WASTER" in connection with the 36TH DIVISION. Relief by D.D.M.S. and A.D.M.S. (IX Corps and 36TH DIVISION) to review Survey Stations, apparently much pleased by what they had received. Completed holes in Pantry & put fire extinguishers. Received Heavy rain at night. O.C. set working party to INDENHOEK (10 men) everything in good order. Obtained 600 gallons petrol for enemy cab of heavy work. It is necessary to build a store for this away from other buildings. Kept to best corrugated iron covered with felt. Also carried sectional corrugated iron covered with felt for motor loading party. O.C. accb 10 men from 150th Company R.E. and sent these to new to INDENHOEK. This morning the daily working party here to 20 men. Completed building of Bivies & need of Pantry's a very good piece of work, bytes Bivies are now ready for use. Obtained canvas with which to finish Pantry walls. Sent at 1:15 p.m. by an officer personal to the Division Engineer General Batts Q.D. St Inyds, IX Corps. at 1:30 p.m. Enemy shells fell 10 yards from our huts making a large hole but little most of all	

2449 Wt. W14957/M90 750,000 1/16 J.B.C. & A. Forms/C.2118/12.

WAR DIARY / INTELLIGENCE SUMMARY

Army Form C. 2118.

(Erase heading not required.) **108 the FIELD AMBULANCE**

Place	Date	Hour	Summary of Events and Information	Remarks and references to Appendices
DRANOUTRE	17.5.1917		Hot and grand. Flying about us. Day unpleasant. Received orders from D.D.M.S. IX Corps not to keep carts but to evacuate all to Rest Station or to C.C. Station. Began to build Brick Incinerators.	
	18.5.1917		Fine and warm. Visit by A.D.M.S., who sent about 100 horses looking round. The place, but could find nothing wrong. Began to build Pitch fires, wooden frames covered with 6in. corrugated iron roof dovetailed with sods. Went out with rake, and waiting for more bricks in order to complete incinerators.	Began to build fires. Frames covered. Began to build 480 fires.
	19.5.1917		Tuesday. Slightly overcast, pleasant, but very bright. Kept of Trees and hedges and planted young corn very luxuriant. Considered shelling of one side Ypres by the Germans with the 6.9" shells which make a tremendous noise.	Statistics from Thielt.
		10.30	Visit by IX Corps Commandant Asst: General O HAMILTON GORDON with his Chief Staff Officer, Inspected places of work & appeared to know the details that he was quite satisfied with what he had seen. Four Prisoners trained and marched at E. end of camp. Conference at A.D.M.S. Offices at 3 P.M.	
	20.6.1917	9.45 am	Rode with Capt D. G. W. REA to Transport lines. Rode to Divisional Headquarters & then Reports at A.D.M.S, rode with Major	

Army Form C. 2118.

WAR DIARY
or
INTELLIGENCE SUMMARY
(Erase heading not required.) 108th FIELD AMBULANCE.

Place	Date	Hour	Summary of Events and Information	Remarks and references to Appendices
DRANOUTRE	20.6.1917 (cont.)		to Nieuport Lines. Rode back by way of KEER & BROHM, BOESINGHE, JANSEN & VRAIMD. Two bulgues received and published. Regiser more staff for the ensuing two weeks. Offices in the Marquee. Filled stores completed week. Taken into use. Received 100 stretchers from 110 & 7 Amb, also received small articles. Sent requirement in on move went to O.C. 109th Fd Ambulance. Received prescribed eliminated cards (6) for sets of quality event for good work performed by N.C.Os and men of this Unit - cited Scope to other units in order.	
	21.6.1917	10 A.M.	Rode to Nieuport lines and back by tanks through fields. Heavy rain overnight.	
	22.6.1917		Heavy rain during the morning. Visit by D.D.M.S. and D.A.D.M.S. 12. noon. LIEUT. RAMSBOTHAM on land with me to "NO EARLIER" by the upper road which I think might be used for lower patients we came nearer home for motor ambulances. Walked by the line, vested back to DRANOUTRE by top cart through "SWINDON JUNCTION". LIEUT. RAMSBOTHAM and Capt J.H. DUNLOP, M.C. took all available wheeled stretchers to LINDENHOEK by motor ambulance & me at night.	

Army Form C. 2118.

WAR DIARY
or
INTELLIGENCE SUMMARY

(Erase heading not required.) 108th FIELD AMBULANCE.

Place	Date	Hour	Summary of Events and Information	Remarks and references to Appendices
DRANOUTRE.	22.6.1917.	9.45 a.m.	Rode to BAILLEUL by way of KACKE through field count at CROIX POPERINGHE. Bought a half nib. chews so as to fetch some work of superintendence for wite carts alongside over to carry extra water. began work on shed to hold stretches and blanks to for exchange as expected this eving.	
		2.45 p.m.	Visit by 2nd army Commander – General sir HERBERT PLUMER, K.C.B./Heavy rain at night.	
	24.5.17 1917.	10. a.m.	Rode with Capt. S.P. REA to HEAD QRS., 109th FIELD AMBULANCE, and field count of inspiring our cases sent by a through farmer on a ridge army service corps. Rode back by track through the fields. Capt. PRATT, R.A.M.C. joined the field ambulance in place of 4.15017. A. GRANT evacuated to the BASE. Fine day, chilly at night. Two years today since I took over command of this Field Ambulance. Completed Muster and blankets.	
	20.5.17 1917.		Heavy Torkish gun fire most of today. Beautiful bright clear warm, with very little wind. began second blanket and established their completed Musty, an excellent fine – new gun fire at night, Hulls of works far on-	

Army Form C. 2118.

WAR DIARY
or
INTELLIGENCE SUMMARY

(Erase heading not required.) 108th FIELD AMBULANCE

Instructions regarding War Diaries and Intelligence Summaries are contained in F. S. Regs., Part II. and the Staff Manual respectively. Title Pages will be prepared in manuscript.

Place	Date	Hour	Summary of Events and Information	Remarks and references to Appendices
DRANOUTRE	25-6-17		Another 1½ mile E. of DRANOUTRE — NEUVE EGLISE ROAD. Completed staining of marquees with the exception of tops. Weather fine, warm, wind Easterly. Rode to Transport Lines, held 2 hours one Employment Company men at 3 p.m., most of them are unfit for the trenches. Capt J.H. DUNHOP, M.C. returned 5 pm LINDENHOEK, Capt A.W. REA proceeded to LINDENHOEK. Fairly heavy British gun fire all day with little reply from the Hermans. The Rev. C.C. MANNING returned from the Corps Rest Station, BAILLEUL, completed nine Inoculations.	10
	26-6-17		Weather fine, hot and dusty. Rode round recently past transport Lines and 109th Field Ambulance. Heavy Bosche gun fire all day. at 9 p.m. Heavy German artillery fire began over our trenches and at 9.30 p.m. shells began to fall in DRANOUTRE in considerable numbers, having fairly close over our camp, sent all men not required for duty to the trenches near by for shelter, at 9.45 p.m. sent too motor Ambulances to Divisional Headquarters front S. of DRANOUTRE where many casualties were occurring. Three NCOs and men killed in Divn Headquarter coach and Hotel. as well as Pt Jones, E. R. E. killed during the night.	

WAR DIARY or INTELLIGENCE SUMMARY

Army Form C. 2118.

(Erase heading not required.) 108th FIELD AMBULANCE.

Instructions regarding War Diaries and Intelligence Summaries are contained in F.S. Regs., Part II. and the Staff Manual respectively. Title Pages will be prepared in manuscript.

Place	Date	Hour	Summary of Events and Information	Remarks and references to Appendices
DRANOUTRE.	27/6/1917.		Shelling stopped at 1.p.m. Recd very rapid shelling again at 3.30 p.m. Stopped at 3.45 p.m. Sixty eight casualties occurred amongst troops in the village and its neighbourhood during the night. These casualties behind village billets. Evacuated by pieces of shell. Seven cases major. Eighteen, R.A.M.C. by this unit, slightly wounded, no single by piece of shell.	
	28/6/1917.	9.30 a.m.	Walked up to ANDENHOEK with the Captn DUNHOP. One pte. to R.A.P. (B) Slightly wounded by gas in one shell last night at ANDENHOEK. Returned by motor ambulance to DRANOUTRE at 2. p.m. Twenty three men not Dit. wd E.S.E., light duty. Heavy rations 9 am Repetition of Monday. Throughout the day but there was no notification in so as to give any warning. Many shells dropped on the camp just over to the united Trenches; Shelling of roads in neighbourhood of the village continued till 10 p.m. After 2.p.m. Two men killed, nine other casualties, rode by own country tracks round about way to transport lines. Repetition of wagons is now newly completed. Country too dry lovely; but constant noise. Feel the military roads wonderful over men encircle of nature. Oriental, and newtownships, road.	

| | 29/6/1917. | 10.30 a.m. | | |

2449 W.: W4957/Mg0 750,000 1/16 J.B.C. & A. Forms/C.2118/12.

WAR DIARY

INTELLIGENCE SUMMARY

(Erase heading not required.) 108th FIELD AMBULANCE.

Army Form C. 2118.

Instructions regarding War Diaries and Intelligence Summaries are contained in F. S. Regs., Part II. and the Staff Manual respectively. Title Pages will be prepared in manuscript.

Place	Date	Hour	Summary of Events and Information	Remarks and references to Appendices
BRANDHOEK E.	29.8.17	cont	Engaged to build concealed new shelters to mess writing room, officers sleeping quarters to form a communicating trench between mess hut and advanced dressing station. Visit to camp by Brigadier General RICARDO, 109th Infantry Brigade, at 6 p.m. Camp and village shelled at night.	
	30.8.17 10 a.m. and		Rode to Divisional Headquarters & ordered to maintain gas shelter in newly known offices on night duty etc. Started to re-erect former shelters & to build up front of village shelled at night, village billets slightly damaged by the fire, weather fine, bright, Wind S.W. Chilly at night.	
	31.8.17 10 a.m. cont		Rode to Transport Lines, MILLE FARM, and severence of Headquarters. Obtained additional material for the two theatre cases, placed boy upright and horizontal in position in cellar so as to maintain the wages of filling memory. KITE BALLOON burnt by German supply guns at 9.15 p.m. Weather fine, very chilly at night.	

W.H. Fincastle Lt.
108th In Field Ambulance
O.C., 108th In Field Ambulance, Colonel

COMMITTEE FOR THE
MEDICAL HISTORY OF THE WAR
Date - 7 AUG. 1917

No. 108. T. A.

WAR DIARY or INTELLIGENCE SUMMARY

Army Form C. 2118.

Vol 21

16

108 III FIELD AMBULANCE

Place	Date	Hour	Summary of Events and Information	Remarks and references to Appendices
TRANOY Fm.	Feb 16 1917		Weather hot, everything now ready for tomorrow. Where lying on bed at midnight, 5.9 in shell landed 20 yards from myself, got into small dugout. Several shell landed within 15 yards, covered one with rubble & grass, empty stores hut (tenet) by fragments of shells, newly persons left shell scenes within ten feet; burst by fragments of shells; whole clung to the ground, got into old repwater trench (by art) and stood in thin rope, shell momentarily burst close but beyond immediately followed by another which burst right opposite me at distance of 4 1/2 yards, knocked a decent blow on the top of the head from a large stone, steel helmet twisted on one but head somewhat bruised, got out of trench as a couple of minutes apart went round camp, allowed herd to come tea. Turned in at 3.30 am. All men and patients; turned in at 2.30 am. Revelles for the night	

Army Form C. 2118.

WAR DIARY
or
INTELLIGENCE SUMMARY

(Erase heading not required.) 105th FIELD AMBULANCE.

Place	Date	Hour	Summary of Events and Information	Remarks and references to Appendices
DRANOUTRE	2.6. 1917	2.30 P.M.	Rode to MONT NOIR and arranged with D.D.M.S. IX Corps to attach a 2nd Divisional Headquarters if necessary. Its became intensely fierce shellfire. Quiet at night.	
	3.6. 1917		Fine weather. Quiet except for a few shells at night.	
	4.6.1917	4 p.m.	Motored up to LINDENHOEK and then Capt. BOYD CAMPBELL and CAPT. ST. REA. Rode to BAILLEUL in the afternoon with Capt. ST. REA. Heavy shells falling in the neighbourhood of the town. On return 5.9 inch shells falling in neighbourhood roads one mile S. of DRANOUTRE, waited for a comparatively quiet moment and then rode rapidly back to the village. A few shells over camp at night.	
	5.6. 1917		Still wind extremely hot. BAILLEUL and its neighbourhood shelled by guns of heavy calibre, a large store of gun ammunition up W. of LE RAVETSBURG blown up by a bomb from an enemy aeroplane.	
	6.6. 1917	4 p.m.	Went up to LINDENHOEK by car. Returned at noon by car with A.D.M.S. 8th Division. Rode to 109th Field Ambulance at 3. P.M. and attended Conference.	

Army Form C. 2118.

WAR DIARY
or
INTELLIGENCE SUMMARY

(Erase heading not required.) 108TH FIELD AMBULANCE

Instructions regarding War Diaries and Intelligence Summaries are contained in F. S. Regs., Part II. and the Staff Manual respectively. Title Pages will be prepared in manuscript.

Place	Date	Hour	Summary of Events and Information	Remarks and references to Appendices
DRANOUTRE	7/6/1917		A few wounded in during the early part of the day. At 8 a.m. Messines exploded at 8 a.m., not very much fired by the ground and bed trembled considerably. Barometter began becoming in fairly large numbers from 9 a.m. onwards, being all day. Over 700 casualties through the field ambulances. MESSINES and WYTSCHAETE taken from the Germans, one of our men (MADDISON) killed, two wounded. Numbers of casualties were coming through very fresh.	MAJOR W. REDMOND 6TH Bn. ROYAL IRISH, died of wounds in this ambulance.
	8/6/1917		BAILLEUL slightly shelled in the morning. Attended funeral of MAJOR W. REDMOND at LOCRE at 6.30 p.m., very few casualties, chiefly Germans, beginning to hand over, began to clear camp.	
	9/6/1917		Handed over to 34TH FIELD AMBULANCE. 11th Divission marched from DRANOUTRE at 2.40 p.m. through LOCRE and WESTOUTRE to a farm 1½ miles S.E. of BOESCHEPE, a beautiful place comparatively quiet, accord a pleasant change from the recent shell.	
	10/6/1917		Only necessary work done. Rode to MONT NOIR in the afternoon and drew ₣1000 with which to pay men. Paid out partly recently at LINDENHOEK, at 6 p.m. Weather fine and hot. (COQUERELLE FARM).	

2449 Wt. W14957/M90 750,000 1/16 J.B.C. & A. Forms/C.2118/12.

WAR DIARY or INTELLIGENCE SUMMARY

Army Form C. 2118.

10 S.A. FIELD AMBULANCE

Place	Date	Hour	Summary of Events and Information	Remarks and references to Appendices
12/6/1917			Sticking of Infantry by section Commanders in the morning kept me busy in the afternoon.	
	12/6/1917	2.30 pm	Rode to DIVISIONAL HEADQUARTERS, SJANSCAPEHE. Heavy Thunderstorm shown H.Q. over T.E.O. 6th D.W., T.E.O. 8th D.B. CAMBEEH viewed our temporary billets with the 12th Royal Welsh Rifles.	
	13/6/17		In the afternoon, Rode in direction of BOESCHEPE and BERTHEN with Capt S.P. REA round country, bound of this country here are almost as pretty as those in ENGLAND, but I much, no quite so pretty.	
	14/6/17	8.30 am	Heavy firing by our guns and enemy guns. Two I believe 9 machine enemy aeroplanes to be them to be our as well returned to harbour.	
	15/6/17		Proceeded to gallop in the morning. the men are having a glorious and well deserved rest in this beautiful place. Rode through BOESCHEPE and about neighbouring country, kept in careful list of names for honours and rewards (Immediate)	
	16/6/17		I ever very hot. proposed to be D.M.S. II Army at 4.15 pm. (5.15 pm to 8 pm) went to front to night DES.EA. 78	
	17/6/17		Made to front E.7. S.JANS CAPEHE by way of BERTHEN, returning visibility by Electric Flash light by candlelight	

Army Form C. 2118.

WAR DIARY
or
INTELLIGENCE SUMMARY

(Erase heading not required.) 108th FIELD AMBULANCE

Place	Date	Hour	Summary of Events and Information	Remarks and references to Appendices
	17.6.17		(Cont) Large numbers of troops moving up from METEREN area. Received orders to move tomorrow to MERRIS AREA. The orders were cancelled at 10.p.m.	
	18.6.1917		Heavy raids during the day. Some shells passed over the camp, other shells must have been fired from a point more than 10 miles away. Received orders to hold a party in readiness to return to WINDENHOEK. Detailed Capt. S.P. REA and Capt. E.S. SOWERBY with the N.C.O. and 36 men with 8 motor ambulances. They two the party to WINDENHOEK at 11.30.p.m. Saw O.C. 35th Field Ambulance and arranged to take over from him in the morning. Remainder of camp moving party on journey at KEMMEL for the night, at 12.45 p.m. Field Ambulance ordered to return to DRANOUTRE tomorrow.	
	19.6. 1917	11.15 a.m.	Marched to DRANOUTRE arriving there at 1.p.m. took over again from 3/4 the Field Ambulance, where relieved us when we marched out on June 10th. Sent N.C.O. and 23 men to PATR RAIN FARM, 3/4 mile N.E. of WINDENHOEK to	

2449 Wt. W14957/M90 750,000 1/16 J.B.C. & A. Forms/C.2118/12.

WAR DIARY or INTELLIGENCE SUMMARY

Army Form C. 2118.

(Erase heading not required.) 108 (1/0) FIELD AMBULANCE.

Place	Date	Hour	Summary of Events and Information	Remarks and references to Appendices
DRANOUTRE	19.6.17 (Cont)		Received forty where received there last night. Sent up a photo motor ambulance for duty at ok E.O. PATRAIN FARM. A large number of shells passed over the camp at night; falling in or near WESTOUTRE, 3 miles	DRANOUTRE
	20.6.1917	10 am	Rode to LINDENHOEK. The field ambs. covering to PATRAIN FARM. Saw Capt S.T. REA. Thank you. Temporarily but to hand. Went to BAILLEUL act 5.30 p.m. took one officer to the Isolation Hospital, and one to the 18. Corps Rest Station, three shells fell in the town this morning fired from a distance of 10,000 yards. A few shells burst fairly near camp this afternoon. Sent a FORD MOTOR AMBULANCE for duty at LINDENHOEK and arranged to send a horsed ambulance daily to patient road from LINDENHOEK, two Captive Balloons burnt by German aeroplanes (2) at 4.55 p.m. Heavy rain at night.	
	21.6.1917		In camp all day attending to various matters. Heavy rains all night. German high velocity guns spasmodically shelled our neighbourhood with such severity literally. Some [?] at night.	
	22.6.1917	6.10 am	Walked to PATRAIN FARM. Had to go by STUD ROAD and YONDE STREET as KEMMEL was being shelled. Showers during the morning and overcast. Walked with Capt. E.S. SOMBY through WYTSCHAETE and returned via to. Heavy shelling by the Germans	

Army Form C. 2118.

WAR DIARY
or
INTELLIGENCE SUMMARY

(Erase heading not required.) 108th FIELD AMBULANCE.

7.

Place	Date	Hour	Summary of Events and Information	Remarks and references to Appendices
DRANOUTRE	22.6.1917 (cont.)		especially in OOSTAVERNE WOOD our reply much heavier, in returning had to lye on road and run to the dug-outs and which wind moving to some shelling by 5.9" shells, several the ruins of WYTSCHAETE 3 minutes before shells were bursting in the middle of it. In many places a vile smell is very apparent. I believe a large number of Germans are buried by our shell fire. Examp of German uniform protruding in many places. We have just inspected a 15" gun just E of the large crater (mine crater) and I believe there to be another one beside it in WYTSCHAETE there is scarcely a building standing a foot above the level of the ground. Returned to DRANOUTRE at 8 p.m. German high velocity guns rather annoying at night. A little mortar in the afternoon and evening. Refilled FORD CAR from LINDENHOEK. Some shelling by Germans in neighbourhood with high velocity gun at night.	
	23.6.1917		Weather cool, casual shots from but number of high morning. Many of the men having temperatures of 102°. Three of our Captive Balloons burnt by German aeroplanes at 4.50 p.m. Usual shelling in neighbourhood at night.	

Army Form C. 2118.

WAR DIARY
or
INTELLIGENCE SUMMARY
(Erase heading not required.) 108th FIELD AMBULANCE

Place	Date	Hour	Summary of Events and Information	Remarks and references to Appendices
DRANOUTRE	24.6.1917		The thirteen (?) aeroplane of Captain Bellew's burnt by a German aeroplane 1½ miles S.E. of this camp. Shelling in neighbourhood of DRANOUTRE at night, also of BAILLEUL which caused a fire considerable size but not far from this town. No casualties. Patrols midnight onwards till 2 a.m.	
	25.6.1917		No casualties from midnight to 8 a.m. Bellew immediately S.O.S. was shewed at intervals during the day without any effect. No further casualties at Field Ambulance and killed amongst other Staff Sergeant Palmer of this unit for 18 learning as patients. This is the first Court Martial on any man of the Field Ambulance since I took over command over two years ago and despite the fact it will be the only one. In note of the Royal Australian Travelling Company was accidentally killed when riding on a motor Bicycle by collision with a motor lorry 1½ mile S.W. of DRANOUTRE at 11.10 a.m. Cause of death extreme fracture of right side of skull. Weather cool and overcast. Rain at night.	
	26.6.1917		Heavy rain during the greater part of the night. Several wounded in during the night, there shaky and Menebo accidentally wounded by explosion of a German bomb, not much shelling during the night. Haphazard reconnaissance for divisional breaks.	

Army Form C. 2118.

WAR DIARY
or
INTELLIGENCE SUMMARY
(Erase heading not required.) 108TH FIELD AMBULANCE

Place	Date	Hour	Summary of Events and Information	Remarks and references to Appendices
DRANOUTRE	26.6. 1917. (cont)	11 a.m.	LIEUT. TEWKESBURY proceeded to STRAZEELE and to arrange about billeting O.C. Still Field Ambulance arrived to relieving Futher over. Major J. A. BOWKER; J. A. BOWKER sent to No. 2. Corps Rly Receiving Station suffering from anaemia and debility. German aeroplanes active.	
	27.6. 1917.		Half of advanced Post relieved by 50TH Field Ambulance. Rode to MONT NOIR with Capt. A.W. REA and drew money to pay leave men with Capt. A.W. REA. Heavy hostile gun fire in front of us at night. Capt. T.S. P/REA and half of bearers returned at 7.p.m.	one of our Balloons burnt at 3.45 p.m 2 miles N.T. This camp.
	28.6.(?)20. 1917. Cont		Non-lighted sentence about marshal one Staff Sergeant in P/MER reduced to Mes and HS. Went to FLETRES with LIEUT. TEWKESBURY and arranged new billets ½ mile S. of FLETRES, ½ mile S. OF FLETRES, parties of our bearers attached to parties completed and Capt. SOMERBY and second half returned to main body arriving there at 11 a.m. Main body of 50TH Field Ambulance arrived at 2 p.m. and began to take over. Weather fine, warm. Somewhat cloudy and a rifle of evening.	
	29.6. 1917.	2:30 p.m.	Completed handing over main Dressing Station by 11 a.m. Moved from DRANOUTRE by way of CROIX de POPERINGHE, S. JANS CAPELLE, METEREN and FLETRES, arriving at BILLETS ½ mile S.W. of FLETRES at 6.10 p.m., Major MEREDITH joined the Field Ambulance.

Army Form C. 2118.

WAR DIARY
INTELLIGENCE SUMMARY

(Erase heading not required.) 108th FIELD AMBULANCE

Place	Date	Hour	Summary of Events and Information	Remarks and references to Appendices
FLÊTRE.	30/6/1917.		Heavy rain following a thunderstorm which began at 9.30 a.m. 30/6 is a godsend to be only able to hear the guns comparatively faintly thro' the raining most of the afternoon and gun fire much heavier from 5 p.m. onwards. No premises in present Billets for washing or latrines, and no materials available with which to make these structures. I shall have to "borrow" a few pieces of timber from the inhabitants.	

B F Fawcett
Lieut. Colonel:
O.C. 108th Field Ambulance.

COMMITTEE FOR THE
MEDICAL HISTORY OF THE WAR
Date   10 SEP. 1917

Army Form C. 2118.

Vol 22/1

WAR DIARY
or
INTELLIGENCE SUMMARY
(Erase heading not required.) 108th FIELD AMBULANCE

Instructions regarding War Diaries and Intelligence Summaries are contained in F. S. Regs., Part II. and the Staff Manual respectively. Title Pages will be prepared in manuscript.

Place	Date	Hour	Summary of Events and Information	Remarks and references to Appendices
PLÊTRE	1.7.1917		Weather wet.	
	2.7.1917	10 a.m.	Hot and sultry. Rode to MONT NOIR and thence 76960.00	
		2 p.m.	Paid men. Paid out 76820.00.	
	3.7.1917		Hot and sultry. Received orders to march to LA KREULE Std 6 TH instant	
	4.7.1917		Slight showers. Rode to LA KREULE	
	4.7.1917	10.30		
	19.17	p.m.		
	5.7.1917	8.15 a.m.	Marched from LE BEURRE — PLETRE — arrived at LA KREULE at 10 a.m. Military accommodation insufficient, 8 officers in tents.	
	6.7.1917	6.20 a.m.	Marched from LA KREULE. Arrived at BLOMART at 10.30 a.m. Beautiful fine country. Weather fine, bright moonlight, night about 25 Boards dropped by Germans unexploded at 10.30 to 11 p.m. and 2nd batch at distance of 2 miles from camp.	
	7.7.1917	5.50 a.m.	Marched from BLOMART through BLENDECQUES, WIZERNES, HALLINES, SETAUES, QUELMES, CARME NOIR, to WHEOSE, arriving at 11.45 a.m. Billeting material all over used Doriers. LIEUT. TEWKESBURY preceded on leave, went to (officers in tents, country very fine concerning forth 500 with which to pay leave men)	

S. OMER
2449 Wt. W14957/M90 756,000 1/16 J. B. C. & A. L. Forms/C. 2118/12

Army Form C. 2118.

WAR DIARY
or
INTELLIGENCE SUMMARY

(Erase heading not required.) 108th FIELD AMBULANCE.

Instructions regarding War Diaries and Intelligence Summaries are contained in F. S. Regs., Part II. and the Staff Manual respectively. Title Pages will be prepared in manuscript.

Place	Date	Hour	Summary of Events and Information	Remarks and references to Appendices
NIEUW S.E.	9.7.1917.	(Contd.)	Heavy rain with lightning at night. Lance Corporal GIBSON awarded the Military Medal for gallantry at MESSINES.	
	8.7.17.		Overcast and threatening rain. Rode to MOURE	
	9.7.17.		Cool and threatening rain.	
	9.7.17.	9.30 am	Route march through BARBINGHAM, MORINGHEM, Pt DIEQUES, COPMETTE and ZUDAUSQUES, out two hours and the pace got the whole time. Hut in accommodations for immediate removal for period June 19th to June 29th 1917, where our Teams were at rest beyond WYTSCHAETE. Birrelie? Rain in the afternoon.	
	10.7.17.	9.30	Route march. Handed over to Major Ineson, R.A.M.C. and proceeded on 10 days' leave.	

H.F. Ainsworth
Lieut. Colonel.
O.C. 108th Field Ambulance.

Army Form C. 2118.

WAR DIARY
or
INTELLIGENCE SUMMARY

(Erase heading not required.)

Place	Date	Hour	Summary of Events and Information	Remarks and references to Appendices
Dickebusch	24/7/17		Capt H. L. Burton 110th Field Ambulance arrived in morning & temporarily attached to unit. Capt Dunlop & Capt Swaby with one Tent Sub division proceeded to HAVENSQUERQUE Farm to run a rest station. Lt Tuskerby and S/Sgt men proceeded to WINNEZEELE as advance party & took over billets from 113 Field Ambulance. Capt G W Rea left at 7.30 am with Field Ambulance transport en route for WINNEZEELE Area. Rest Part attached to report at No 2 Canadian CCS. Left this morning at 6 am. Ambulance arrived at 9 am and marched to entraining point. W2A30 Sheet 27 where S.E. landed over & Capt H L Burton and proceeded on 10 days leave.	
	25.7.17		very wet	A.W. Campbell Capt RAMC
	25.7.17		Ambulance arrived at WINNEZEELE 25.7.17.	
	26.7.17		Should back to Col Jewitt, and did not proceed on 10 days leave.	Signed Capt RAMC

WAR DIARY
or
INTELLIGENCE SUMMARY

Army Form C. 2118.

Place	Date	Hour	Summary of Events and Information	Remarks and references to Appendices
LIHEUSE	21/7/17	—	At rest. Training, route marches, gas-drills & bathing parades. Handed over to Capt Ondey. R.A.M.C.	
	21.7.17	3 P.M	Marched from LIHEUSE to BARBINGHEM. All men and officers accommodated in billets. Officers marque pitched for mess.	Renewed field Ranks
BARBING HEM	23/7/17		Received instructions from A.D.M.S. to detail 1 M.O.R. for duty with No 2 Canadian C.C.S. also to detail 3 Officers and one Tent Subdivision with Transport - two motor ambulances for duty with 5th Army first station at HAVENSKERQUE FARM. Instructed 2nd Lieutenant & the above four and then 2 Hope. ? VIII Corps at ESQUERLESQUES and interviewed D.D.M.S. VIII Corps. Detailed Capt. E. S. SOWERBY and myself for this duty on 23.7.17. Handed over command of the Ambulance to Capt. S. B. B CAMPBELL.	

23/7/17

J. Sopwith Smith
Capt. R.A.M.C.

Army Form C. 2118.

WAR DIARY
or
INTELLIGENCE SUMMARY

(Erase heading not required.)

Instructions regarding War Diaries and Intelligence Summaries are contained in F. S. Regs., Part II. and the Staff Manual respectively. Title Pages will be prepared in manuscript.

Place	Date	Hour	Summary of Events and Information	Remarks and references to Appendices
NINNEZEELE	26.7.1917	11.30 a.m.	Returned from leave and took over from Capt D.G.W. BEA. Weather very hot, walked 10 miles to Graase Hunt. Capt P.R.E.A. reported from 107 R.A. Rifled.	
	27.7.1917		Norenmhs regiment proceeded to POPERINGHE to a Conference.	
	28.7.1917		Norenmhs.	
	29.7.1917		Norenmhs.	
	30.7.1917		Regt S. P. Ran proceeded to 8th Army Rest Stations in relief of Capt E.S. SOWERBY who proceeded with 1/9 men to WAAMERTINGHE for duty at a Walking wounded Station, marched at 8.30 p.m. to L.13.d.3.2. (Sheet 27) 2½ miles S.S.E. of WATOU.	
	31.7.1917		Heavy rain all afternoon. Capt. J.N. DUNN,O. reported from 8th Army Rest Station at noon. Reinforcements of 178 men, drawn to draw.	

2449 Wt. W4957/M90 750,000 1/16 J.B.C.&A. Forms/C.2118/12.

Army Form C. 2118.

WAR DIARY
or
INTELLIGENCE SUMMARY 108 TH FIELD AMBULANCE
(Erase heading not required.)

Instructions regarding War Diaries and Intelligence
Summaries are contained in F. S. Regs., Part II.
and the Staff Manual respectively. Title Pages
will be prepared in manuscript.

Place	Date	Hour	Summary of Events and Information	Remarks and references to Appendices
L.13.D.3.2. Sheet 27. 1/4n. 2/4o m/to S.S.E of WATOU	31/7/17		Applied for 6 extra Bell Tents. Heavy firing again at night.	
			H. Fitzwoy H. Lieut. Colonel, O.C., 108th Field Ambulance	

B.E.F.

SUMMARY OF MEDICAL WAR DIARIES OF 108th F.A. 36th Div.

8th Corps 5th ARMY.

19th Corps from 26th July.

4th Corps 3rd ARMY from 23rd August.

Western Front Operations - July-August 1917.

Officer Commanding - Lt.Col.R.F.M.FAWCETT.

SUMMARISED UNDER THE FOLLOWING HEADINGS:-

Phase "D" 1. - Passchendaele Operations-"July-Nov. 1917"

(a) - Operations commencing July 1917.

B.E.F.

2.

108th F.A.   36th Div.   Western Front.

19th Corps 5th ARMY.   July-Aug. 1917.

Officer Commanding - Lt.Col.R.F.M. FAWCETT.

PHASE "D" 1. - Passchendaele Operations - "July-Nov.1917".

    (a) - Operations commencing July 1917.

Headquarters at Winnezeele.

July 26th.	Transfer. To 19th Corps.
30th.	Moves. Detachment. 1 & 19 to W.W. Station.
	Moves. To L. 13. d. 3.2. (Sheet 27) 2½ miles South of Watou.

B.E.F.

1.

<u>108th F.A. 36th Div.</u>   <u>Western Front.</u>
<u>8th Corps 5th ARMY.</u>   <u>July 1917.</u>
<u>Officer Commanding - Lt.Col. R.F.M. FAWCETT.</u>

<u>19th Corps from 26th July.</u>

PHASE "D" 1. - <u>Passchendaele Operations "July-Nov.1917."</u>
    (a) - <u>Operations commencing July 1917.</u>

Headquarters at Liheuse.

July 7th.   <u>Transfer.</u> Transferred from 2nd Army.

              <u>Decoration.</u> L/Cpl. Gibson awarded M.M. for gallantry
                          at Messines.

8th-20th. <u>Ops. R.A.M.C.</u> Training etc., in Rest Area.
21st.   <u>Moves.</u> To Barbinghem.
23rd.   <u>Moves.</u> Detachment. O & 19 to No. 2. Can. C.C.S.
24th.   2 & 1 T.S.D. to 5th Army R.S.

           Haversquerque Fm.

25th.   <u>Moves.</u> To Winnezeele.

26th.   <u>Transfer.</u> To 19th Corps.

B.E.F.

108th F.A.   36th Div.   Western Front.
8th Corps 5th ARMY.   July 1917.
Officer Commanding - Lt.Col. R.F.M. FAWCETT.

19th Corps from 26th July.

PHASE "D" 1. - Passchendaele Operations "July-Nov.1917."
    (a) - Operations commencing July 1917.

Headquarters at Liheuse.

July 7th.	Transfer.	Transferred from 2nd Army.
	Decorations.	L/Cpl. Gibson awarded M.M. for gallantry at Messines.
8th-20th.	Ops. R.A.M.C.	Training etc., in Rest Area.
21st.	Moves.	To Barbinghem.
23rd.	Moves. Detachment.	O & 19 to No. 2. Can. C.C.S.
24th.		2 & 1 T.S.D. to 5th Army R.S. Haversquerque Fm.
25th.	Moves.	To Winnezeele.
26th.	Transfer.	To 19th Corps.

B.E.F.

2.

108th F.A. 36th Div.   Western Front.

19th Corps 5th Army.   July-Aug. 1917.

Officer Commanding - Lt.Col.R.F.M. FAWCETT.

PHASE "D" 1. - Passchendaele Operations - "July-Nov.1917

(a) - Operations commencing July 1917.

Headquarters at Winnezeele.

July 26th.   Transfer.   To 19th Corps.
     30th.   Moves. Detachment.   1 & 19 to W.W. Station.
              Moves. To L. 13. d. 3.2. (Sheet 27) 2½ miles
              South of Watou.

COMMITTEE FOR THE
MEDICAL HISTORY OF THE WAR
Date -1 OCT. 1917

No. 108. 7a.

WAR DIARY

INTELLIGENCE SUMMARY

108th FIELD AMBULANCE

Vol 1 2 3

Army Form C. 2118.

Place	Date	Hour	Summary of Events and Information	Remarks and references to Appendices
L.13, D.3, 1.8. 2½ miles S.S.E. of WATOU	1.9.14.		Very heavy rain throughout the day. A.D.M.S. returned to do leave. Instructed Ambulance at 2.45 p.m. Detailed Capt J.H. DUNLOP, M.C. and 36 men & 1 N.C.O. to be held in readiness to move forward at short notice.	
	2.8.1914.		Heavy rain throughout the day.	
	3.8.1914.		Major MEREDITH returned from leave. Heavy rain. Camp kept in much. Received orders to send 2 officers and 2 bearer subdivisions to Corps main Dressing Station at 9 am tomorrow (RED FARM. 2 miles E. of POPERINGHE.)	
	4.8.1912		Sent Capt J.H. DUNLOP. & Capt J.W. REA with 2 bearer subdivisions as ordered. Weather damp with some rain. A.D.M.S. went south and was evacuated to the Base.	
	5.9.17		Weather fine and during afternoon somewhat. Some shelling in neighbourhood from heavy German guns. Went to Divis Hdqrs camp 2½ miles beyond POPERINGHE, also to VLAMERTINGHE.	6 men of unit gassed. 3 wounded, evacuated to C.C.S.
	6.9.17		Weather very damp and foggy. Sent 3 clerks and two G.S. waterly motor ambulances to Corps. Walking Wounded Station at Bicael through fence & took (arm ornament) and placed their for as possible under cover of this. Major MEREDITH proceeded to Corps main Dressing Station, RED FARM. Capt J.W. REA.	

H.J. Rugles.

Army Form C. 2118.

WAR DIARY
INTELLIGENCE SUMMARY

(Erase heading not required.) 108th FIELD AMBULANCE.

Instructions regarding War Diaries and Intelligence Summaries are contained in F. S. Regs., Part II. and the Staff Manual respectively. Title Pages will be prepared in manuscript.

Place	Date	Hour	Summary of Events and Information	Remarks and references to Appendices
6.1.B.d.2.2. 2 1/2 miles S.E. of WATOU.	7.8. 1917.		Weather damp but no rain during the morning. Fine in afternoon. Heavy artillery fire from 9.30 p.m. till midnight. Many trains troops trains passing.	
	8.8. 1917.	10 am	Sent 19 N.C.Os and men to do temporary duty at Corps Rest Station. Two men of this unit slightly gassed yesterday afternoon and evacuated to C.C.S. Weather mild but misty. No remarks.	
	9.8. 1917.		Weather unsettled. Bombs dropped near camp at midnight.	
	10.8. 1917.		Visited A.D.M.S. Office and received orders to proceed to WIELTJE. Obtained the necessary maps.	
	11.8. 1917.			
	12.8.17.	3 pm	Visited A.D.M.S. Office in company with Capt. J.G. DUNLOP, M.C.	
	13.8.17		Orders to proceed to WIELTJE cancelled. Received orders to proceed to RED FARM and Take over MAIN DRESSING STN.	
	14.8.17.		Found Transport lines and accommodation were RED FARM, returned to camp (MILK Cuts Camp) packed transport wagons and marched at 9.20 p.m.	
	14.8.17.		At destination at 9.20 p.m., packed transport in square near farm	

Army Form C. 2118.

WAR DIARY
or
INTELLIGENCE SUMMARY

(Erase heading not required.) 1/08th FIELD AMBULANCE   No. 3

Place	Date	Hour	Summary of Events and Information	Remarks and references to Appendices
RED FARM, 2 miles NE of POPERINGHE	14/8/1917		Took over command of main Dressing Station; Casualties occurring day and night about 100.	
	15/8/1917		O.C. 1/9 Fd. Ambulance and his officers proceeded to W.15.A.7.S.E. Dug up nearly all kit of their unit.	
	16/8/1917		Severe attack but Dressing Stn caught the heavy day & night. Capt. S. ECCLES R.A.M.C. (unposted 13th R.S. Rifles) killed 5 Capt. DUNDEE Bomb with R.S. Rifles wounded. Capt. RAWLINS R.A.M.C. 110th Fd Amb. Both continued till they were relieved. Stretcher Bearer Officer wounded.	
	17/8/1917		Division began to be relieved. Our men returned to their Dressing Station during the night, having been relieved by ambulance of 67th Division. 110th Field Ambulance returned to RED FARM. 110th Fd ambce new Strength Advance Party of another field ambulance 67 Division arrived.	
	18/8/1917			
	19/8/1917			
	20/8/1917		Handed over RED FARM, and loaded our men passing Station, arrived at 4.10 p.m., and marched to a point just outside E.J. WINNEZEELE 8.80 p.m. pitched camp; the men marched extremely well.	

Army Form C. 2118.

WAR DIARY
or
INTELLIGENCE SUMMARY
(Erase heading not required.) 108th FIELD AMBULANCE.

Instructions regarding War Diaries and Intelligence Summaries are contained in F. S. Regs., Part II. and the Staff Manual respectively. Title Pages will be prepared in manuscript.

Place	Date	Hour	Summary of Events and Information	Remarks and references to Appendices
WINNEZEELE	26.8.1917		Weather warm. The crew rested, but a guard in attendance to rear areas to get organs where necessary.	
	22.8.1917.		Rode over to 110th Field Ambulance. Lieut. RICHMAN U.S.A. joined for duty. Capt. J.L. DAMP presented on return to Base from area. Went to CASSEL Station to engage rd entrainment.	
	23.8.1917.		Heavy rain at night. Packed wagons.	
	24.8.1917.	9.45 am	Marched to BAVINCHOVE STATION and entrained; horses entrained and twice and whilst entrained in two horses arrived at MIRAUMONT (7 miles W.S.W. of BAPAUME) at 8.30 p.m. Detrained. Men went in lorries to camp immediately S. of BEAUNEVOORT, leaving Station at 10.30 P.M.; Rode to camp with Quartermr arriving at 4 A.M.. Feeling ill with throwings & catarrh. Capt. A.W. REA also ill suffering from asthma and bronchitis. Weather fine. Checked all Equipment left S.P. REA detailed for temporary duty with 11th Batt R.B., 2 Rifles. Rode through VILLETS an FMO S and LE TRANSLOY.	
	26.8.1917.		Received orders to take over from 27th Field Ambulance 9th Division at FREGNECOURT.	

WAR DIARY
INTELLIGENCE SUMMARY

108th FIELD AMBULANCE

Place	Date	Hour	Summary of Events and Information	Remarks and references to Appendices
BEAUENCOURT	27.8.1917	9.30 a.m.	Sent advanced party of 1 Officer (Capt. BOYD CAMPBELL) and 20 other ranks to ROYON EFFORT to begin training crew. Proceeded to ROYON COURT at 10.20 am and drew a.e. 27 To field ambulance and A.D.M.S. 9th Division. (COLONEL EASNER, R.A.M.C. 9th Division, enclosed to Lieut. RIGHTMAN, U.S.A. Medical Corps to join Capt. I. Campbell. Heavy rains at night with regarding work.) Capt. G.W. REA examining 42nd Labour Company at YPRES for classification as to fitness for service. Capt. C.P. REA with Capt. G.W. REA proceeded to YPRES to continue examination of men of 42nd Labour Company, during the day. Walked to WHER & ODEBY with Pre. e.e. MANNING, the place is a perfect scene of desolation but has been a very pretty village.	5
	29.8.1917	8.50 a.m. 9.19 a.m.	Marched off from BEAUENCOURT; arrived at ROYON COURT at 11.20 a.m. Went to advanced pumping station. Returned at 4 p.m.	Capt. Campbell at 2.30 p.m.

Army Form C. 2118.

WAR DIARY
or
INTELLIGENCE SUMMARY

(Erase heading not required.) 108th FIELD AMBULANCE.   6

Instructions regarding War Diaries and Intelligence Summaries are contained in F. S. Regs., Part II. and the Staff Manual respectively. Title Pages will be prepared in manuscript.

Place	Date	Hour	Summary of Events and Information	Remarks and references to Appendices
REMILLY-WIRQUIN	30.8.1917	10 am	Route to Advanced Dressing Station, Mont noir, and all Posts Reconnoitred on our two return's left. Examined the Advanced Dressing Station with a view to making improvements by the Field Ambulance detailed on Oct. 9/10. and the Captain UNDERHILL	Capt. J.h. DUNLOP proceeded on leave.
	31.8.1917	10.30 am	went to Advanced Dressing Station with 19th FIELD AMBULANCE for instruction. (Returned from 19th FIELD AMBULANCE for instruction.) Returned at 12.30 p.m. Heavy showers during the morning. Went out extreme for entertaining music during Pierrots.	

31/8/1917

B Whitwell
Lieut: Colonel
O.C., 108th Field Ambulance.

Aug. 4th.	Moves. Detachment.	2 & 2 Br. S.Ds. to C.M.D.S. Red Farm.
6th.	Moves. Detachment.) Moves Detachment Transport.)	O & 3 and 5 M. Ambs. to C.W.W.C.P.
8th.	Moves. Detachment.	O & 19 to C.R.S.
	Casualties R.A.M.C.. Gas.	O & 2 gassed.
14th.	Moves.) Medical Arrangements.)	To Red Farm and took over C.M.D.S.
15th.	Moves. Detachment.	All bearers sent up to front line.
16th.	Operations.	36th Division attacked but were repulsed.
	Casualties.	Heavy.
18th.	Moves. Detachment.	Bearers rejoined Headquarters.
20th.	Medical Arrangements.	Red Farm handed over to F.A. of 61st Division.
	Moves.	To Winnezeele.

B.E.F.

<u>108th F.A. 36th Div.</u>   Western Front.
<u>19th Corps 5th ARMY.</u>   August 1917.
<u>Officer Commanding - Lt.Col. R.F.M. FAWCETT.</u>
<u>4th Corps. III. Army.</u>

<u>PHASE "D" 1. - Passchendaele Operations - "July-Nov.1917"</u>
   (a) - <u>Operations commencing July 1917.</u>

<u>Headquarters at Winnezeele.</u>

Aug. 23rd.   <u>Moves and Transfer.</u>   To 4th Corps 3rd. Army and commenced move to New Area.

B.E.F.

<u>108th F.A. 36th Div.</u>　　　　　　　<u>Western Front.</u>
<u>19th Corps 5th ARMY.</u>　　　　　　　<u>August 1917.</u>
<u>Officer Commanding - Lt.Col. R.F.M. FAWCETT.</u>
<u>4th Corps. III. Army.</u>

<u>PHASE "D" 1. - Passchendaele Operations - "July-Nov.1917"</u>
　　　(a) - <u>Operations commencing July 1917.</u>

<u>Headquarters at Winnezeele.</u>

Aug. 23rd.　　<u>Moves and Transfer.</u>　To 4th Corps 3rd Army and commenced move to New Area.

B.E.F.

SUMMARY OF MEDICAL WAR DIARIES OF 108th F.A. 36th Div.

8th Corps 5th ARMY.

19th Corps from 26th July.

4th Corps 3rd ARMY from 23rd August.

Western Front Operations - July-August 1917.

Officer Commanding - Lt.Col.R.F.M.FAWCETT.

SUMMARISED UNDER THE FOLLOWING HEADINGS:-

Phase "D" 1. - Passchendaele Operations-"July-Nov. 1917"

(a) - Operations commencing July 1917.

Aug. 4th.	Moves. Detachment.	2 & 2 Br. S.Ds. to C.M.D.S. Red Farm.
6th.	Moves. Detachment. Moves Detachment Transport.	) O & 3 and 5 M. Ambs.) to C.W.W.C.P.
8th.	Moves. Detachment.	O & 19 to C.R.S.
	Casualties R.A.M.C. Gas.	O & 2 gassed.
14th.	Moves. Medical Arrangements.	) To Red Farm and took over) C.M.D.S.
15th.	Moves. Detachment.	All bearers sent up to front line.
16th.	Operations.	36th Division attacked but were repulsed.
	Casualties.	Heavy.
18th.	Moves. Detachment.	Bearers rejoined Headquarters.
20th.	Medical Arrangements.	Red Farm handed over to F.A. of 61st Division.
	Moves.	To Winnezeele.

No. 108. 7. a.

COMMITTEE FOR THE
MEDICAL HISTORY OF THE WAR
Date -5 NOV.1917

Army Form C. 2118.

WAR DIARY
INTELLIGENCE SUMMARY
of 108th FIELD AMBULANCE

(Erase heading not required.)

Instructions regarding War Diaries and Intelligence Summaries are contained in F. S. Regs., Part II. and the Staff Manual respectively. Title Pages will be prepared in manuscript.

Vol 24

Place	Date	Hour	Summary of Events and Information	Remarks and references to Appendices
ROYANCOURT	1.9.1917		Began to erect first NISSEN BOW HUT; an advance party away assisting and seems to make a Reception Hut. Leaving from the south. Walked to YPRES and interviewed C.R.E. re Stores for enlargement of Main Dressing Station. Rode to 110th Field Ambulance (N. of BUS). Capt. WILSON joined from 8/9th Rifles. Lieut. TEWKESBURY went to AMBERT for stores.	
	2.9.1917		Weather showery. Continued clearing ground for Reception Hut. Continued work at NISSEN BOW HUT. Proceeding on "Gas Palette". Lieut. TEWKESBURY proceeded to AMBERT for Hospital Equipment. Heavy firing throughout the night.	
	3.9.1917		Two large B.G.x'L beams by hand and Tackle into Field Ambulance Compound for purpose of reinstating Reception Hut. Rode to ETRICOURT and seen R.T.O. with which to pay two men. Weather misty but clearer at 11 am. Paid men.	
	4.9.1917		Rode to Headquarters at 5.45 pm. Weather cleaned fine, warm, very little wind. German aeroplanes active. Rode to Advanced Dressing Station and fined two men. Completed work on first Nissen Bow Hut with exception of lining. Began to put upright in position for Reception Hut.	
	5.9.1917		Work proceeding well with second Nissen Bow Hut, began to put uprights in position for Reception Hut.	
	6.9.1917 2.30 pm		Rode to YPRES and obtained order from C.R.E. for timber, iron, sheeting and nails. Work as usual.	

2449 Wt. W14957/M90 750,000 1/16 J.B.C. & A. Forms/C.2118/12.

Army Form C. 2118.

WAR DIARY
or
INTELLIGENCE SUMMARY.
(Erase heading not required.)

108th FIELD AMBULANCE.

Place	Date	Hour	Summary of Events and Information	Remarks and references to Appendices
RUYAULCOURT	7.9.1917	10.30 a.m. and	Rode to Advanced Dressing Station, HAVRINCOURT WOOD, and paid remainder of men there, tents were up to expect for the day in making framework of shelter for officers. Began roof of Reception Hut.	
	8.9.1917		Continued work on Reception Huts and Miners Bow Huts, containing Reception of Sick. Rode to YPRES in the afternoon.	
	9.9.1917		Discovered officers tent pegs very well, rode to advanced dressing station, reached new framework in HAVRINCOURT WOOD, had 2 shelters now in running. Capt. E.S. SOWERBY returned from leave, began work on 2nd MINER BOW HUT. Made to DIS. and attended payment of men from ordnance. Held memo at 5.30 p.m. on Divis. A.S.C. for services as Infantry. Capt. E.S. SOWERBY joined 11th Nor. R. commanding FUSILIERS at BERTINCOURT on temporary duty.	
	11.9.1917		Rode to EQUANCOURT and YPRES, saw A.D.M.S. who stated that he would recommend one for promotion. A few enemy shells falling in neighbourhood of village from 2 p.m. until 5 p.m. on Shelter tents to E.A. camps nearly finished. Overcast with slight showers which cleared up at noon. Wind fresh, northerly. Tiled roof of Reception kept covered. Tacwelta called the accel erected. Root of Reception tent half completed.	

WAR DIARY
INTELLIGENCE SUMMARY

Army Form C. 2118.

108 2nd FIELD AMBULANCE

Remarks and references to Appendices: **3**

Place	Date	Hour	Summary of Events and Information
FUTRAHENTAIT	12.9.1917.		(cont) Had board on officer for Indian Army Reserve etc. - completed shuttle tunnels for men E. of camp. Road to advanced dressing station in the afternoon and continued work in progress, also ambulance of shell fuzzy shells. Indented for Remount Supplies for advanced dressing station. Captain J.T. DUNLOP, M.C. returned from leave. Occupied most of the day. Col. ROSS to Divisional Headquarters. Major General O.S.W. NUGENT, commanding 36th Division visited our camp at 12.30 p.m. and informed us that our work reflected the greatest credit upon us. Work going on well.
	13.9.1917.		
	14.9.1917.		Cool. Showered during the morning. Completed the V of 3 Sgt. NISSEN Doll. Hut and heavy rains at night. Captain J. ROSS returned to 11th R.J. Rifles in relief of Capt. COWELL, RAC.
	15.9.1917.		Showers throughout morning. Went out & got NISSEN Hut and Spindle surface of two width earth to cover it. Capt. UNDERHILL, Capt. COWELL sent down sick and evacuated to LIEUT. R/B/H M.R.W. Rode to Ordnance Depot beyond DVS and ordered Dumpsters to purchase two large iron kettles for cook-Pits. Fulfilled letter of instruction. OpD HQ W/A 80M /16.

Army Form C. 2118.

4.

WAR DIARY
or
INTELLIGENCE SUMMARY

(Erase heading not required.)

108th FIELD AMBULANCE.

Instructions regarding War Diaries and Intelligence Summaries are contained in F. S. Regs., Part II. and the Staff Manual respectively. Title Pages will be prepared in manuscript.

Place	Date	Hour	Summary of Events and Information	Remarks and references to Appendices
ROYAL COURT.	16.9.1917.		Weather unsettled. Continued work. Major RUSSELL and Capt. STAHLMAN, U.S.M.C., joined for 7 days' instruction.	
	17.9.1917.		Showers during morning, work progressing well with 4 Battns. Completed reorg and regn. log of Reg'tal Aid Posts. Advanced Dressing Station and Collected Waters with regard to requirements in cases of wounded reaching Theatre Iron Josh dome scheme that, Rode through EVRANCOURT to ETRECOURT with Major RUSSEL, U.S.M.C., and Capt. STAHMAN, U.S.M.C., prescribed & advanced Dressing Station for a three days tour. Obtained 2 large covered Motor Vehicles for use this Reserve from AMIENS.	
	19.9.1917.		Beautiful mild weather. Major RUSSELL and Capt. STAHMAN U.S.M.C.	
	20.9.1917.	9.30 am.	Rode to NEUVILLE and had home at Divisional Hd qrs, YPRES on Lieut. BRADY, 12th R.J. Rifles, a candidate for the Section Army. Not Work as usual, got Neuville for Roof on own House. Began Huts to be used for Night duty Belly used as a Breach Emergency Ward.	

WAR DIARY or INTELLIGENCE SUMMARY

Army Form C. 2118.

108th FIELD AMBULANCE.

Place	Date	Hour	Summary of Events and Information	Remarks and references to Appendices
RUYAULCOURT.	21/9/17.	10 am	Rode to ETRICOURT and drew 71000 w. th which to pay men going on leave. All MESSEN HUTS Named (14) all now erected. Carpenters from putting up more became the R.E. are slow at what is supplying materials. Continued painting & inside of Recreation Room and walls of Reception Room. These are really fine, keep to own building into the others. Wrote a total keep of 1400 ft. Got running lights in position for Res. Room Roof. Weather beautifully fine.	
	22/9/17.		Perfect meal cooks. Enemy aeroplane overhead eventually got so near, took to advanced Dressing Station. Continued work on huts.	
	23/9/17.		Work as usual. Major RUSSELL and Capt. 87th LANMAN v. S. M. C. left the Field Ambulance and Proceeded to No. 21, C. C. S., YPRES, Weather beautiful.	
	24/9/17.		Held Board to classify certain men at Divisional H.d Qr. Weather beautiful. Sky cloudless, hot, and no wind. Box ward completed as hut for night duty party to be used as an emergency theatre.	

WAR DIARY

INTELLIGENCE SUMMARY

Army Form C. 2118.

108th FIELD AMBULANCE

(Erase heading not required.)

Place	Date	Hour	Summary of Events and Information	Remarks and references to Appendices
RUYAULCOURT	25.9.1917	10:30 am	Rode to advanced Dressing Station. Officers Mess completed and work being pushed. Work proceeded at Headquarters. Repairs to furniture, Officers' Ward with beds, mattresses, crockery etc.	
	26.9.1917		Began Erecting 4 additional NISSEN BOW HUTS for accommodation of men. Finished painting inside of roof of Receiving & Dressing Huts. Night Duty Party (Emergency Hut) nearly completed. Capt J.L. DUNLOP proceeded to No. 19 C.C.S. on temporary duty. Lieut. Capt. ———— a good Medical officer, he may not rejoin this unit, having applied for an appointment where he may have an opportunity to do surgery. Received a notification from the War Office that Capt. A.W. REA is sick at home, and will not rejoin. Rain at night.	
	27.9.1917		Overcast during the greater part of the day. Five wounded evacuated from METZ, struck by one shell which also killed three. Began to put Pugain corrugated into Dressing Hut, the roof of which is all painted white which gives it more light and looks extremely well. Receiving Hut is having a second coat on its roof and shelves are being put into it. Capt. SOWERBY proceeded to Advanced Dressing Station in relief of Captain BOYD Campbell. Lieut. McTavish with thirteen other rank proceeded to build thirteen but Munich huts. Lieut. McTavish writes to say that he is getting on well with constructing another steel nissen.	

m1821 W 0141/484 750M 6/17 D.D.& L.   A.D.S.S./F9147/C 2118

WAR DIARY

INTELLIGENCE SUMMARY.
(Erase heading not required.)   108th FIELD AMBULANCE

Army Form C. 2118.

Place	Date	Hour	Summary of Events and Information	Remarks and references to Appendices
ROUADCOURT			Completed posting of Sergeant Officer who was proceeding Hosp.	
	28/9/1917		Held Board on Officer for Indian Army Reserve. Rode to Divisional Headquarters and held round and memo for distribution. Orderliest Seargt begat at intervals. Capt. S.P. REA returned from leave.	108th FIELD AMBULANCE
	29/9/1917		Rode to Advanced Dressing Station, officer in charge complete and went nearly so. The group fence in addition the various shelts used for casualties but exposed to interning at the [?]. Capt. S.P. REA proceeded to Advanced Dressing Station.	S.P. REA
	30/9/1917 10.30 a.m.		Rode to Divisional Headquarters and obtained orders for troops. Weather very close, constant shelling throughout afternoon and night in neighbourhood. Enemy German gas.	

H.Fitzacrett
Lieut. Colonel
O.C. 108th Field Ambulance

30/9/1917

COMMITTEE FOR THE
MEDICAL HISTORY OF THE WAR
Date -8 DEC. 1917

Army Form C. 2118.

WAR DIARY
INTELLIGENCE SUMMARY.

(Erase heading not required.) 108th FIELD AMBULANCE.

Instructions regarding War Diaries and Intelligence Summaries are contained in F.S. Regs., Part II. and the Staff Manual respectively. Title pages will be prepared in manuscript.

Place	Date	Hour	Summary of Events and Information	Remarks and references to Appendices
RUYAULCOURT.	1.10.1917.	5.45 p.m.	Rode to ETRICOURT and drew 7.6700 with which to pay the men. Paid out at 6.45 p.m.	
	2.10.1917.		Rode to advanced Dressing Station and fixed new ground there.	
	3.10.1917.		no remarks.	
	4.10.1917.		no remarks.	
	5.10.1917.		Heavy shelling to E of camp by German guns from 1.45 p.m. till 7 p.m. auto medic light completed. Steps from road to Receiving Hut.	used as new Duty room.
	6.10.1917.		Opened Receiving Hut for patients, using E end for Medical Inspection Room. Began to roof Stables. Heavy rain storms.	
	7.10.1917.		Heavy rain during day. Began to build Drying Room.	
	8.10.1917.		Continued work on Orderly Room, Officers Beds, Drying Room, lining walls of Cook House, roof of Stables. Worth of Dummies Hut, first stoves in a ward. Receiving Hut used during night.	
	9.10.1917.		Heavy normal protected road during last night but new buildings not damaged by it. Rode to ETRICOURT and drew 7.100 with which to pay men going on leave.	
	10.10.1917.		Retired firmly. Proceeded to AMIENS and bought bolts, hinges, and calico for use in building huts. Pte MULCAHEY, R.A.M.C. died of wounds received firmly. Pte PORTER, R.A.M.C. killed by shell fire.	

Army Form C.2118.

WAR DIARY
OF
INTELLIGENCE SUMMARY.
(Erase heading not required.) 1/08 2⁰ FIELD AMBULANCE.

Instructions regarding War Diaries and Intelligence Summaries are contained in F. S. Regs., Part II. and the Staff Manual respectively. Title pages will be prepared in manuscript.

Place	Date	Hour	Summary of Events and Information	Remarks and references to Appendices
BUYANCOURT.	11.10.19.17.		Rode to Divisional Headquarters and held General's Officers and men. Redeau Army Reserve - Officers Dispensation - general in the Killyanjel awaited, attended funeral of the late and Pte MULCAHEY at 3. P, our heavy command day, bath with strong S.W. wind.	
	12.10.19.17.			
	13.10.19.17.		So ruin during morning but weather milled wind they switted, cleared chilly, went to PERONNE in the afternoon. Some old and haf seen beautiful but thoroughly disturbed in many parts by the Germans.	
	14.10.19.17.			
	15.10.19.17.		White frost in the night, am now putting up 7 TD. NISSEN BOW HUT, two could have been completed long ago if materials had been available, attend conference at Divnl. HQrs at 10. am re authority of patients.	
	16.10.19.17.		Rode to Divisional Headquarters and obtained order for CAMP's SHELTER 45"×11". To instigate us shelters for the men io cover this village is shelled. I have got trenches in various parts of the camp but think it advisable to have better protection.	
	17.10.19.17.		Village shelled from 8.15. and RB 9.30 and with 4.2" shells, about 30 shells fell in the village, two of our men slightly wounded and one infantry 2 cer/ two civile wounded dispersed men to shelter and turned horses out onto the neighbouring lay as much	

W 2354—K 34 W 25+1/1454 508,000 5/15° D. D. & L. A.D.S.S./Forus/G.2118

Army Form C. 2118.

WAR DIARY

INTELLIGENCE SUMMARY

(Erase heading not required.) 108TH FIELD AMBULANCE.

Instructions regarding War Diaries and Intelligence Summaries are contained in F.S. Regs., Part II. and the Staff Manual respectively. Title pages will be prepared in manuscript.

Place	Date	Hour	Summary of Events and Information	Remarks and references to Appendices
RUYAULCOURT	17/9/1917		Heavy morning ground shell which only earned a burial. Began excavating the CRAB'S SHELTER. Went to ETRICOURT in the afternoon and drew 9,1000 with which to pay men going on leave.	
	18/9/1917		Rode to ETRICOURT, went to C.R.E. (as ronds E & W of HAYRINCOURT WOOD which require repair) wrote to C.R.E. requesting the repair of these roads with sleepers or R.E. Props, our men dig the roofs of contained excavation for shelter. This is now 6 feet in all. Visit by A.D.M.S. at 6.30 p.m.	
	19/9/1917		Weather unsettled. Began to bed flooring of shelter together and fixed in anatomies. Rode through B U 8 and BARASTRE returning partly across country.	
	20/9/1917		Continued work on shelter, worked to lower dimensions of the latrine completed.	
	21/9/1917		Both exercised. Heavy shelling by enemy of HAYRINCOURT WOOD.	
	22/9/1917		Two convivial officers joined for a days tour. Surveying some during the day. Made Friday good progress with the TCC. Relief ordered to Wagons R.E.O.	
	23/9/1917		Relieved troops remaining in newfeer on Red Post W. side of HAYRINCOURT WOOD went other W.231HY154 700 Sept 9/15 D.D.&L. A.D.S.S./Form/C. 2118. Obtained under for Cullins Patrol for A.D.G.	

Army Form C. 2118.

WAR DIARY

INTELLIGENCE SUMMARY.

(Erase heading not required.) 108th FIELD AMBULANCE

Instructions regarding War Diaries and Intelligence Summaries are contained in F. S. Regs., Part II. and the Staff Manual respectively. Title pages will be prepared in manuscript.

Place	Date	Hour	Summary of Events and Information	Remarks and references to Appendices
ROYAULCOURT	23.10.1917 (cont)		Capt. BRIDGMAN and Lieut. WHARTON U.S.M.S.R. who joined in a few days for instruction proceeded to the advanced Dressing Station at 9.30 a.m.	
	24.10.1917.		Fine in forenoon; wind strong N.W. Roads to ETRICOURT. The Undertaking Heavy Car on right to the gun emplacement completed and roundway roof of shelter. Many were at night.	
	25.10.1917.		Rain at intervals during morning and afternoon after the gun emplacements from S, went to Corps Headquarters (VILLERS AU FLOT) and then 4,000 with whirls to buy men going on leave. Went with A.D.M.S. and HERMIES as far as broken CANAL BRIDGE, from there along road to RESERVE AID POST; N.W. of HAVRINCOURT WOOD, walked from there to WADON POST. W.of HAVRINCOURT WOOD and to MOTOR AMBULANCE back to Headquarters. Heavy rain at night, began to place log roof on shelter. Third to go are obtained from a German Dug out S.W. of this village.	
	26.10.1917.		Weather chilly and uncertain. Continued discovery of dugout, German dugouts.	

WAR DIARY

INTELLIGENCE SUMMARY

(Erase heading not required.) 108½ FIELD AMBULANCE.

Army Form C. 2118.

Remarks and references to Appendices: 5.

Instructions regarding War Diaries and Intelligence Summaries are contained in F.S. Regs., Part II. and the Staff Manual respectively. Title pages will be prepared in manuscript.

Place	Date	Hour	Summary of Events and Information	Remarks and references to Appendices
BUSSUCOURT	27.10.1917		Reconnaissance work. Rec'd wire from Divn. Shelter to cross road W. of HAVRIN COURT WOOD. Capt. BRIDGMAN and Lieut. WHARTON; V.S. M.T.O returned from Advanced Dressing Station. Capt. BOYD CAMPBELL-here. Capts. S.P. REA at advanced dressing station. Work continued on Shelter, orderly room completed, built of recovered corrugated iron.	
	28.10.1917		Capts. BRIDGMAN and Lieut. WHARTON left for AMIENS on completion of their tour of instruction. Rec'd mockingly; Staff front least weight. Orders to VILLERS AU FLOS in the afternoon in search of timber for making of road from MATHESON ROAD to WAGON POST E. of HAVRIN COURT WOOD. There is considerable amount of timber in the German trenches but it would need a great deal of excavations before much of it could be recovered.	
	29.10.1917		Wind W. Cold. Went through ALBERT to AVELUY and HAMEL. This village was the scene of our work in the Spring of 1916. The Shelters built by us which accommodated, bye evacuated our wounded are now running. The trench running by this side of the road from the wood tenable to HAMEL, were no field dug, but use to trench by sap. NVIIIL E. now in care HAMEL. The Shelter built by Sergt. NVIIIL E. at the entrance of the village is still standing. The communicating trench-dug they have also disappeared.	

2355 Wt. W.3041/454 750,000 5/15, D. D. & L. A.D.S.S./Forms/C. 2118.

Army Form C. 2118.

WAR DIARY

INTELLIGENCE SUMMARY.

(Erase heading not required.) 108th FIELD AMBULANCE.

Instructions regarding War Diaries and Intelligence Summaries are contained in F. S. Regs., Part II. and the Staff Manual respectively. Title pages will be prepared in manuscript.

Place	Date	Hour	Summary of Events and Information	Remarks and references to Appendices
BUSVILLERS.				6.
	29.10.1917.		Issued large quantities of Heavy Trench Standards No. 9. the village without cost. One officer was present. Could not negotiate. Convoy reached 4 p.m.	
	30.10.1917.		Weather chilly; showing S.W. wind. Rode to YPRES to see C.R.E. But two officers there, returned by way of BUS near BERTINCOURT.	
	31.10.1917.		Obtained orders for troop for making of road to Wagon Posts. Attended Conference at A.D.M.S. Office at 4 p.m.	

K.J. Fawcett
Lieut: Colonel
O.C. 108 Field Ambce

31
10
1917

COMMITTEE FOR THE
MEDICAL HISTORY OF THE WAR
Date   17 JAN.1918

No. 108. T. A.

WAR DIARY

INTELLIGENCE SUMMARY

108th FIELD AMBULANCE

Army Form C. 2118

Place	Date	Hour	Summary of Events and Information	Remarks and references to Appendices
ROYAUCOURT	1.11.1917	8.45 am	Rode to VILLERS AU FLOS and drew $160.40 with which to pay the men. Paid out at 12 noon. Handed over to Capt. S.P. REY and proceeded on 14 days leave.	

R.P. Inwood Tt
Lieut. Colonel.
O.C. 108th Field Ambulance

Army Form C. 2118.

WAR DIARY
or
INTELLIGENCE SUMMARY.

(Erase heading not required.)

108th FIELD AMBULANCE

Place	Date	Hour	Summary of Events and Information	Remarks and references to Appendices
RUYAULCOURT	28/11/17		Took over command of the 108 F.A. from Lt. Col. R.J.H Fawcett on the 1st NOVEMBER 1917. Shelter shelters for stretcher ambulances. Continued work on the dugout for the personnel of F.A. & also continued work on the new Canteen and Recreation Room.	

E.P.Ree
Captain
O.C. 108th Field Ambulance

WAR DIARY
or
INTELLIGENCE SUMMARY
(Erase heading not required.)

Army Form C. 2118.

108º FIELD AMBULANCE

Place	Date	Hour	Summary of Events and Information	Remarks and references to Appendices
RUYAULCOURT	3/11/1917		Continued the work of interments.	
			COL. WEEK A.D.M.S. Corps. called this morning & discussed the nature of arrangements and	
		3.30 pm	proceeded further on, to the left magazine at P.12.13.50 SHEET 57C. to see the track from it, F.A. moving the road for convenience by motor Ambulance.	
			CAPT. C.C.GIBSON I.R.A.M.C. 109 F.A. returns home for temporary duty G. 30Q. to Anthony A.D.M.S.	

Alfred Cuppin
O.C. 108º Field Ambulance

Army Form C. 2118.

108th FIELD AMBULANCE

WAR DIARY
or
INTELLIGENCE SUMMARY.
(Erase heading not required.)

Place	Date	Hour	Summary of Events and Information	Remarks and references to Appendices
RUYAULCOURT	4/11/1917	13 a.m.	The wounded of yesterday still give us anxiety. Sixteen received 9 R.I.B. so stretcher Co. went in making the lighter wounded walk & not through the MEATH-ENCOUTURE - RUYAULCOURT ROAD for enemy by motor ambulance of sick and wounded, they take during return and return here in the evening.	

SPRBa
Captain
O.C. 108 F/AMBULANCE

Army Form C. 2118.

WAR DIARY
or
INTELLIGENCE SUMMARY.
(Erase heading not required.)

108TH FIELD AMBULANCE

Place	Date	Hour	Summary of Events and Information	Remarks and references to Appendices
RUYAULCOURT	5/10/17	6.30 am	Attended flour store, night mist, enemy aeroplanes went down trying Aspect wall not enemy aircraft. S. HELLITE T.G. and search party leaving mats for ambulances stand by - came to A.D.S. at Q 14.a.7. Thence from there to METZ-EN-COUTURE. Improving situation. Went to A.D.M.S. office YPRES Q 36 h.i. as A.D.M. seemed to have gone slightly different route to there went, much thing etc night and returned 2 F.A. CAPTAIN C.G. GIBSON R.A.M.C. 109 F.A. previously O.i/c 1st R.IR.FUS. for 13 hours trying duty by today A.D.M.S. CAPTAIN E.S. SOWERBY M.C. R.A.M.C. returned to duty out. Enq wrote after Company duty with 12TH R.IR. RIFLES. Saw A.D.M.S. 31st Division St.A.D.S. and should be the minimum places for men and makes & regrets. CAPTAIN J.L. DUNLOP M.C. R.A.M.C. & this for returning stud 19 C.C.S. billed dead leaving 1st F.A. Saw CAPTAIN SIR B. CAMPBELL MO% ADS Ammunition well.	

S.P.? Supple
O/C 108. F.A.

Army Form C. 2118.

WAR DIARY
or
INTELLIGENCE SUMMARY.
(Erase heading not required.)

106 FIELD AMBULANCE

Place	Date	Hour	Summary of Events and Information	Remarks and references to Appendices
RUYAULCOURT	6/11/1917		The enemy commenced severe shell at 10 A.M. about 150 yards from the Cemetery which is about 400 yards N.E. of F.A; the horses were immediately removed at once to Ytres. Bombardier Smythe enters the village and at right range a safety shot which confidence was seen on fire as an incendiary was falling. Bright shrapnel came in from (8-11-17). The Shelter or Relief a shelter has been quilt. CAPTAIN C.C.G. GIBSON R.A.M.C. 109 F.A. attained Q. Ric unit after he was put until for R.I.R. FUSILIERS. there was no funds during the villages was one truck admitted for minor 8th stellen.	

L.P.H.C. Birthin
108th Fd A.M.B.

Army Form C. 2118.

108 FIELD AMBULANCE

WAR DIARY
or
INTELLIGENCE SUMMARY.
(Erase heading not required.)

Place	Date	Hour	Summary of Events and Information	Remarks and references to Appendices
RUYAULCOURT	7/11/1917	8.45	Worked transport this morning owing to the inclemency of the weather, a slight snowstorm occurred. No route march. CAPTAIN H.G. WILSON R.A.M.C. & the unit returned to duty on expiration of temporary leave. 2 FIELD CASHIER at the Bank and drew one thousand francs. Owing to the mud. He reports that 2. CAPTAIN H.G. WILSON started with 9 men. He being senior O. me.	

S.P. Rea
CAPTAIN
O.C. 108 Fd.A.M.B.

Army Form C. 2118

WAR DIARY
or
INTELLIGENCE SUMMARY.
(Erase heading not required.)

108th FIELD AMBULANCE

Instructions regarding War Diaries and Intelligence
Summaries are contained in F. S. Regs., Part II.
and the Staff Manual respectively. Title pages
will be prepared in manuscript.

Place	Date	Hour	Summary of Events and Information	Remarks and references to Appendices
RUYAULCOURT	8.11.17	9.15 p.m	Took over command of the unit from CAPT. S. P. REA yesterday on return from leave. The usual improvements are being carried out. The enemy (German) shelled the village at 5.30 p.m. One shell dropped near the officers quarters, a second drifted close to the reception room. Personnel & patients immediately took refuge in the horse dugout. Horse & mules were immediately cleared. There were no casualties. The shelling lasted about half an hour.	

H Bowden Cpt
O.C. 108th Field Amb

Army Form C. 2118.

WAR DIARY
or
INTELLIGENCE SUMMARY
(Erase heading not required.)

100th FIELD AMBULANCE

Place	Date	Hour	Summary of Events and Information	Remarks and references to Appendices
RUYAULCOURT	9.11.17		Owing to the inclemency of the weather, outside work was hampered. Capt GALE (D.A.D.M.S.) (P) called & inspected accommodation for wounded, & found everything satisfactory.	
		6.30 p.m	CAPT. S. P. REA & self walked up to & inspected P.12.B.50 used where the huts & road for wheeled stretchers is being made to Receive R.A.P. (No 4) also inspected P.18 Central to clearing place for erection of advanced dressing place for walking wounded	

A.H. Lundon Cpl
R.A.M.C.

WAR DIARY
INTELLIGENCE SUMMARY

108th FIELD AMBULANCE

Army Form C. 2118.

Place	Date	Hour	Summary of Events and Information	Remarks and references to Appendices
RUYAULCOURT	11.11.17	7pm	CAPT. S.P. REA + self went up to Lieutenant WOOD to inspect pelet site for marquee tents. P.18.D.22 Sheet 57c was chosen as a likely spot for collection of walking wounded. Then we also went to wagon post (P.17.B.50) + inspected the hundred yards of loft road to there to R.A.P. (J.36.D.8.3) We went to three in the afternoon + interviewed the A.D.M.S. (COL BRAY) + informed him of the state in the wood which we had selected. Was informed by letter from A.D.M.S. Office that CAPT. J.L. DUNLOP. M.C. R.A.M.C. had been taken on the strength of No.19 C.C.S. + struck off the strength of this unit, by order of D.M.S 3rd ARMY.	

J. Rendoon Capt
R.A.M.C. O/c 108th F Amb

Army Form C. 2118.

WAR DIARY
or
INTELLIGENCE SUMMARY.
(Erase heading not required.)

105th FIELD AMBULANCE

Place	Date	Hour	Summary of Events and Information	Remarks and references to Appendices
RUYAULCOURT		11.11M	Went to A.D.S (Q.14.d Sheet 57c) with officers of 2/3rd (WEST RIDING) Fd AMB and DA.D.M.S 62nd Div who accompanied an N.C.O. inspected the R.A.P.s of the Right and Centre Brigades of our division. The methods of Evacuation of wounded from the site to R.A.P and from R.A.P to A.D.S + M.D.S were fully explained to them. The day was sunny and warm	
		1pm		

H. Lewden Cpl
R.A.M.C i/c of 105th F.A.

WAR DIARY
or
INTELLIGENCE SUMMARY

108th FIELD AMBULANCE

Army Form C. 2118.

Place	Date	Hour	Summary of Events and Information	Remarks and references to Appendices
RUYAULCOURT	12.11.17		One thousand stretchers and three thousand blankets were received to-day by this unit. The work of placing huts & stores on the site of the large dugout was proceeded with. I drove to interview the D.A.D.V.S. about the exchange of a heavy draught horse whose hind leg have become badly swollen. He was not in his room at inspection so we left a note with the Serjeant explaining what we wanted. Capt. D. KELLY C.F.C.E. reported to this unit for duty and was taken on the strength	

S. Wilson Cpt
R.A.M.C. O/C 108 F.A.

Army Form C. 2118.

WAR DIARY
or
INTELLIGENCE SUMMARY.
(Erase heading not required.)

108th FIELD AMBULANCE

Place	Date	Hour	Summary of Events and Information	Remarks and references to Appendices
RUYAULCOURT	13.11.17		The motor load from ADS (Q.14.d.Pivot S.P.) to METZ-EN-COUTRE for motor ambulances made by the personnel of the F.A. was completed to-day. Broken bricks are being used up in levelling slowly to fill shell holes in the various tracks to the posts for evacuation of wounded. Lt. Col. BRAYE A.D.M.S called this afternoon & ordered (?) experts over from the extra Divisional Lines moving the extrication & deep dug outs.	

H Studon(?) Cpt
R.A.M.C. o/c 108th F. Amb.

Army Form C. 2118.

WAR DIARY
or
INTELLIGENCE SUMMARY
(Erase heading not required.)

108th FIELD AMBULANCE

Place	Date	Hour	Summary of Events and Information	Remarks and references to Appendices
RUYAULCOURT			LIEUT. S.H. RICHMAN U.S.M.R. proceeded from duty to 36th D.A.C. by orders of A.D.M.S.	
	9th		MAJOR. J.F. McINTOSH R.A.M.C and CAPT. R.T. BRUCE R.A.M.C 1/2nd HIGHLAND FIELD AMBULANCE 51st DIV + fifty other ranks arrived to-day to inspect and were being familiarized with the unit for the night COL. BRAY A.D.M.S 36th DIV called this morning in tour of inspection. he found everything in order the lamp dugout for the personnel in the event of shelling was completed to-day The Mens canteen and recreation room were finished a concert was held in the latter 6-8 p.m.	

H/Lewden Cpl R.A.M.C
o/c 108th F.O. Amb.

Army Form C. 2118.

WAR DIARY
or
INTELLIGENCE SUMMARY

(Erase heading not required.)

106th FIELD AMBULANCE

Place	Date	Hour	Summary of Events and Information	Remarks and references to Appendices
RUYAULCOURT	16.11.17		CAPT. GORRIE H.G. R.A.M.C. and CAPT LAING A.C. R.A.M.C. with fifty other ranks of the 1/2nd HIGHLAND FIELD AMBULANCE arrived in accordance with previous recent instructions from 51st DIV.	
		7 p.m	to take ordinary work. Conditions normal Weather foggy	

J. Euan Gd
R.A.M.C. 16/11/17

Army Form C. 2118

WAR DIARY
~~INTELLIGENCE SUMMARY~~
(Erase heading not required.)

108th FIELD AMBULANCE

Place	Date	Hour	Summary of Events and Information	Remarks and references to Appendices
RUYAULCOURT	17.11.17		The 2/3rd West Riding FIELD AMBULANCE 62nd DIV relieved Nos 2, 3 + 4 R.A.P.'s PLACE MONT. MARE and the LEFT ~~Place Mont Mare~~	
		1 p.m.	WAGON POST (Pt. B 50 Sheet 57C) The 1/3rd HIGHLAND FIELD AMBULANCE 51st DIV took over the stores and equipment to be left behind at RUYAULCOURT CAPT. C. G. GIBSON and 4 men proceeded to the new area at BARASTRE as advance party (O15. B99 Sh 57C)	

H. M. Sanderson Capt
R.A.M.C.
O/C 108 F.Amb.

Army Form C. 2118.

18.

WAR DIARY
or
INTELLIGENCE SUMMARY.
(Erase heading not required.)

108th FIELD AMBULANCE

Place	Date	Hour	Summary of Events and Information	Remarks and references to Appendices
RUYAULCOURT	15.11.17		The A.D.S (9.14.d.93 Sh 57C) was taken over by 2 officers and 50 O.R of the 2nd HIGHLAND FIELD AMBULANCE this unit (108th F.d AMBce) left RUYAULCOURT at 12.45 p.m and marched by BERTINCOURT, many all available tracks, reached BARASTRE at 3 p.m the remainder of the 1/3rd FIELD AMBULANCE 51st DIV left BARASTRE after being relieved by us to join the rest of their party at RUYAULCOURT at 4.15 p.m Departure and arrival notices were sent to A.D.M.S	
		1 p.m		

H. Emden Cpl
108th F. AMBce

Army Form C. 2118.

WAR DIARY
or
INTELLIGENCE SUMMARY.

(Erase heading not required.) 108th FIELD AMBULANCE.

Instructions regarding War Diaries and Intelligence Summaries are contained in F. S. Regs., Part II. and the Staff Manual respectively. Title pages will be prepared in manuscript.

Place	Date	Hour	Summary of Events and Information	Remarks and references to Appendices
BARASTRE	18.11.17	8.30 a.m.	Returned from Mine Rescue Drainage of Unit.	
	19.11.17	8.30 a.m.	Marched to VELU WOOD by way of BERTINCOURT.	
	19/10/1917		Marched through BERTINCOURT to Stay Head Qrts. Capt. E.C. SOWERBY proceeded with 40 Rank & File of 107 th Brigade, and Capt. GIBSON with 40 Rank & File of 108 th Brigade relieved members of HAVRINCOURT, FLESQUIÈRES, RIBÉCOURT.	
	20.11.1917	6 a.m.	N. of HAVRINCOURT and area ground to the west taken from the ANNEUX and area ground to the west known as Canal and Humard.	
			Marched at 4 p.m. under orders to new Canal and Trenches a heavy barrage taken in or near HAVRINCOURT eventually dug themselves in round by the enemy. Eventually day Head Quarters detailed Capt. H.9. WILSON in Returned to Duty. Capt. GIBSON posted to 2nd Rifles in lieu of relief of Capt. GIBSON resigned. Neither black with smoke & Keep Capt. LINDSAY resigned.	
			Every situated a few tests for the night.	
			March to HERMIES and bivouaced at Railway Station.	
	21.11.17	4 p.m.		
	1917			

WAR DIARY or INTELLIGENCE SUMMARY

Army Form C. 2118.

108TH FIELD AMBULANCE

Place	Date	Hour	Summary of Events and Information	Remarks and references to Appendices
HERMIES	2	6:45 AM	Rode through DEMICOURT to BOURSIES. German aeroplane dropped one year ["years"] and fired down at HQ over BOURSIES and DEMICOURT while I went through. Rode to Canal Bank ½ mile north of HAVRINCOURT with A.D.M.S. and examined Capt Campbell who is something and advanced dressing station's and [?] east of Canal in Bright side. Capt Campbell Wilson's last of night sent Capt Wilson worked in charge of A.D.S. Received urgent message at midnight from Capt Wilson to say that he was short of men, wounded, sent up all remaining men as bearers leaving only 24 at Halyweemetery [?]. The Sergeant in charge up to A.D.S. right entering dusk, left foothold [?] where left 100 or so nearby [?] so suitable shell free dugout each A.D.S. at 2 men frequently came which deep ravine ? sent up entire about 90. He later move there ? sent up entire also who ensure others too very used heavily and Capt Wilson returned back at 5 am.	

WAR DIARY
or
INTELLIGENCE SUMMARY
(Erase heading not required.)

Army Form C. 2118.

102nd FIELD AMBULANCE

Place	Date	Hour	Summary of Events and Information	Remarks and references to Appendices
HERMIES	23.11.1917		Sent up 160 stretchers might 800 blankets to C.C.S. who continued to clear until midnight. The day people up their at 9 a.m. & extremely thankful. Tpl. A.P. M.S. yesterday and conveyed orally that our hospital was rendered R.A.M.C. untenable, they did not agree. HAVRINCOURT but they stop no degree. Received orders ready to move to BOURSIES in entry Noncthe cold wonderfully Hospital / Ambulance Wagon is definitely staying in House Col. M.	
	24.11.1917		Marched to BOURSIES by way of DEMICOURT had to go through fields for some distance as road steepest by shellfire just S. of DEMICOURT, arrived at BOURSIES at 9.15 a.m. parked Wagons fancy W. on roadside, the place dangerous and heavily shelled. Thought to be difficulty in getting transport away, cleaned out old house for reception of patients. Shells began to fall in village at 10.30 a.m. Sent W/Lieut. THWAITES to 1FLO Carrying returns via BATAUME - CAMBRAI road in	

Army Form C. 2118.

WAR DIARY
or
INTELLIGENCE SUMMARY.
(Erase heading not required.)

108TH FIELD AMBULANCE.

Place	Date	Hour	Summary of Events and Information	Remarks and references to Appendices
BOURSIES.	24/11 1917		In direction of CAMBRAI intermittently, probably through CAMAI, presently shells bursting on road roughly opposite one thousand yards heavily shelled. Attempts on very hasty journey were for their most part unsuccessful on account of their deep cut hay concealment had on every side. Dug outs beg conspicuous had on either west turned walked out both banks when laying down to avoid shells walked to W. end of village with OC R.F.A. Shells dropped in village throughout the day. Wounded [being] evacuated from ADSS proceeded at 5 p.m. to MTRB from CAMBRAI via S. of situation as I have been informed. ADMS all day used therefore no supplies yet off from A.D.S. received orders to move back at once, horseback received orders passed 8 horses shelled by shrapnel on widen [turning] passed on BAPAUME — CAMBRAI road, passed out of BOURSIES at 9.30 p.m. Shells burst in village street 2 minutes after we cleared the village.	

Army Form C. 2118

WAR DIARY
or
INTELLIGENCE SUMMARY.
(Erase heading not required.)

108th FIELD AMBULANCE.

Place	Date	Hour	Summary of Events and Information	Remarks and references to Appendices
BOURSIES	24.11.17	10.30 p.m.	Marched through DOIGNIES and HERMIES to 1/2 mile S.W. of Hwy Heap; arriving there at midnight. Pitched tents and had some tea; turned in shortly after 2 a.m.	
SHAG HEAP (Camul du NORD)	25.11. 1917		Neither billets sheet and rain falling. Rode to YTRES and MÉTZ and HQs. returned through HAPLINCOURT and BERTINCOURT. Remained pitched except for tents; sent up supplies to Capt. Camp Well, unified up to A.D.S. with Capt. U.S.P. TEA. Bitter weather with piercing wind. Food to receive with no change in heavy mud; and feet blistered and ulcerated.	
	26.11. 1917		Unable to walk to A.D.S. today owing to condition of feet; sent up supplies as usual.	
BARASTRE	27.11. 1917	9.30 a.m.	Marched to BARASTRE by way of BERTINCOURT and HAPLINCOURT. Took over Field Ambulance camp there. Bearers returned from A.D.S. with Capts. SOWERBY, CAMPBELL, and WILSON.	

Army Form C. 2118.

WAR DIARY
or
INTELLIGENCE SUMMARY.
(Erase heading not required.)

108th FIELD AMBULANCE.

Place	Date	Hour	Summary of Events and Information	Remarks and references to Appendices
BAPAUME	28/11 1917		Rested whole day as far as possible, men got a wash and changed of clothing. Received orders to move off tomorrow to HEBUTERNE area.	6.
	29/11 1917	10 AM	Transport marched at 8.11. Bd. am. to ACHIET-le-PETIT, to move on next day to SIMENCOURT. Troops marched at 10:45 am under Capt S.P.REA to BATAUME and entrained for BEAUMETZ les LOGES, from camp closed and followed 108 Fd. Brigade to YPRES Station to push up may sick no rich arrived at SIMENCOURT at 9:15 pm.	
SIMEN- COURT.	30/11 1917		Rested for the day, infantry returned to HOMIECOURT and ACHIET-le-PETIT at 2:15 pm. Received no orders to move to stand fast, arranging to receive tomorrow at 5:45 am.	

M Fenton-Jones
Lieut. Colonel
O.C. 108th Field Ambulance

30/11/17

No. 108. F.A.

COMMITTEE FOR THE
MEDICAL HISTORY OF THE WAR
Date -1 FEB. 1918

WAR DIARY

INTELLIGENCE SUMMARY

(Erase heading not required.) 108th FIELD AMBULANCE

Army Form C. 2118.

Instructions regarding War Diaries and Intelligence Summaries are contained in F.S. Regs., Part II. and the Staff Manual respectively. Title pages will be prepared in manuscript.

Place	Date	Hour	Summary of Events and Information	Remarks and references to Appendices
SIMENCOURT	1.12.1917	12.30 a.m.	Received orders to march at once to ACHIET LE GRAND. Marched at 2 a.m. Snow and hoarfrost, 18 men had to be carried on motor ambulance cars, 4 men sent to C.C.S. suffering from exhaustion. Arrived at ACHIET LE GRAND at 9 a.m. Got breakfasts for the men who only dumped, until one M.O. and two horsed ambulances to follow, 108 FA proceeded to ROCQUIGNY and one horsed ambulance to follow. 107 FA proceeded to BANCOURT 1½ miles S.E. of BAPAUME. Marched at 12.45 p.m. Arrived at ROCQUIGNY at 8 p.m. Bitter weather, freezing hard, strong wind, bivouacked therefore in open over in badly built huts.	
ACHIET LE GRAND	2.12.1917		Refitting and collecting kits etc.	
ROCQUIGNY	3.12.1917	10 a.m.	Had to move out onto ROCQUIGNY - BUS road, worked over to see the room for 112 to fill ambulance, after he however proceeded there bound to MARICOURT. Received orders to march to BERTINCOURT, marched at 4 p.m. 3 times after proceeding six hundred yards ordered counter ordered to return to ... ... lights, but not face[d] ... ... very high. Got billets for my ... ... tired.	BERTINCOURT

WAR DIARY
or
INTELLIGENCE SUMMARY.
(Erase heading not required.)

108th FIELD AMBULANCE.

Army Form C. 2118.

2

Place	Date	Hour	Summary of Events and Information	Remarks and references to Appendices
RUCQUIGNY	4/12/1917		9am Collected stuff from BERTINCOURT. Received orders at 12/15 p.m. to march to MOISLAINS and take over III Corps Rest Station. Fitz from 62nd Field Ambulance, 20th Division. Advance party (Capt BOYD CAMPBELL with an advanced party) collected stuff from MOISLAINS by motor ambulance, marched at 2 p.m., by way of LEWEBNIK and MANANCOURT, arrived at MOISLAINS at 4. Took over from 62nd Field Ambulances. This Rest Station is much overcrowded owing to the fact that the Convalescent Depot is now closed, so that the only outlet is by discharging to C.C.S. or duty, about 700 patients in this Station.	
	5/12/1917		62nd Field Ambulance marched at 8 am. Some difficulty over the butterly dinners, there being 87 heavy men for dinner. Rooms every extremely cold in spite, harvey offices short of food. The leave depôt at STAYKEY for the lorries, the huts we have heard for, for two years.	

WAR DIARY

INTELLIGENCE SUMMARY
(Erase heading not required.) 1/8 2ND FIELD AMBULANCE

Army Form C. 2118.

Instructions regarding War Diaries and Intelligence Summaries are contained in F.S. Regs., Part II. and the Staff Manual respectively. Title pages will be prepared in manuscript.

Place	Date	Hour	Summary of Events and Information	Remarks and references to Appendices
MOISLAINS	6/12/1917		Began to build rickers across & wound, dividing patients suffering from scabies from other patients. I came also going to build another Dining Room as soon as possible. Number of patients in Rest Station 900. Visit D.D.M.S. at TEMPLEUX le FOSSE, saw D.A.D.M.S. to Corps on return and arranged to try and obtain materials to rebuild to ensure that ladies put to the copse is fallen. Hard frost but wind has fallen.	
	7/12/1917		Frost has gone, consequently roads are becoming muddy, sent requisitions to D.M.S. for materials for huts. Finished partitions in Dining Ward. Visit by D.D.M.S. 2nd [?] Dealt 400 cases today, 330 to C.C.S. 70 to duty. Rain during the night. Heads out. I think that this place is improved since we arrived, though done with [?] now system. This is due to the efforts of Capt. BOYD	
	8/12/1917		CAMPBELL and Capt. TEWKESBURY. Indented for cement to complete [?] began in wards by out sister the D.	

Army Form C. 2118.

WAR DIARY
or
INTELLIGENCE SUMMARY.
(Erase heading not required.)

108th FIELD AMBULANCE.

Instructions regarding War Diaries and Intelligence Summaries are contained in F. S. Regs., Part II. and the Staff Manual respectively. Title pages will be prepared in manuscript.

Place	Date	Hour	Summary of Events and Information	Remarks and references to Appendices
MOISLAINS.	8.12.1917	2.30 pm	Rode to Corps Headquarters, TEMPLEUX LeROSSE, heavy showers on the way. Rev'd. BARRETT, S.J., C.F., left for duty on the series of Communications.	
	9.12.1917		Work as usual.	
	10.12.1917		Obtained stationery and bedding lotion for FM.S. Ports SAMS. SA 1st Ed.	
	11.12.1917		Rode to Corps Headquarters and saw 7970 with whom to pay the men. Patrol move to "G.m."	
	12.12.1917		Began to build hut for treatment and accommodation of Scabies Patients. Rode to Corps Headquarters.	
	13.12.1917		Slight frost last night (ointment work on Scabies hut) also work at dressings. Heavy snow walks, Rode to DOINGT, and saw mode of treating Scabies.	
	14.12.1917		Sent by A.D.M.S. who inspected patients of 36th Division. Rode to MANANCOURT.	
	15.12.1917		Advanced party of 2 Officers and 20 N.C.O's and men arrived to take over. Capt. Hill. Received orders to move to SUS-ST-LEGER.	

Army Form C. 2118.

WAR DIARY
INTELLIGENCE SUMMARY.
(Erase heading not required.)

Instructions regarding War Diaries and Intelligence Summaries are contained in F. S. Regs., Part II. and the Staff Manual respectively. Title pages will be prepared in manuscript.

Place	Date	Hour	Summary of Events and Information	Remarks and references to Appendices
MOISLAINS	15/12/1917	—	On 17th and 18th instant Capt. J. TEWKESBURY proceeded on 14 days' leave. Frost at night.	5.
	16/12/1917	10 am	Began to thaw over night. Station to 62nd Field Ambulance. Heavy fall of snow at nights. Freezing sharply.	
	17/12/1917	7 am	Capt. S. P. REA marched with Transcos and entrained at ETRICOURT for MONDICOURT; Capt. B. BOYD CAMPBELL left by MOTOR CAR at 8.30 am for SOS – S. LEGER to obtain billets in new area. Sent limber wagon by train at 3 pm from YPRES with blankets. Completed handing over. Freezing and roads bad.	
	18/12/1917	7 am	Tent off. Horsed Transport by road. A two days' journey at the halt of James. Marched at 9 am with the help of new van Capt. H. A. WILSON, entrained at ETRICOURT in trucks bitterly cold, and had to wait 3/4 hour before train moved. Journey took 7 hours, detrained at 3.30 pm, and marched from MONDICOURT to WATHORET, snow deep in places and had to take to the fields at known stretches.	LIEUT. WOODHRIDGE joined 153rd Brigade, R.F.A., in lieu of Capt. Hays.

Army Form C. 2118.

WAR DIARY
INTELLIGENCE SUMMARY
(Erase heading not required.) 108 to FIELD AMBULANCE.

Instructions regarding War Diaries and Intelligence Summaries are contained in F. S. Regs., Part II. and the Staff Manual respectively. Title pages will be prepared in manuscript.

Place	Date	Hour	Summary of Events and Information	Remarks and references to Appendices
WARLUZEL.	19.12.1917.		Capt. S. BOYD CAMPBELL proceeded on 14 days leave to ENGLAND. Walked to ADEHEUX with Capt. S.P. REA. Weather cold and MOTOR AMBULANCES stuck in snow during the morning on the road, one received told here that Wilstone very bad.	
	20.12.1917.		Received motor ambulances arrived. Horse transport arrived HUMBERCOURT, left it there no one more in that direction. Went to COUTURELLE and looked round. Motor billets there in WARLUZEL. Visited SAMBRIN and COUTURELLE with Capt. S.P. REA, arranged to move into COUTURELLE tomorrow morning, feeling very ill with bronchitis. Weather better with strong N.E. wind. Visit by A.D.M.S. in afternoon; showed him billets.	
	21.12.1917.			
	22.12.1917.	9.30 am	Sent Capt. S.P. REA in advance to COUTURELLE to obtain billets. He sent back a cyclist when billets had been obtained. Ordered Horse transport from HUMBERCOURT to COUTURELLE. Marched from WARLUZEL at 10.30 am. Arrived at COUTURELLE at 11.15 am. Still feeling very ill.	

Army Form C. 2118.

WAR DIARY

INTELLIGENCE SUMMARY
(Erase heading not required.) 108th FIELD AMBULANCE.

Place	Date	Hour	Summary of Events and Information	Remarks and references to Appendices
COUTURELLE	22.12.1917.		Visit from A.D.M.S. in afternoon who otherwise accommodation for sick in SAULTY 2 miles away. SAULTY is the place that the FIELD AMBULANCE ought to have been sent to as there is in it decent accommodation for many patients and horses. This is probably the reason we were not sent here.	
	23.12.1917.		Weather colder than ever, feeling a bit better, sent 2 N.C.O's and 20 men to SAULTY to open a temporary Hospital. Capt. S.P. REA went to SAULTY to superintend the work. Unable to obtain chickens or pigs locally for the men. Christmas dinner. Went to C.R.E. for envelopes and felt with which to repair billets.	
	24.12.1917.		Weather dull, less cold, and looks like a change. Capt. S.P. REA, Capt HQ. WILSON and STAFF Sergt. A MEN'S in motor ambulance to try to get materials for Christmas Dinners. Went to SAULTY and new hospital huts, no traces of heating crates for Sailies patients. Went to A.D.M.S. for horses or horses dens undoubtedly and takes cold.	

Army Form C. 2118.

WAR DIARY
of
INTELLIGENCE SUMMARY
(Erase heading not required.) **108th FIELD AMBULANCE.**

Place	Date	Hour	Summary of Events and Information	Remarks and references to Appendices
COUTURELLE	24/12/1917		Pte Rawmich sent to C.C.S. DOULLENS and 4 to SADLTY. Sent Sergt McMULLEN to DOULLENS to enquire into some tent equipment for tomorrow for the mens Toilets. One Motor Ambulance badly broken up, sent out, but bought returning with Stores reed kitchens MOISLAINS, sent to Divisional Supply Columns Workshops. Received order for Canvas, wood, and nails; sent to LUCHEUX for that. Item and obtained by Sergt McMULLEN. Returned 20 grease trap from AMIENS for men's dinner tomorrow. Snow at night but not much.	
	25.12.1917		Walked to SAVLTY and saw Patients, A.D.M.S. (Lieut Colonel ROCH) returned. Remembered as D.A.D.M.S. 28th Division at YPRES in February 1915. Considerable snow during the day through it now Thursday. Capt SOWERBY came overland from IVERGNY to dinner. Heavy snow fall at night. Started Capt S.P. REA and 2 Motor Ambulances to Albert at Brigade Headquarters at 8.45 am. tomorrow to go to new billeting area.	

Army Form C. 2118.

WAR DIARY
INTELLIGENCE SUMMARY

(Erase heading not required.) 108th FIELD AMBULANCE.

Place	Date	Hour	Summary of Events and Information	Remarks and references to Appendices
COUTURELLE	26.12.1917.		About 4 inches of snow fell during last night and there were frequent and heavy showers during the day. Freezing. Unit not ready. Two motor ambulances up the Cart. S.P.R.E.A. and convoys Regule Staff employees left for new area after keeping cars workshop for archives. Went sound transport until stables. We have only a Ford Car available for the collection of sick. Today, there is Workshop Cart being in the Workshop for repairs, and two out with the Regular Staff; the other Ford Car was sent to the Base, including from MORLANS.	
	27.12.1917.		Weather continued very cold; Horsed Transport with exception of 2 Water Carts, 3 G.S. Waggons, and 1 Limbered Waggon marched by road at 9 a.m. for BOVES 4 miles S.S.E. of AMIENS.	
	29.12.1917.	7.30 am	Marched from COUTURELLE, arrived at MONDICOURT at 8.15 a.m. Bitter N.E. wind blowing, entrained at 9.45 a.m. Left at 10.15 a.m. arrived at BOVES at 2.20 p.m. Marched to LE PARACHETS 1½ miles S.S.W. of BOVES a large agricultural school but with little accommodation for patients. Transport wheels entrained at MONDICOURT at 1.15 a.m. are removed out at _____ no billets.	

Army Form C. 2118.

10.

WAR DIARY

INTELLIGENCE SUMMARY

(Erase heading not required.) 1/08 2nd FIELD AMBULANCE.

Instructions regarding War Diaries and Intelligence Summaries are contained in F. S. Regs., Part II. and the Staff Manual respectively. Title pages will be prepared in manuscript.

Place	Date	Hour	Summary of Events and Information	Remarks and references to Appendices
LE PARACQET'S.	28.12.1917.		Arranged rooms for Quartermasters Stores, Bootmakers and Tailors Shops; General Room; ward for sick; Billets for transport drivers. Found billets very difficult to get, no fires &c.	
	29.12.1917.		Began to take in patients, only accommodation for 12. Method of Entry.	
		2 p.m.	Went to AMIENS with the Capt. HQ. W/A 80N and bought 300 kilograms coke and 11 Stoves. Distributed stoves to Officers Rooms, 2 in Mens Ward Room, and Tailors Shop. No fuel except coke purchased today.	
	30.12.1917.		Thawing slightly. Capt. I.F.S. SOWERBY reported from 8/9 Rd R.D. Rifles on temporary attach[ment]. Owing to heating arrangements of ambulance and fuel difficulties no baths. I have ordered fuel with which to heat & water no bottles applied for bath and boiler.	

31/12/1917

R.H.M. Fawcett
Lieut Colonel,
O.C., 1/08 2nd Field Ambulance.

Army Form C. 2118.

WAR DIARY
INTELLIGENCE SUMMARY

(Erase heading not required.) 108th FIELD AMBULANCE.

Instructions regarding War Diaries and Intelligence Summaries are contained in F.S. Regs., Part II. and the Staff Manual respectively. Title pages will be prepared in manuscript.

Place	Date	Hour	Summary of Events and Information	Remarks and references to Appendices
OLLEZY.	21/1/1918.	9.30 a.m.	Took a G.S. Waggon and rode to E. of MARSH (S. SIMON – ANNOIS Road), got a load of French Wounds from old Jungle shelter. Sent for bricks to TUGNY. Rain throughout the morning. Rode to Divisional Headquarters in search of our Interpreter – none available. Heavy rain at night.	
	22/1/1918.		Showers during the morning. Lied French Rounds obtained yesterday. Worked at Stand for Motor Cars and Roll of House, also in repairing high paths. Sent for more bricks. Went by Ar. Rec. S. at 11.30 a.m. Rode to DURY in afternoon, also to ESTOUILLY.	
	23/1/1918.		Showers during morning. Continued work on motor ambulance Stand and Bath House. Visit by D.D.M.S. and A.D.M.S. at 12.30 p.m. Rode to CUGNY in the afternoon and saw French ambulances. Rain at night.	
	24/1/1918.		Drizzling rain till 10 a.m. when sky cleared. Rode to PITHON in search of timber for upright with two servants. Sent for bricks as usual, continued work on Motor Ambulance Stand. Sent waggon to HAM in the afternoon and obtained Felt, planks, Iod, and cement.	
	25/1/1918.		Foggy morning but turned very bright by 11 a.m. Rode to HAM in every tambees, nearly struck near HAM by Aeroplane antenna of Shell whistle fell by wireless frightening horse so good deal, obtained order for canvas. Three waggons of timber. Bright moonlight.	

WAR DIARY
INTELLIGENCE SUMMARY.
(Erase heading not required.) 108th FIELD AMBULANCE.

Army Form C. 2118.
6.

Place	Date	Hour	Summary of Events and Information	Remarks and references to Appendices
DHUZX	26/1/1918		Weather foggy all day and chilly. Carried some old German timbers and finished Motor Ambulance Stand with this.	
		2.30pm	Rode to CUGNY with A.D.M.S., Lieut. Colonel Magill and Capt. CHRISTIE, Senior O.C. Field Ambulance there.	
	27/1/1918	8 a.m.	Sent N.C.O. & 2 men to join convoy at OLLEZY (remainder) to proceed to AMIENS to draw timber purchased on 18th instant.	
		8.30 a.m.	Sent 3 G.S. waggons and a party of men to remove hut from field off Rode road near junction of S. SIMON-ANNOIS and S. SIMON – MARCEL LE FAY Roads. Rode there and found work progressing well at 10.30 a.m. Rode to ARTEMPS in the afternoon. Very foggy in the evening.	
	28/1/1918		Sharp frost in the night. Timber arrived from AMIENS; began to build Reception Hut, which is to contain Medical Inspection Room, room for Bootmaker and Tailor, also Barber and Guard Room. Began to build hut for men in rear of Hospital 6 Huts. Held Inspection by Rev. Register and had talk with them at 8.30 and Parade. Weather clear. Capt. KING; V.S.M.R.C. proceeded on temporary duty to 11th/3rd Rifles. Capt. E.S. SOWERBY. Lieut. Fitzpatrick from an A.D.S. 110th Field Ambulance.	

Army Form C. 2118.

WAR DIARY

INTELLIGENCE SUMMARY.
(Erase heading not required.) 108th FIELD AMBULANCE.

Place	Date	Hour	Summary of Events and Information	Remarks and references to Appendices
OLLEZY	29/1/1918		Sharp frost in the night. Village bombed last night by aeroplanes. Aeroplanes could be heard passing over camp very distinctly. Sun C.B.E. re stores. None available to make huts furphier in winds. Continued work on two new huts beyond yesterdays one hut, new felt on one wood roof. The roof had a long portion of its felt stripped off in the recent gale. German aeroplanes over at night and dropped bombs in OLLEZY.	
	30/1/1918.		Sharp frost in night, clear, continued work on huts Bath House and Cook House Range. Visit by D.D.M.S. who did not help us much. Rode to KAVENSE.	
	31/1/1918.		Sharp frost, weather foggy. German aeroplanes passed over camp last night, flying low, but no bombs dropped in our neighbourhood. These could be heard hesitating in the distance. Work as usual.	

R.F.M.Fawcett
Lieut: Colonel,
O.C., 108th Field Ambulance.

31/1/1918.

CONFIDENTIAL.

WAR DIARY.

OF

108th FIELD AMBULANCE.

FROM 1st FEBRUARY 1918.   TO. 28th FEBRUARY 1918.

VOL. XXIX.

Army Form C. 2118.

WAR DIARY
INTELLIGENCE SUMMARY.
(Erase heading not required.) 108th FIELD AMBULANCE.

Instructions regarding War Diaries and Intelligence Summaries are contained in F.S. Regs., Part II. and the Staff Manual respectively. Title pages will be prepared in manuscript.

Place	Date	Hour	Summary of Events and Information	Remarks and references to Appendices
CHUZY	1.2.1918.		Continued work on Huts. Weather sharp, hard frost, foggy. Road to HAM. Numerous aeroplanes overhead at night apparently flying very low. R79. Russell Lieut. Colonel	
	2.2.1918.		Weather cold, clear. Continued work as usual. Road to HAM as the afternoon and then 710,000 notes which to pay the men. Parcel out at 5.30 p.m. German aeroplanes fairly close over head at night. R79. Russell Lieut. Colonel	
	3.2.1918.		Bright weather, hard frost. Staged order in our power of removing Rancho to take pillow roof of Reception Hut. Continued work on Hut. Good progress is being made. Night dark and cloudy. No German aeroplanes overhead during the waiting. R79. Russell Lieut. Colonel	
	4.2.1918.		Cloudy and milder. Continued work. Orderlies Hut for some in the village. A good hut left by the French troops in the worst state of neglect. Conditions of dirt, filth, floors if any material even showing the grossness of remembers. Though the habits and the total disregard of sanitary and neatly thought they apparently though their methods of sanitary and sanitary fit the whole look healthy and most therefore there is no doubt I like the French people but can say nothing in defence of their neglect of cleanliness. It has been stated they may not be Christians.	

WAR DIARY

INTELLIGENCE SUMMARY

Army Form C. 2118.

108th NEW AMBULANCE. 2.

Place	Date	Hour	Summary of Events and Information	Remarks and references to Appendices
OLEZY	4.2.1918		affected by it but I must I hope to believe that they will not interfere with this after what I know so often read of their weakness, and need military.	Lt. Intwrwett. Field Colonel
	5.2.1918		Continued work, weather fine without frost, wind E.S.E.	Lt. Intwrwett. Field Colonel Ordered 45 doses Red Head Bedycco too N. CO and men
	6.2.1918		Decent morning, clear, no a furor. Mild. Rode to HAM and attended conference at D.M. & Office at 10.30 a.m. Seen 1,000 French holdbodies togeth men going on leave and returned to hospitals for patients here.	
	7.2.1918		Heavy rain in the night. Decent, stormy S.W. wind. Begun to build loop and walls to new stations, continued workers receptions hut and men's hut.	
	2.30 p.m.		Met O. 64, 109th and 110th Field Ambulances and arranged situations of new advanced dressing stations. Rode to TURNY. Heavy rain in the night.	Lt. Intwrwett. Field Colonel
	8.2.1918		Frosty and threatening snow. Third field performance; this roof is 80 p'us length and of corrugated iron. Reception hut quite a fine performance, this hut which I hope will be completed tomorrow now will greatly assist my the efficiency and cleanness of this place. But as I now hard to entrance Dimmingfs Rest Station and Red Head very effected.	Lt. Intwrwett. Field Colonel

Army Form C. 2118.

WAR DIARY
or
INTELLIGENCE SUMMARY.
(Erase heading not required.) 108th FIELD AMBULANCE.

Place	Date	Hour	Summary of Events and Information	Remarks and references to Appendices
OLLEZY	8.2.19.18		(Cont.) Regns Patients/Walton/Meek, as accommodation in Buffs. Mess is insufficient; continued work on drainage scheme, continued records on large lorris load, and on mens huts. Visit by D.A.M.S. at 4 p.m. Heavy hard day.	W.7 Fawcett Lieut.Col. enlisted
	9.2.19.18		Weather fine with fresh S.W. wind. Sent to HAM for 50 sheets of corrugated iron with which to finish roof of huts for men, completed walls of Reception Hut, a very fine and roomy hut.	W.7 Fawcett Lieut.Col.
	10.2.19.18		Heavy rain in the night, fine but wind strong throughout the day. Proposed to put windows in men hut and take Y.M.C.A. room into occupation. First section of ground under hangars ready to make. New S.F.O. & Portecroft battles.	W.7 Fawcett Lieut.Col.
	11.2.19.18		Sent for cement from HAM used for gravel for ground from AVESNES with which to make a concrete floor on which to stand baths for general cases. Weather fine, no frost, fresh southerly breeze. Hail board our Majors S.V.S. CLEMENTS, + to Box; Royal Irish Fusiliers, evacuated him as fit for general service. Vitamin examined and entered continued work in department for treatment of gassed cases. Strained and ordered for 30 sheets of corrugated iron with which to finish men's hut. Captain S.P. REA returned from temporary duty with 10th R.J. Rifles. Yeomaner aeroplane overhead today.	W.7 Fawcett Lieut.Col.

Army Form C. 2118.

WAR DIARY

INTELLIGENCE SUMMARY.
(Erase heading not required) 108th FIELD AMBULANCE.

Instructions regarding War Diaries and Intelligence Summaries are contained in F. S. Regs., Part II. and the Staff Manual respectively. Title pages will be prepared in manuscript.

Place	Date	Hour	Summary of Events and Information	Remarks and references to Appendices
OU EZY	12.2.1918.		Foggy and very damp. Began to floor Reception Hut with chalk. Rode to HAM and drew £2,000 with which to pay men going on leave.	R.F.Truswell Lt Colonel
	13.2.1918.		Heavy rain during the night. Weather milder. S.W.A.D.M.S. returned from leave. Sanitary squad. Completed two trenches and tailors shop, and installed them in this hut. Continued flooring of Reception Hut with chalk. Continued brick and cement to Bath House which will be completed today. Began to write huts in front of camp quite effective in appearance and useful. Continued drainage scheme for carrying off slops next to second Bath House. At thirteen stated with working squad completed roof of men's hut.	R.F.Truswell Lt Colonel
	14.2.1918.		Rain during the night, wind N. completed stands for butts for gassed cases. Began to dig walls of tents, continued wire fencing in front of huts, began to dig new ground in which to plant potatoes.	R.F.Truswell Lt Colonel
	15.2.1918.		Bright, colder. Rode to HAM and attended Conference at D.D.M.S. Office. Drew £1,000 with which to pay men. A.D.M.S. visited camp. 2 Boys NC provided and held round on horses two hrs, branch interior lines groomers and ploughs overhead a twilight. Two riding attaches to be of course.	R.F.Truswell Lt Colonel

Army Form C. 2118.

WAR DIARY
INTELLIGENCE SUMMARY.
(Erase heading not required.) 108 FIELD AMBULANCE.

Instructions regarding War Diaries and Intelligence Summaries are contained in F. S. Regs., Part II. and the Staff Manual respectively. Title pages will be prepared in manuscript.

Place	Date	Hour	Summary of Events and Information	Remarks and references to Appendices
OMEZY	16.2.1918.		Freezing hard with pouring east wind continues even at jarring, turning walls of huts, roofs of Marquee hut for many attention. Sheet flies of Reception Hut, which is now nearly furnished, and furnishings of Resident Inspection Room, McParker is now at work in his hut, many German aeroplanes overhead at night and several bombs dropped not far from this camp.	W.F.Furnivall Lieut Colonel
	17.2.1918.		Cleared cold moonlight, S.S.E., but shower at daybreak, German aeroplanes stopped bombing in neighbourhood. Continued work at new Gas Dispensary. Finished laying roofing felt. Huts feel in the night and raining midday.	W.F.Furnivall Lieut Colonel
	18.2.1918.		Reception Hut, an excellent piece of work. Capts. T.P.Waters invalided to 11/13 F.Mbce. Seedings. Continued turning of huts. Capts.T.P.Waters marked duty with us. Began	W.F.Furnivall Lieut Colonel
	19.2.1918.		Freezing hard but bright sunshine day with no wind. Began to build huts for our men do. Large Marquee, continued work on men's hut.	W.F.Furnivall Lieut Colonel
	20.2.1918.		Fine but gradually clouding over and becoming milder to-day by 2 p.m., it was no longer freezing, tracked men's hut teeth began covering, finished bamboo fence hut to front of camp. There place now looks more like a workman-like thorough the usual attempt to catch the eye of the inspecting officer. Visit by D.D.M.S. 1 A.D.M.S. Heavy Shell at night.	W.F.Furnivall Lieut Colonel

WAR DIARY
INTELLIGENCE SUMMARY
(Erase heading not required.) 108TH FIELD AMBULANCE.

Army Form C. 2118.

Instructions regarding War Diaries and Intelligence Summaries are contained in F. S. Regs., Part II. and the Staff Manual respectively. Title pages will be prepared in manuscript.

Place	Date	Hour	Summary of Events and Information	Remarks and references to Appendices
OLLEZY.	21.2.1918.		Mild and overcast. Put 32 men into their new huts. Continued work on Baths in Hangar for treatment of gassed cases.	
	22.2.1918.		Completed Baths in Hangar; dull and overcast. Visit by D.M.S. V Army.	Note forward pass to Colonel 1/4th Staffs.
	23.2.1918.		Got up journey to Boileo in Hangar; completed path to Reception Hut Side door, and continued pavings of paths to Reception hut on improvements. Visit by A.D.M.S. at 11.30 am, to see progress of the work, he was much pleased with our improvements to Baths. Genl ward with 27 beds with spring mattress dull and misty. Genl ward is nearly full. N.F. Infantry moon at night though it is nearly full.	Lieut E. Colonel 1/4th Staffs.
	24.2.1918.		Dull and overcast; worked W.S.W. fresh, mild and threatening rain. Continued Training hut and painting of fumes mts, begun to put ventilating flats in 18 fields of Reception Hut; this will much increase the amount of light as very few be kept open in mild weather and can be closed and keep out workmanlike.	
	25.2.1918.		Rain during the night. Overcast and fresh W. Begun to said to forms. went moved Redoubt Lines. Continued Training and said buggy of hut walls, front of camp is now finished and huts including M.S. A.O.W.W.W.D.S.D. are now completed, the Lines only regd.	147. N. Fusiliers Lieut E. Colonel. W.F. James Lt. Colonel.

Army Form C. 2118.

WAR DIARY
or
INTELLIGENCE SUMMARY.
(Erase heading not required) 108th FIELD AMBULANCE.

Place	Date	Hour	Summary of Events and Information	Remarks and references to Appendices
	25.2.1918		Enemy in over the dawn has a layer of barbed wire on the forward. This is followed by a layer of barbed wire, and further to fields above the field. Continued work on the canteen.	
	26.2.1918.		Continued work on wire B. Placed Spray Bath is positioned. Road a tonight. 27 M Farrewitt Lieut Colonel. Burnt and oiled. Carpenters nearly ready to open. Sent in recommendations for Birthday Honours Lieut B. Rumbolt. 27 M Farewitt Lieut Colonel	
	27.2.1918.		75 Fritowcit Col. Shower during the day, mild, completed concrete work in Hangar tonight. 75 Fritowcit Lt Colonel. 108 Field	
	28.2.1918	10.30am	Attacked at A.D.M.S. Office with O.B.s 109 & 110 Field Ambulances and discussed medical arrangements in case of a German attack. A.D.M.S. visits completed. New dental cases. Lieut: y. MARKETTE. M.O.R.C. sent to 61 C.C.S. suffering from Bronchitis. 75 Fritowcit Lieut Colonel	

75 M Farewitt.
Lieut: Colonel
O.B., 108th Field Ambulance

140/2900

108th Field Ambulance.

Dec 1918

COMMITTEE FOR THE
MEDICAL HISTORY OF THE WAR
Date 6 JUN 1918

CONFIDENTIAL

WAR DIARY

OF

108th FIELD AMBULANCE.

From 1st MARCH 1918   To 31st MARCH 1918.

VOL. XXX

H S Roch
Lieut-Colonel,
R.A.M.C.
Commanding.

WAR DIARY

INTELLIGENCE SUMMARY

(Erase heading not required.) 108th FIELD AMBULANCE.

Army Form C. 2118.

Instructions regarding War Diaries and Intelligence Summaries are contained in F. S. Regs., Part II. and the Staff Manual respectively. Title pages will be prepared in manuscript.

Place	Date	Hour	Summary of Events and Information	Remarks and references to Appendices
OLLETY	1.3.1918.	R.J.J.hrt	Sharp frost during the night. Wind N.E. Took over wounded and stretcher-handed, at present the balance of ward work, a total of over 150 patients, is being done by Capt. S.B. BOYD CAMPBELL, a most capable and zealous officer whose name has gone forward for promotion to entity rank of Major. The men paraded for two moments washing with the B.O.O.R. Relic totals 016. Heavy cannonade on our right front from 8.30 p.m. to 10.30 p.m. J. M.J.Frit	18.F.M.J.
		7.S.M.J.		
	2.3.1918.		Stormy N.E. wind, snow during morning. Drew 79,000 from Caphus XVIII Corps. Paid crew at 2.30 p.m. by W2 of A.D.M.S. at 12.35 p.m. M.F.M.J.	M.F.M.J.
	3.3.1918.		Wind light, N.N.E. Mustering service at 10.30 am. The Recreation Room is very comfortable and is much appreciated by patients. Staff Sergeant is at present being trained by one of our men. "Guard." Drum and fife under Bandmaster Bent by Cott. M.S.R. 36th Division with A.D.M.S. 20th Battalion. Milled at night. M.F.M.J.	18.F.M.J.
	4.3.1918.	1 p.m.	Visit by German aeroplane in early morning, a fairly large mobile of bombs were dropped but of these none went very near. It began to snow slightly at 10 am. A black day, freezing slightly. The circulations for the treatment of every "not feeling at score complete and ventilation" Stoves and good. Completed but outside Hangar for Separator. Rain in afternoon but by D.D.M.S. at noon. 18.F.M.J.	
	5.3.1918.		Wind fresh S.E. Snow has disappeared. Campress completed but as two yet available 18.F.M.J.	
	6.3.1918.		Checked bright. Wind light, E. Continued training and disinfecting of huts.	18.F.M.J. Lieut Colonel
		2 p.m.	Took out a J.S. wagons and small party of men 1000 yards in rear of camp and got a load of dead wood. Job fine C. 18.F.M.J.	

WAR DIARY
or
INTELLIGENCE SUMMARY.

Army Form C. 2118.

(Erase heading not required.) 108th FIELD AMBULANCE.

Place	Date	Hour	Summary of Events and Information	Remarks and references to Appendices
OUEZY	7.3.1918.	10 a.m.	Rode to HAM and their F. 2000.00. with the which to pay men. 78.7.Fawcett.	
	8.3.1918.	8.10.45 p.m.	Rode out in search of Tiddies but did not obtain any. Wind fresh, E, clear. 78.7.Fawcett. Concert at night in Recreation Room, attended by the a.D.m.S.	
	9.3.1918.		No wind, but clear. German aeroplanes received a good part of the night well supported, flying very low. N.F. McFawcett, Lieut. Colonel. Wind light. N.E. Early with Sergt. LeTonglit. Got up night in	
		2.30 p.m.	proceeds for exhibition to Courtiers. A.D.m.S, who was pleased with its appearance. N.F. Fawcett, Lieut. Colonel. Inspection of Transport by A.D.m.S.	
	10.3.1918.	10.45 a.m.	Inspection of Camp by Deputy Director General A.m.S. (Major General MACPHERSON, and Major General SKINNER, D.M.S, 5th ARMY.	
		11.30 a.m.	Inspection by Divisional Commander (Major General O. NUGENT). Weather fine, wind light. W. 78.7.Fawcett, Lieut. Colonel.	
	11.3.1918.		Wind light: N.W. frost for the night.	
		10 a.m.	Road to HAM with A.D.M.S. and attended conference of officers D.D.M.S, XVIII Corps. Many German aeroplanes passed over & next night but apparently did not drop bombs in this neighbourhood. Stunned a new heavy gun to the (Cerrisière), 78.7.Fawcett, Lieut. Colonel.	
	12.3.1918.		Clear; frost in the night. Wind light. W. Francs and walls of rooms from completely began symphonised. Leaving floors, which brought Price to W. and gave day to take field in no good and found to be very unspiritual. 78.7.Fawcett, Lieut. Colonel.	

Army Form C. 2118.

WAR DIARY
INTELLIGENCE SUMMARY.
(Erase heading not required.)

Instructions regarding War Diaries and Intelligence Summaries are contained in F.S. Regs., Part II. and the Staff Manual respectively. Title pages will be prepared in manuscript.

Place	Date	Hour	Summary of Events and Information	Remarks and references to Appendices
OLLEZY.	13.3.1918.		Clear; wind light N.E. slight frost in the night; routine duty; visit by A.D.M.S.; at noon, R.F. Falconer, Lieut: Colonel.	
	14.3.1918.		Fine Weather; Wind N.N.E., light; Inspection by A.D.M.S. Captain J.ROBB joined for duty; Handed over documents and cash to Captain S.B. BOYD CAMPBELL prior to proceeding on leave. R.F.Falconer Lieut: Colonel. 14/3/1918. C., 108th Field Ambulance	

Army Form C. 2118.

WAR DIARY
or
INTELLIGENCE SUMMARY.
(Erase heading not required.)

Instructions regarding War Diaries and Intelligence Summaries are contained in F. S. Regs., Part II. and the Staff Manual respectively. Title pages will be prepared in manuscript.

Place	Date	Hour	Summary of Events and Information	Remarks and references to Appendices
HUSY.	15-3-18		Took over temporary command from Lieut Colonel R.F.M. FAGGETT. D.S.O. who proceeded on leave to England from 15-3-18 – 14-4-18. Visited "DDMS XVIII Corps" & ADMS 30th Divn at 12.30 pm. Divisional band performed from 2.30 – 4.30 pm to troops of the palatute. Capt J.C. Robb took over command of Transport	AMC.
	16.3.18.		Bright sunny day. Usual ceremonial about 6 a.m. I went over to 110th FA at ANNOIX to see Then bathed & camped Thursao Splint in Wire Ambulance. ADMS paid visit at 5.30 pm to see Dental Laboratory. Given room attached to but B recreation room below stairs.	SAME
	17.3.18		St Patricks day and a Divisional holiday. G.O.C. Presbyterian Service at 11 am & C.B.E. service at 11.45 am. The A'Subs & DA'Sups attended the latter. Ambulance football team played Divisional Signal Company at 2 pm & were beaten. Head Colonel Tignere & Capt McCready went away on 14 days leave to England.	SAME
	18.3.18		Rev W. Rickerton. C.F. proceeded on 14 days leave to Ireland. 5 got 5mm embanked have & pickets from the R.E. to make particular barricades between hire horses in Transport lines. Day was kept sunny throughout.	SAME

WAR DIARY or INTELLIGENCE SUMMARY

Army Form C. 2118.

Place	Date	Hour	Summary of Events and Information	Remarks and references to Appendices
Ollezy	19.3.18		A cold wet day. The Carpenters of unit started to make a sanctuary. A small hut 12' × 12' was emergency our canvas side. The "Henry Mawes" (36th DW troops) gave a concert to the patients from 2.30 pm – 4 pm. It was much appreciated.	PMR
	20.3.18		Huns was wet but weather improved towards evening. I went to see ADMS at his office re arrangements about this gas centre. In the afternoon I detailed the men for their various duties in the gas centre and lectured to them on the treatment of gas cases. Capt Sowerby went up to Grougis with the ADMS to arrange about huts in a new aid post. Two deserters from the enemy have information to the British that the Germans were going to attack that night about 10 pm. On Huns bombarded the German lines very heavily for an hour	Possible

Army Form C. 2118.

WAR DIARY
or
INTELLIGENCE SUMMARY.
(Erase heading not required.)

Instructions regarding War Diaries and Intelligence Summaries are contained in F.S. Regs., Part II. and the Staff Manual respectively. Title pages will be prepared in manuscript.

Place	Date	Hour	Summary of Events and Information	Remarks and references to Appendices
Villery	21.3.18		About 4.30 am we were all wakened by a heavy bombardment left by command of the Enemy's guns. This continued to several hours at 6 am the order to man battle positions was received from CO A.D.M.S. and soon afterwards we had a most from the A.D.M.S. who was on his way up to round learcut to take charge of a party of 3 detailed Capt. E.S. Smeeth to take charge of a party of 60 Stretcher bearers then reported to O.C. 107 F.A. at Raud. Sent a cart for duty. Lieut J. Scott Raud took charge of the receiving room in the far centre. and the remaining orderlies went to then appointed posts at 7.30 am everything was in readiness to deal with any Gassed cases. Mi. suppt Lieut Cott & I had Breakfast & we moved all Annie. The Irish then wanted B the Patients to clear CCS in readiness as far carts to keep Rame personnel a case might be. all Stretcher cases and 3 from Ambulance took 8 Sitting case were sent to CCS at Cepoy. At 6 am however the CCS closed	

A5834 Wt. W4973/M687 750,000 8/16 D.D. & L. Ltd. Forms/C.2118/13.

WAR DIARY or INTELLIGENCE SUMMARY

Army Form C. 2118.

Place	Date	Hour	Summary of Events and Information	Remarks and references to Appendices
01625J	21.8.18		and the remaining cases had to be sent to 61 C.C.S Ham. By 8.30 am all the sick had been evacuated. The remainder having been sent to Ham in P.S. wagons. 20 No. M.A.C. cars had turned up. St Simon about 2 Kilometres from the hospital was shelled at frequent intervals and a few shells were dropped in the trenches rear of Orcarsh. about 400 yards away. Wounded & gassed cases began to come in about 8 A.S. am. The trains were then sent in the depth backward. Provs? J the cannon were kept busy. The gassed cases were chiefly of the phosgene variety, only 4 cases had to be battled as they were Knt? full altogether. There were 1 mus & 3 a O.R. Gassed cases. Two J the vain? serums and all shewed here a few signs J eyanness? difficulty in breathing it is admitting Ency? case was taken with the oxygen and given the usual ¼ - 1 hour antonunia? oxygen and Riven ten Set J orgyen apparatus allied up. a Holdaue? apparatus	

A8834 Wt.W4973/M637 750,000 8-16 D.D.&L.Ltd. Form/C.2113/13.

WAR DIARY
or
INTELLIGENCE SUMMARY.
(Erase heading not required.)

Army Form C. 2118.

Place	Date	Hour	Summary of Events and Information	Remarks and references to Appendices
Ollezy	2.7	8.18	A modified American mode of an oil river and the strelzy Ruyple device which worked the 2 gels. [sketch showing oxygen cylinder, plano trial, plano trial, oxygen cylinder] oxygen cylinder in centre with tubing leading to from a T plan tube to each side and from them a noble tube 2 plans trial ran as each end. The pateutulo shine him a thick carrier weather can be made of the holdane shirt was performed on exercise them to an unnecessary extent. All the case improved considerably except the died after he - I him in the oxygen and they were taken to a res horse used his tube and after being put with bygrines was air twice them not before being taut 2 c.e.s. The number 3 connected other than passed but has was so. Capt. J.C. Robb returned from the unit from the D.A.C. South large. J. The hauper at 11 am been kept Amphurge returned to duty in this return from the different rating Capt Iletchie the Rent & sketch thereon mills. Charge I the mgm toal. about 7 pm as hand for a cent toad. Capt I Smith returned	

A 5834 Wt. W 4973/M687 750,000 8/16 D. D. & L. Ltd. Forms/C.2118/13

WAR DIARY or INTELLIGENCE SUMMARY

Army Form C. 2118.

Place	Date	Hour	Summary of Events and Information	Remarks and references to Appendices
Olley	21.3	1 P	to be evacuated & kept from 2 & 6 men had remained in Ramp. Lieut Cenral known after the others & left & succeeded in getting a few more wounded in. They were about captured by the enemy. Men up at the 2nd R.I.R. R.A.P. at 11.30 p.m. Received order to report to the ADMS 9th Div the ndvn. There we met the unit was & come to Villers St Christophe and there SS unit Met with O.C. 93rd F.A. I went in conjunction with him Capt Sneeks had in wit 2 men to arrange beds etc while the remainder of the returned started to try and salve as much of the medical equipment as possible. Capt C. All the wards were emptied of stretchers, blankets & other stores and a large through the wards at entrance. Quar J Vivs Chumps was salved as 6 Cars Ambulance Cars were 8 2 Lorries were sent in to take Col Lupot and 2 send Corps back at 8 am in the morning. 1000 complete suits of Kharki dress and a large quantity of Stretchers, blankets medical comforts were salved.	
Olley	22.3	1P	At 2.30 a.m. The unit (all except a left of 6 men who were left behind to load the lorries) marched at where 76 men were billeted in the Camp Adrian huts in Villers St Christophe at 4.4.15 a.m. I at unit	

WAR DIARY or INTELLIGENCE SUMMARY

Army Form C. 2118.

Place	Date	Hour	Summary of Events and Information	Remarks and references to Appendices
Villers St Christophe	22.3.18		Got out and met Lieut Colonel Rawlins DSO OC 97th FA who had already established an ADS there. He sent him in bearing his wd of canal from Happencourt towards Tugny at Pontru. On reaching a narrow part there were four wounded men. Hopkinson I sent with Lanson & two Ambulance cars to collect them. They were unable to do any of the relap as it was hot in German occupation. The Ambulance went up to where in their a furneer was firing and got all the wounded in that area away. 15 in all. As in line was shelling back top I received men from the ADS to send out transport and cars of personnel to Somerly Hallon. Capt Tesdale being sent charge of this party. Capt Sorrel and I remained with 30 ord 3.30 pm when we were unable to leave the village. We established an ADS at Ppy but left here in a tho hours and returned not of ceut Sorrel Hallon from the I sent back to Wabally cars of Ppy and there went to & of Pho from there all the wounded were cleared. Arrived in Tielis at La Fene Hosptal about 2 Kilometers. Sent I Sorrey Hallen at 7 p.m. Chief fam. we shared with 110 x L A At 6 am Hgy with Colliet reported that Bridge over canal at Ppy had been blown up and that there were no wounded left there a clue were received from the A Surg to send via Etreicount	OK/l
Le Fique Hosptal Consley Hallon	23.3.18		

A5834 Wt. W4973/M687 750,000 8/16 D.D.&L.Ltd. Forms/C.2118/13

WAR DIARY or INTELLIGENCE SUMMARY

Army Form C. 2118.

Place	Date	Hour	Summary of Events and Information	Remarks and references to Appendices
	23.3.18		Freincke. Fetry to Chateau and to back in a field near the Fetry - Beaulieu road. While halted here with the 109th & 110th Field Ambulances we saw a fight between 4 German planes & one of ours. The latter was forced to land as the pilot was wounded. We observed this wound & kept him to the O.C.S. at Bagni. The German planes flew very low at a height of a few hundred feet but did not fire on the R.A.M.C. personnel in any form. 3 of the British planes took to the Air. Dropped the Ambulance to a Cage d'Am. to two sergts Samuels 66 D. & 15th A.3. There there was Cage Dames & Sergt. J. Shaw to the Queen of the ———. At 5 p.m. we returned to about the 109th F.A. We were to do Capt Smith's evacuation. I informed from the new Lieut taken up by the Divn RAMC he was not P. He went for ready to award. If at Short Willie - Adsv. were received from the A.D.M.S. Via Beaulieu to Amiens. He arrived at Catlin Place at 5 p.m. but as we were so exhausted after the rain we turned to the Hotel Willap. Army where we were able to get a good nights rest.	
Amy to Corbie	26.3.18		Adsn were received in the afternoon to that march to Corbie via Beauraignes - Villers Bretonneux. Marquillen Querbigny Du Broken & Vitulir into 108th BCs in a Cage German Prisoners camp at which we arrived at 12 midnight.	

WAR DIARY or INTELLIGENCE SUMMARY

Army Form C. 2118.

Place	Date	Hour	Summary of Events and Information	Remarks and references to Appendices
Orches	26.3.18		Thinking that the Germans were still well away the Lt Col had gone to bed at 9 am. Lieut Colonel Kell, 9th R knot Fusiliers came into the tent but to get his hat held attended to. It does no let the Germans had advanced considerably during the night having passed back the front trench opposing them. The German patrols were then only about 2 miles away. I saw nothing to have all the wagons ready + he was to ready to move at once. I then went down to Querbigny to see the A Dn/S. He gave me orders to send the transport and hort 2 the personnel under Capt Tattersburg to Hanfcourt. This unit was detailed to make arrangement for the wounding. The wounded of the Division. 3 large Ambulance Cars of the 110th and 2 of the 109th were attached to us to keep in the evacuations. The Division was supposed to hold a line in front of Andechy running South to Eckelles St Aurin. but the infantry were unable to get out. The forward village and troops been as that the I trenches horst Pst. I detailed Capt E.S. Smith M.C. to take charge of the advanced posts. He went out with two Ambulance Cars carrying hort Inglebigh Cpl Hearn and 8 men with Stretcher blankets dressings etc. to post there in Andechy this Gring up the trenches Andechy were they ran into a German	

WAR DIARY
or
INTELLIGENCE SUMMARY

Army Form C. 2118.

Place	Date	Hour	Summary of Events and Information	Remarks and references to Appendices
Enches	26	3.18	German outpost which immediately fired on [illegible] with a machine gun. An ambulance car was riddled with bullets but miraculously only two men were wounded. The Driver, Pt Cave, & D Griffiths showed great courage & when in getting the Ambulance turned & bringing them out of danger zone. As Amalechy was in German occupation Capt Swietz M.C. found Lieut Inglish & party at Enches. When they got in touch with 108th Infantry Bde. an ambulance car was posted his & Caen way cleared to MDS at DAVESCOURT. Lieut Scott (10th FA) Sergt Sytlle D.C.M. and 15 O.R. were posted at Ennee road. Q.18.C.4.2. Sheet 66.E. When they got in touch with 109th Infantry Bde. an NCO & 4 men of the Bearer party were posted at RAP of 9th Royal Inniskilling Fusiliers. With the Party, a large Ambulance car was also stationed and it cleared the cases & MDS at DAVESCOURT. Sergt Beedum MT Sergt 108th FA was put in charge of an ambulance relay post which was formed at Q 15 a 3.2. Under 109th Bde Headquarters from this post cars were sent up to the two advanced posts to evacuate cases which brought down wounded & formed MDS at School known in DAVESCOURT and her Capt	

WAR DIARY or INTELLIGENCE SUMMARY

Army Form C. 2118.

Place	Date	Hour	Summary of Events and Information	Remarks and references to Appendices
DAVENSCOURT	26.3.18		J.C. Ruth to assist. There were 15 D.R. at the post and a rescue party of 20 under Staff Sergt Byron in case men were picked up after ADS. The ADMS 31st Div. arrived about 12 noon and I went up with him to go round the ADSs. The ADMS stayed with Capt Smith for some time while I returned to the MDS. This scheme of evacuation worked very well till about 6.30 p.m. At that hour Capt J.C. Ruth had gone up to the car relay post and found when he got there that the Germans had occupied Beaufort Inches. The Ambulance Sections were trying to get round a corner was attended but another Ambulance of the 110th FA came up & I thought the Germans were within sight, & was able to turn this damaged car back. Dr Kennedy 110th FA shared great nerve in doing this car and saving its occupant. Two of the party under Sergeant Loughridge succeeded in getting back to the wagon post but the remainder I found another ADS. Near the village and continued to work there. Unfortunately a Staff German patrol came round in their flank and captured Lieut Loughridge, 7 OR. Capt Ruth & Capt Lindsay MO i/c 2nd RIR were at relay post at 6.30 p.m. and having seen the 108th Infantry Bdr. were cut off they tried to get in touch with them they had	

WAR DIARY or INTELLIGENCE SUMMARY

Army Form C. 2118.

Place	Date	Hour	Summary of Events and Information	Remarks and references to Appendices
DAVENSCOURT	26.8.18		They had to return to the ulan post. Soon afterwards machine gun bullets began to whistle past this post and as there was a great danger of the Corps being captured Capt. Ross decided to withdraw the Corps to DAVENSCOURT about & form several of the 108th Bde Head Quarters Staff came with us to H.Q.S & reported that a Staff Runner Patrol had captured their Headquarters and had invited its way between our Infantry towards Guerbigny. A message from Brigadier General Griffiths to the British confirmed this. Sergt Beadman M.T. Sergt. went up in a motor cycle to try and find out definitely but enemy shrapnel was not to be cured near the German shelling to each other in front of them. 107th Infantry Bde had taken up a position between Ercheu & Amiens and their Headquarters were at Q8 & 4.9. To clear the wounded Patient I came here left up. DAVENSCOURT - AVILLERS ROAD as no Cars had ever moved from 109th Bde for two hours & sent the M.T. Sergt. & 109th T.M. with the Car Bany - with orders to return not Guerbigny as I considered then the enemies line & Will decrease of the 109th Bde. In cases to find out how things stood. I sent my motor cyclist to try and get in touch with HeadQtrs & Posts and not 109th Bde Headqtrs the south at Berguigny would not allow them to take their bicycle	

WAR DIARY
or
INTELLIGENCE SUMMARY
(Erase heading not required.)

Army Form C. 2118.

Places	Date	Hour	Summary of Events and Information	Remarks and references to Appendices
DAVENSCOURT	26.3.18		Carry further S. to heat to proceed in front. & ultimately to put in truck with the Brigade. As this was a great foretells of DAVENSCOURT being captured at any moment I sent Lieut Evans & two men to Contoire to prepare a place for another ADS. The ADMS Y D.A.D.M.S. visited us again and stayed in the area for some considerable time.	
	27.3.18		No information had reached us as of the situation of 107 Brigade, but we were told in truck with 107th Bde. I went to France situation was thus. The car stationed with Lieut Evans's party. Mr Humphrey a wounded man driver & the M.D.S. was captured. The Germans took the driver & newly prisoners and made them form a stretcher party with several infantrymen of the Division to carry a German wounded back to their lines. The foot Pte Thompson Rowe and & Mr Humphrey had arranged that the party they set out captured. The car meanwhile then arranged till the men prisoners that if they met a British patrol he would call out to him to fire at the Germans behind and that all of them to know their labour in the French. This ruse succeeded & the two Germans as were their escort were killed, Harry then then rescued the car driver Dr Macgowan also & Lieut Eclit Dr. McCullogh. Major General		10 pm

WAR DIARY or INTELLIGENCE SUMMARY

Army Form C. 2118.

Place	Date	Hour	Summary of Events and Information	Remarks and references to Appendices
Davenscourt	27.3.18		Tried to get up to the Ambulance and below it at Dan(?) by proceeding in mostly of and near the Faucitel of German P.O.W. in the way back to our lines they saw a Staff Car (which had been captured from the E.S.O.) of the Division on captured and stopped they attacked a two nights & it & brought it back also. In this car they found several very valuable Court Documents, which were seen by the French armoured to the Germans. When they were guarding the American. So at last I managed and brought them to the C.C.S. had staff & Points, Guarding that they were cut. The decision to try and make their way back via Montdidier. The men brought 14 wounded back with them carrying them several wounded were in unformed Stretchers. first as done, to Hargicourt. The total distance they carried them being about 18 miles. At DAVSNSCourt at 2.30 am Brigadier General Riflet came in to the Divisory Station to tell this what they heard and to strongly advise us to leave the place at once as to tie about several have dropped. The German between Exkus of Davencourt & Therfus were supplying to Captain and to a few times moved again to Hargicourt.	
			Also at 11 am he was joined by the party which was still there wounded 109^ Bde. Being informed that there	

Place	Date	Hour	Summary of Events and Information	Remarks and references to Appendices
Hargicourt	27.3.18		At Bergugny I took up two Ambulance Cars & cleared the A.D.S. on the 26th. We had 2 Pruin & 49 Queen. I on rue Shop. Through the weary Station & 2 O.R. were sent direct from the French Division. A fresh enemy now-attack was taking place and this did not I kept in touch parts to the A.D.S. and this did not I kept in touch Capt J. C. R.A.P.C. took 2 Cape Ambulance Cars up to Davencourt and patrolled the road to Aurilles Bergny in touch with 107th Acc and the road to Bergugny keeping in touch with 109 Bde. He remained in Davencourt till 3.30 pm when he had to leave very suddenly as the Germans were coming down into end of the street while he & his car escaped at the other end. The unit was moved to Aubvillers where the transport was parked & A. Dressing Station was established in a farm house and Ambulance Cars were sent to Hargicourt to bring the wounded in. Capt Tewkesbury Lieut Scott with all the H.T. transport and most of the then proceeded to Chirmont via Thory & Sourdon, where they parked the night. The A.D.M.S. visited the Dressing Station & stayed till we till about 12 pm when the became very dark.	

WAR DIARY or INTELLIGENCE SUMMARY

Army Form C. 2118.

Place	Date	Hour	Summary of Events and Information	Remarks and references to Appendices
Aubillers	27.3.18		Most of the wounded were slight cases. The total number was 62	
	28.3.18		I came B4 we Duftin was relieved in the line by the French we got orders to move back to their unit. First of all 3 sent ambulance cars round the roads that the Duftin would witness along & see if there were any sick to be picked up. we of the ambulance wells Capt Togen 1st UA. had a narrow escape as they ran into a small patrol of Germans but successfully away took a billet went through one type and arithe through the town & the cars Capt Snouts, Capt Ross and 3 then proceeded to Clermont there we found ital, the transport had left to its brow while the Clap & Capt Tuckering and the rest of the personnel had already reached up to Lawardi house. Here we billeted for the night.	SM&C
	29.3.18		Next day we had a great rest most till the evening when we got orders to march via Ifers, Breuilly, Wally, to Haumpes, the journey was a long tedious me, as all the transport in front of us Britt in a deep hill notoria Wally, which backs at the foot of the hill in was bad teas... A fine transport luring tried to Arrulle track the column and train in hot trocti in thin effort.	

WAR DIARY
or
INTELLIGENCE SUMMARY

Army Form C. 2118.

Place	Date	Hour	Summary of Events and Information	Remarks and references to Appendices
	29.3.18		Capt E.S. Smith had [?] us to arrange billets but found on arrival that all the available billets were occupied by French Cavalry. The troops parked on the wagons in a field and Men & Men kept in a wood. Tents, that was no rain during the night.	R.A.M.C
Naurpès	30.3.18		The French cavalry having left the village we were able to get into the town at 9am. In the afternoon news was received to send the transport to the 3 Field Ambulances under Capt R.M. & Capt Russell on W[?]. While the personnel were to entrain at 12 midnight at Saleux. The 3 Ambulances were [?] at 8pm under the charge I went [?] [?] Rouaple and marching via Ruenand they reached Saleux about 11pm & found a good bit empty. Sent some had gone ahead & found all 3 Ambulances. The rest had been moved to them from the Australian Supply Column & Men marched up to [?] head when they had to spend the night in the Saleux railway station.	R.A.M.C
Saleux	31.3.18		All of this day was spent in the Saleux railway station.	R.A.M.C

A 5834 Wt.W4973/M687 730,000 8/16 D. D. & L. Ltd. Form/C.2118/13.

WAR DIARY
or
INTELLIGENCE SUMMARY.
(Erase heading not required.)

Army Form C. 2118.

Place	Date	Hour	Summary of Events and Information	Remarks and references to Appendices
SALEUX	31.3.18		There was no room in the train allotted to us so we had to wait for another and this same thing prevented us going down into the village just now a fast mail preventing us going down into the village to get a place for the men to shelter in. At 2 a.m. on April 1st the train finally arrived and all the men were got in to it. No one got into the train no experience of the "interchard ended. On such a battle one is bound to learn many things from a practical point of view. Amongst mainly the chief thing of relatively little value unless motor ambulances can be kept standing up to the front line. To get wounded away in time. It is necessary to keep the ambulance running to & from the line continuously, and to have M.T.C. cars ready at a fixed point a few miles behind to take the cases in to the C.C.S. Another great advantage to be met was the knowing of trans of the transport in advance up Keeping. except to meet all the daily requirements.	

Army Form C. 2118.

WAR DIARY
or
INTELLIGENCE SUMMARY.
(Erase heading not required.)

Place	Date	Hour	Summary of Events and Information	Remarks and references to Appendices
Salum	31	18	The Sports of the men was wonderful. Capt E S Smoods led & Capt J C Rire both showed fine reserves of energy in running with the warmth of weather. The saddest part of the whole show was to see old Peasant men & women weeling then belongings along the road. There was no confusion in the rout of the lud at least and it was marvellous how refugees softhis etc were	

SMCampbell
Major Ramc
A/oc 108 Field Ambulance.

140/2900

108th Field Ambulance.

COMMITTEE FOR THE
MEDICAL HISTORY OF THE WAR
Date -6 JUN 1918

Secret.

War Diary

of

108th Field Ambulance

From 1st April 1918   To 30th April 1918

Volume XXXI

Army Form C. 2118.

Vol. XXXI / 1.

WAR DIARY
or
INTELLIGENCE SUMMARY.
(Erase heading not required.)

108th FIELD AMBULANCE.

Instructions regarding War Diaries and Intelligence Summaries are contained in F. S. Regs., Part II. and the Staff Manual respectively. Title pages will be prepared in manuscript.

Place	Date	Hour	Summary of Events and Information	Remarks and references to Appendices
Wargnies	1.4.18		We and arrived at Gamaches about mid day and went quiet there to the 57 DMS Capt Johnston & Capt Snively W.C. Then too had arranged that to tennis should take on men to their destination at Longpraint. Capt Robb had arrived 2 hours before us with the transport and he was ready to start to show men an excellent public the men.	
	2.4.18		Had an inspection of the men's feet at 2 p.m. The rest of the day being devoted to cleaning up purposes as all the men's clothes boots etc were very muddy. The French people in the village were very very kind to the British OR of C. Capt Tasker by arrived with rest of transport from Abbeville a nice sunny day.	
	3.4.18		A DMS Rel. We met car to rejoin at Eu in car. We 70 at 8 a.m. — [crossed out: Inspected of kits of things Captn Bedford from the HQ of 36th DS]	
	4.4.18		Reveille & transport was 1.30 am & then started for Reveille & transport war. Capt J. C. Robb Renée to Raure 3 am when command of at 4.30 am. Twas a tram Was 3 am new were marched to marching but unimp over unpleasant to marching.	

Army Form C. 2118.

WAR DIARY
or
INTELLIGENCE SUMMARY.
(Erase heading not required.)

108th FIELD AMBULANCE.

Place	Date	Hour	Summary of Events and Information	Remarks and references to Appendices
Eu.	4.4.18		Arrived at station at 7 am but had to wait till 9 am before our Coes entrain. We journey up but were not heated by steam at 1ph in 10 hrs getting to Herzeele. We arrived at Rehaving Station Proper at 2 am. There Capt Sowerby sent a man to meet us. 5 "Inns took us to Herzeele.	
Herzeele	5.4.18		Arrived at Herzeele at 3 am & woke the transport up. Arrived at 7 am. Then Capt Sowerby and I started off to prepare to meet the A.D.M.S. He had breakfast in the Officers Club and then went on to see the A.D.M.S. at Rr. The A.D.M.S. & D.D.M.S. hired a car to take us to various parts of the A.D.S's & the M.D.S. OC 1st Cat. We went up to see an ambulance car & hut up to Trinity & St Julien A.D.S. Both seemed excellent and we then saw near the M.D.S. at Du Hallis Camp. Which also is a very well equipped dressing Station. The A.D.M.S. arranged us & travel by the Div.Sin to have 4 lorries at 9 am & the 6th & our very own men to Canal Bank.	

Army Form C. 2118.

109th FIELD AMBULANCE

WAR DIARY
or
INTELLIGENCE SUMMARY.
(Erase heading not required.)

Place	Date	Hour	Summary of Events and Information	Remarks and references to Appendices
Du HALLOW Camp	6.4.18		Transport left Herzeule at 7.45 am under charge of Capt Robb. Capt Snively M.C. & Capt Tuckey M.C. left in the Ambulance on Sept at 9.30 with a few men as advance party to take over with the wounded of the men in the line. The A.D.S. at Minty & St Julien were taken over at 12 noon. The A.D.S. at Minty & St Julien were taken over by Capt. Snively M.C. & Capt Tulloch M.C. 110th F.A. Relay posts in connection with these A.D.S. were also taken over. The main Dressing Station was taken over at 6 p.m. from h.q. Field Ambulance. Sent in recommendation to Brigade to work our change the acute infection. Capt S.S. Snively M.C. & M Robb & M.C. Sr Mc Gowan recommended for D.C.M. for very excellent work during but he Sabres his own Ambulance and a Staff-car Litany valuable Sweet taking. Pte Stewart Thompson recommended to M.M. Dr Mc Cullock Jr M.M. Sr Griffiths for M.M. & Capt Dempsta for M.M. all the men did excellent work and all are well worthy of recognition. All of this Ambulance were seen in desperation. I cannot to camp on ten had not received marching order.	
	7.4.18			

Army Form C. 2118.

WAR DIARY
INTELLIGENCE SUMMARY.
(Erase heading not required.)

108 TF FIELD AMBULANCE.

Place	Date	Hour	Summary of Events and Information	Remarks and references to Appendices
Du Hallop Camp.	7.4.18		Capt S.D. Rea reported. Lieut T. Browne went to Wimereux Major H.S. Dainder FRCS 109 F.A. General on "Surgical Specialist."	RAR
	8.4.18		On Field Ambulance marched off at 6 p.m. No.1 St Julien A.D.S in the forenoon. Day was dull & wet.	MSC
	9.4.18		Went up to Specialist Mintz with A/DMS & S/A Surg. and a/the the same has Special Time A.D.S Capt Sneed M.C. took up to the RAP B W 1st Rifles B which Capt Anderson relay post working with in Emotions B. Ree MC Rawe is in charge. The Stretcher water and many lay wounded own Such the is per B we came back via St Julien knees and numbers were to be seen the relay posts in but time did not permit of us visiting the Medical Men D on arrival at Dr Macphersons we found Emaction with it there there were forces in has Medical Men D Stevenson M.O R.C 1st Lieut J E G ? 1st Lieut J & R Stevenson M.O R.C 1st Lieut J E G ? H.R.	RAR
	10.4.18		Mo R C & Lieut & G McGuineis Rawe a few still alpha near the camp in the cocks recovery. Further Staff there on intense Artillery one. The A. Tust arrived about 7 p.m to the own Dr Magruder sun D had Recommended Dr S.C M	RAR

WAR DIARY
or
INTELLIGENCE SUMMARY
(Erase heading not required.)

Army Form C. 2118.

108th FIELD AMBULANCE

Place	Date	Hour	Summary of Events and Information	Remarks and references to Appendices
Du Hallus	11.4.18	8.	Lieut F.G. McGuinness RAMC was posted to ADS St Julien and Lieut T.E. Griffiths MORC to ADS Hunts. I went up in the Ambulance with the two officers & paid the usual Staff visit. Stationed at Thun Dots S. The medical Comdt Three ADS's 30th Div.Sir. (1st Div.Sir in our corps) a that is a possibility of its being taken over by their unit.	MOSR
	12.4.18		a dull day without special report during the day. Major Davidson & I walked over to the Yprein Club Bruden. Snow still lain over in camps about 10.30 p.m.	MOSR
	13.4.18		Capt Turkeley and I went down to 109th FA with the ADMS & DADMS of a conference of O.C.'s & Snowlin matter. The feeling points were discussed in. Surplus equipment to be sent to DADOS & hrs ASC & ASC to be detailed to take charge of same. At Aurulle. Surplus stretchers and blankets at Du Hallus to be sent to 109 FA. Surplus rec 1000 inclined to be withdrawn. The R.A.P.'s moved to at Hunts, C.16.D.3 & Warlty 2 day utes. Ypriin Club Bruilen to be working hunger post & run by this unit.	

WAR DIARY or INTELLIGENCE SUMMARY

108th FIELD AMBULANCE

Army Form C. 2118.

Place	Date	Hour	Summary of Events and Information	Remarks and references to Appendices
Du Hallus	13.4.18		109th & 110th Field Ambulances went each to starr 30 & pullers of Retz Gros farm Field Ambulance Site to be found at an auxiliary post. 2 motor relays to be found at each A.D.S. the A.D.M.S. & D.A.D.M.S. came in & Dr Hallos to lunch & then return from conference. Officers commanding came in about 10 a.m. & dispersed route pink down to gate.	
	14.4.18		Went up to point with A.D.M.S. and arranged with Capt Sinirks m.c. that all surplus equipment should be sent down to Dr Hallos.	
	15.4.18		Capt Sinirks m.c. & Capt Fulleton m.c. came down from A.D.S. to conference with A.D.M.S. Details of plan of withdrawal were then gone into and it was arranged that 4 men should be left at point. Wedge. 7 C 1603.3 (R.A.P. of each battalion). 6 large Ambulance car was also left at point. Capt Turkeling took charge of the surplus equipment at Dr Hallos and as two E.S. wagons from 110th & 109th reported for the purpose most of the surplus equipment was cleared. Lieut Stevenson went to 25 Bee R.G.A. for temporary duty	

Army Form C. 2118.

WAR DIARY
or
INTELLIGENCE SUMMARY.
(Erase heading not required.)

108th FIELD AMBULANCE

Place	Date	Hour	Summary of Events and Information	Remarks and references to Appendices
Du Mallac	15.4.18		Arrival of Lewis CO & Chaplain Lt McGuinness. AD Dismissal transferred was being further back.	note
	16.4.18		Capt Smith M.C. Capt Fullerton M.C. Lieut McGuinness & Lieut Ruffett arrived here about 6 am from the ADS. Capt R.O. & S received Blg. with new ammunition & perfumes & transport to Proven. Here we took over part of site formerly occupied by 12 CCS. I went over to 64 CCS to see their OC with a view to keeping them in their present work. He arranged that he should have 20 NCO & men to clean drive and a Sunday number to report duty. I also distribute 3 men to report to the area commandant & help with the fatigues in the area	JMC
Proven	17.4.18		A bit bleak today. I received news that all Surplus Stretchers & blankets from 80" WFO & new station were to be stored here. 900 Stretchers & 16m blankets arrived in 76C the evening. Capt Tetherby returned from Don Muller.	

A5834 Wt: W4973/M687 750,000 8/16 D. D. & L. Ltd. Forms/C.2118/13.

Army Form C. 2118.

WAR DIARY
or
INTELLIGENCE SUMMARY.
(Erase heading not required.)

108th FIELD AMBULANCE

Instructions regarding War Diaries and Intelligence Summaries are contained in F.S. Regs., Part II. and the Staff Manual respectively. Title pages will be prepared in manuscript.

Place	Date	Hour	Summary of Events and Information	Remarks and references to Appendices
Proven	18.4.18		Carried out day with A ambulance amount B Plat. The A Dress & Stretcher Bearer sector unit at 12 noon. Sent two G.S. wagons to 110th F.A. to bring down B Bearer equipment to this Home to Sharpe. Lieut Colonel R.F.W. Fawcett D.S.O. arrived back from leave in the evening & J. Reviewed men to him.	
			S. Whytampbell Lieut. Major R.A.M.C.	
			R. F. W. Fawcett Lieut. Colonel.	
Proven	18.4.19.18	9.30 p.m.	Returned from leave and took command of unit.	
			R. F. W. Fawcett Lieut. Colonel.	
	19.4.19.18		Weather cold, worth a fall of snow during the night. Enemy aeroplane flew overhead at night (12.15 a.m. till 1 a.m.) dropping bombs, I think in POPERINGHE.	
			R. F. W. Fawcett Lieut. Colonel.	
	20.4.19.18		Weather fine but unsettled, chilly but not unpleasant. Reported A.D.M.S. at DOTHULLOM and other relieved posts WIE 4 P.J.E. and left R.A.T. with A.D.M.S. Returned at 2.15 p.m. M.O.	
			R. F. W. Fawcett Lieut. Colonel.	

Army Form C. 2118.

WAR DIARY
or
INTELLIGENCE SUMMARY.
(Erase heading not required.)

108th FIELD AMBULANCE.

Army Form C. 2118.

Instructions regarding War Diaries and Intelligence Summaries are contained in F.S. Regs., Part II. and the Staff Manual respectively. Title pages will be prepared in manuscript.

Place	Date	Hour	Summary of Events and Information	Remarks and references to Appendices
PROVEN.	21.4.1918.		Bright, cold weather; wind N. Visit by A.D.M.S. at 6.0 p.m. R.J.M. Fawcett Lieut. Colonel.	
	22.4.1918.		Bright, cold day. Wind fresh N.E. Reported advanced Dressing Station at DUHALLOW, N. of Canal Bank 3/4 mile N. of YPRES with Major BOYD CAMPBELL at 9.30 a.m. Lent horse & other material being removed rapidly by G.S. Wagons. R.J.M. Fawcett Lieut. Colonel.	
	23.4.1918.		Rain during the night. Weather fine, mist visible. Heavy gunfire in S.W. directions at twilight. R.J.M. Fawcett Lieut. Colonel.	
	24.4.1918.		Chilly with thick mist. Wind light, N.E. Quiet. Many bombs dropped in Sept 1918 J. Roberts temporarily attached to neighbourhood from 10 midnight to 8 p.m. R.J.M. Fawcett Lieut. Colonel.	Sept 1918 J. Roberts temporarily attached to Infantry.
	25.4.1918.		Warmer, mill. Heavy showers from 2 p.m. till 8.30 p.m. A.D.M.S. visited unit at 12. Wood and held 130 men or more in a Labour Company. R.J.M. Fawcett Lieut. Colonel.	
	26.4.1918.		Attended conference at A.D.M.S's office at 6.15 p.m.; went on from there to DUHALLOW A.D.S. via YPRES. Capt. E.S. SOWERBY asked to withdraw with his party on arrival of party from 109th Field Ambulance, arrived back in Camp at 1 a.m.; roads much congested by heavy gun convoys towards the rear. R.J.M. Fawcett.	
	27.4.1918.	9.30 a.m.	Capt. E.S. SOWERBY and party with motor ambulances (5) returned to HdQrs. Sent B.G.S. Wagons to 110th F. Amb. to assist in removing stores to new camp. Sent 3 horsed ambulances to 109th Field Ambulance to assist in removing stores to the 1110th Field Ambulance. R.J.M. Fawcett Lieut. Colonel.	

Army Form C. 2118.

WAR DIARY

INTELLIGENCE SUMMARY.

(Erase heading not required.) 108TH FIELD AMBULANCE.

Instructions regarding War Diaries and Intelligence Summaries are contained in F. S. Regs., Part II. and the Staff Manual respectively. Title pages will be prepared in manuscript.

Place	Date	Hour	Summary of Events and Information	Remarks and references to Appendices
PROVEN.	28.4.1918		Capt. J. ROBB returned from temporary duty with the 1st Bn Royal Irish Fusiliers. Camp was mainly Shelled all night, one hut destroyed, one N.C.O. wounded, one man of 109th Field Ambulance wounded.	
	29.4.1918		Shells falling in neighbourhood all day. R.Fruitawell Lieut. Colonel scouted H.E. SIXTE (attd. to O.C.S.) and Lusaugud to overnight of the ground and in preparing platoon, if necessary.	
	30.4.1918		Wagons and Intelligently carting materials from former R.Fruitawell Lieut. Colonel Cneles all day from Ruisseau Sidring 1/2 mile N.N.W. of camp to the new site of No 12. C.C.S.	

R.Fruitawell
Lieut. Colonel
O.C., 108th Field Ambulance

30.
/4/
1918.

Secret

War Diary of.

108th Field Ambulance

May 1918.   Volume XXXII

Army Form C. 2118.

WAR DIARY
INTELLIGENCE SUMMARY
(Erase heading not required.) 108th FIELD AMBULANCE

Instructions regarding War Diaries and Intelligence Summaries are contained in F.S. Regs., Part II. and the Staff Manual respectively. Title pages will be prepared in manuscript.

Place	Date	Hour	Summary of Events and Information	Remarks and references to Appendices
PROVEN.	1.5.1918.	10.15 a.m.	Rode to HOOTKERQUE and drew pay for men (Frs. 9000.00). Saw D.D.M.S. and A.D.M.S. on the road. Wet the Villages; received instructions to occupy huts near HARINGHE with a holding party at present; could not, by HARINGHE and made enquiries. But no a holding party of 1 N.C.O. and 4 men in hut occupied by 76th Sanitary Section. R.A. Fawcett Lieut. Colonel.	
	2.5.1918.	10.15 a.m.	Rode to HARINGHE. No men huts vacant yet, started looking around with buying checks to need shelters for transit to B.A.O. They shelter in neighbourhood at 9.80 a.m. my two riding & pack mules & night to Fawcett Lieut. Colonel. with no more shelter.	
	3.5.1918.		Weather fine, wind light. S.E. Rode to BANDAGHEM camp and found that two wards were empty. This afternoon arranged for several to move over to well huts two evenings there shelling at night. R.A. Fawcett Lieut Colonel.	
	4.5.1918.		Attended Conference at Divisional Head Quarters, nothing unusual now at Ouderd[om]. R.A. Fawcett Lieut. Colonel.	
	5.5.1918.		Weather fine & no high morning, heavy rain all day, a few gas shells at night. R.A. Fawcett Lieut. Colonel.	Lt. STEPHENSON joined M.O.R.S. 36th Machine Gun Battn.
	6.5.1918.		Weather milk, unsettled. quiet. Rode to HARINGHE. 101 Field Ambulance established in part of C.C.S. Hts. Capt. E.S. SOWERBY	
	7.5.1918.		Wounded on temporary duty with the 2nd Bn. R.J. Rifles. N.F. Fawcett Lieut Colonel.	
	8.5.1918.		Very heavy rain during the night, much enemy morning; Captain J CLARKE R.A.M.C. went; inspection by A.D.M.S., bombing in neighbourhood at night. R.A. Fawcett Lieut Colonel.	

Army Form C. 2118.

2.

WAR DIARY
or
INTELLIGENCE SUMMARY
(Erase heading not required.) 108th FIELD AMBULANCE.

Instructions regarding War Diaries and Intelligence Summaries are contained in F.S. Regs., Part II. and the Staff Manual respectively. Title pages will be prepared in manuscript.

Place	Date	Hour	Summary of Events and Information	Remarks and references to Appendices
PROVEN	9.5.1918		Night, mild, wind N; light; some bombing at night.	H.F.M.Fawcett, Lieut: Colonel.
	10.5.1918		Cloudy and mild; wind fresh N.E.; quiet. Capt: J. MORHAN, R.A.M.C. travelled yesterday evening.	H.F.M.Fawcett, Lieut: Colonel.
	11.5.1918		Fine; mild; sections recalled at 9.20. a.m. and 10.30. a.m. and damaged walls of Great Room; began to unpair drainage round camp which is in a foul condition and requires a lot of work upon it. Inspected Water Carts which require replacement. Lance J/lodge	H.F.M.Fawcett, Lieut: Colonel.
	12.5.1918		Capt: E.S. SOWERBY returned to Head Q.of Unit. Capt: J. MORHAN.	H.F.M.Fawcett, Lieut: Colonel.
			110th FIELD AMBULANCE.	
	13.5.1918		Strained hard all day.	H.F.M.Fawcett, Lieut: Colonel.
	14.5.1918		Dispatched 5 N.C.Os and 80 men to work under C.R.E., informatory training down Unit.	H.F.M.Fawcett, Lieut: Colonel.
	15.5.1918		Dispatched 15 men to join 110th F.Amb. yesterday; Capt: J.L. JOHNSTON joined the Unit.	H.F.M.Fawcett, Lieut: Colonel.
	16.5.1918		Weather fine; warm; wind light; wind duty. Flies beginning to appear. Continued cleaning of camp and extra lines to prevent development of mosquitos. Made to Divisional H.Q.s and saw the A.D.M.S.	H.F.M.Fawcett, Lieut: Colonel.
	17.5.1918		Warm weather; wind light N.	H.F.M.Fawcett, Lieut: Colonel.
	18.5.1918		Warm weather; wind light N.	H.F.M.Fawcett, Lieut: Colonel.
	19.5.1918		Warm weather; wind light N. A few shells fell in the neighbourhood at 5.30. p.m. German aeroplane over at night but no bombs dropped in the vicinity.	H.F.M.Fawcett, Lieut: Colonel.
	20.5.1918		Weather hot; no wind.	H.F.M.Fawcett, Lieut: Colonel.
	21.5.1918			

Army Form C. 2118.

WAR DIARY
INTELLIGENCE SUMMARY.
(Erase heading not required.) 108th FIELD AMBULANCE.

Place	Date	Hour	Summary of Events and Information	Remarks and references to Appendices
PROVEN 22.5.1918	23.5.1918.		RAILWAY Shelled from 11.p.m. till 1.a.m. one of our huts pierced by a fragment of shell. no casualties in camp. Weather hot and sultry. Books and French wind fresh: W.N.W.	R.F.M.Fawcett. Lieut: Colonel
	24.5.1918.		No casualties.	R.F.M.Fawcett. Lieut: Colonel
	26.6.1918.		Visit by A.D.M.S.	R.F.M.Fawcett. Lieut: Colonel
	26.5.1918.		Visit by D.D.M.S.	R.F.M.Fawcett. Lieut: Colonel. 27.5.1918. Capt J. CLARK attd 153 FA R.F.M.Fawcett Lieut: Colonel
	29.5.1918.		Weather fine, wind fresh N.W. Some Shelling of Railway Station.	
	28.5.1918.		PROVEN. Last night. and Today at 2.30.p.m.	R.F.M.Fawcett Lieut: Colonel
			Occasional shells in village and neighbourhood during the day. Visit by A.D.M.S.	R.F.M.Fawcett Lieut: Colonel.
	29.5.1918.		Weather fine. Part of out "RED CROSS" on roof of hut of O.C.S. now forming part of Reinforcement camp.	R.F.M.Fawcett. Lieut: Colonel
	30.5.1918.		8 - 9.am about 20 shells fell between our camp and village. Weather fine. Very clear. Two German aeroplanes over at 2.25.p.m.	R.F.M.Fawcett Lieut: Colonel
	31.5.1918.		6.30 - 7.15.am. about 15 Shells Littered camp.	
			7.5750. with which to pay. Two others, German aeroplanes, overhead at night.	R.F.M.Fawcett Lieut: Colonel

R.F.M.Fawcett
Lieut: Colonel
O.C, 108th Fd Ambulance

31/5/1918.

CONFIDENTIAL.

WAR DIARY

OF

108th FIELD AMBULANCE

From 1st JUNE 1918.   to 30th JUNE 1918.

VOLUME XXXIII

Army Form C. 2118.

WAR DIARY
INTELLIGENCE SUMMARY.
(Erase heading not required.) **108th FIELD AMBULANCE.**

Instructions regarding War Diaries and Intelligence Summaries are contained in F. S. Regs., Part II. and the Staff Manual respectively. Title pages will be prepared in manuscript.

Place	Date	Hour	Summary of Events and Information	Remarks and references to Appendices
PROVEN	1/6/1918	—	Role of HOUTKERQUE used down. Hqtrs, men found outside 2'Bn'dine. R.F.Hitsworth, Lieut-Colonel.	
	2/6/1918		Had ceremony of men. R.F.Hitsworth, Lieut-Colonel.	
	3/6/1918		No remarks. R.F.Hitsworth, Lieut-Colonel.	
	4/6/1918		No remarks. R.F.Hitsworth, Lieut-Colonel.	
	5/6/1918		No remarks. R.F.Hitsworth, Lieut-Colonel.	
	6/6/1918		No remarks. R.F.Hitsworth, Lieut-Colonel.	
	7/6/1918		Fire from store Hut to inhabited by officers destroyed by fire 4.28 am. Camel in previous an Officers tent well owned by these Kit and equipment. The men worked splendidly used previous Kit The fire from spreading. R.F.Hitsworth, Lieut-Colonel.	
	8/6/1918		No remarks. R.F.Hitsworth, Lieut-Colonel.	
	9/6/1918		No remarks. R.F.Hitsworth, Lieut-Colonel.	
	10/6/1918		No remarks. R.F.Hitsworth, Lieut-Colonel.	
	11/6/1918		No remarks. R.F.Hitsworth, Lieut-Colonel.	
	12/6/1918		No remarks. R.F.Hitsworth, Lieut-Colonel.	

WAR DIARY
or
INTELLIGENCE SUMMARY.
(Erase heading not required.)

Army Form C. 2118.

108th FIELD AMBULANCE.

Place	Date	Hour	Summary of Events and Information	Remarks and references to Appendices
PROVEN	13/6/1918	11 am	Unit visited by A.D.M.S., inspection of horse drawn transport, new saddlery decided upon. W. Fawcett Lieut. Colonel.	
	14/6/1918		horse baths. W. Fawcett Lieut. Colonel.	
	15/6/1918		Medical conference at A.D.M.S. Office at 5 p.m. Visited 10 x VTEI Sgt W. Boulsbery Walker with A.D.M.S. and arranged accommodation for slightly wounded in case of German attack.	
	16/6/1918		Court of Enquiry held at 11 am to investigate circumstances in Officers' quarters; the court found none of fire unknown and held that no one was to blame for the fire. W. Fawcett Lieut. Colonel, President. Oct 2 p.m. Handed report to the War Office.	
	17/6/1918		Received order to proceed to England and claim 72,820 with wheels to pay the men.	
	18/6/1918		Proceeded to HOUTKERQUE and then to HOOGKERQUE. Handed over command to Major E.Y. JOHNSTON, M.C. R.A.M.C.	

W. Fawcett
Lieut. Colonel R.A.M.C.

18
6
1918

WAR DIARY
INTELLIGENCE SUMMARY
(Erase heading not required.)

Army Form C. 2118.

Place	Date	Hour	Summary of Events and Information	Remarks and references to Appendices
PROVEN	19.6.18	9am	Lt. Col. R.F.M. FAWCETT, D.S.O. handed over command of the Ambulance on proceeding to England to report to the War Office.	
"		3pm	Visited ROUSBRUGGE, and inspected the new "Russian" detaining Church, a most excellent arrangement for latering out the sick.	S.L.
"	20.6.18	10am	Visited Divisional H.Q. quarters re Change of Horses, Visited D.A.D.M.S. in reference to new markings for the Divisional Motor Ambulance Cars.	S.L.
"	21.6.18	12.0n	D.D.M.S. I Corps, accompanied by the D.A.D.M.S. visited the Ambce and inspected the Baths in the Camp, owing to the scarcity of water the Supply may have to be cut off for some hours daily. Inspected another type of "Russian" disinfector at 99th Field Ambce. Programme of Divisional Horse Show received.	S.L.
"	22.6.18		Two Ambulance Waggons to be issued from each W.A. Ambulance. Routine.	S.L.
"	23.6.18	10am	Visited Divisional Headquarters requisitioned having order that two sections of this Field Ambulance would move to the CORNETTE AREA with the Brigade, being there for training purposes.	S.L.

WAR DIARY
or
INTELLIGENCE SUMMARY.

(Erase heading not required.)

Army Form C. 2118.

Place	Date	Hour	Summary of Events and Information	Remarks and references to Appendices
PROVEN	2/6/A	11am	ADMS held a conference of O.i.C. and Qr. Masters of the three Field Ambulances here, on the cutting out of Field Ambulance Equipment of articles found to be unnecessary and establishing estimate of the essentials chief of which are two Horrock's disinfectors & one extra Blankets and stretchers. Detailed orders for the move to CORMETTE received - would the personnel of this Field Ambulance to proceed by train from MENDING HEM Station at 6:45 am, the transport will proceed by road leaving at 5 am.	J.F.
"	25.6.18	5am	Major J.C. Roth in charge of Unit transport left PROVEN, proceeding by road to the training area N of St OMER route via WATOU, WINNEZEELE HARDIFORT, CLAIRMARAIS, St OMER, St MARTIN au LAERT CORMETTE CAMP.	
		6am	Personnel of Unit paraded under Major J.R. Johnston & marched to MENDING HEM Station where they entrained at 6:30 am arriving St OMER	
		10:15am	thence by March route to CORMETTE CAMP arriving 12:30 pm	
		4pm	Transport arrived in excellent condition at 4 pm having made a	J.F.

WAR DIARY
INTELLIGENCE SUMMARY

Army Form C. 2118.

Place	Date	Hour	Summary of Events and Information	Remarks and references to Appendices
CORNETTE CAMP	24/6/18	9:30am	Visited the Brigade Camp interviewed the Staff Captain and the three Regimental Medical Officers. Hospital ready to receive sick. The question of Water in this area is a serious one. The Camp supply gives out at 11 a.m. Will have to cart from the RB runway of 2nd DIVISIONS.	
H. Miles W of S.OMER			It will be necessary to send for one The Water Cart to supply the Hospital.	
		1pm	Orders received for Lieut. W. Egan MORC to rejoin the American Army	
	27.6.18		Second Water Cart received Camp plying 12th R.I.R. match draw 1 football	
	28.6.18		The Ambulance Football team plying 12th R.I.R. match draw 1 football. Routine.	
	29.6.18		Routine. Brigade Orders received they return to PROVEN tomorrow. To remain in Charge.	
	30.6.18	4am	Orders recd from ADMS that the Ambulance will return with the Brigade. Kept Ambulance hand over to the Camp W.O.M.s much of Kit.	
		at 8am	Train leaves S.t OMER at 10 a.m. I he arrived at PROVEN	
PROVEN		at 1pm	The transport which travelled by road arrived at 8pm. Capt. Tankerley proceeded on three days leave from 18 to 15th July	

J. Johnston Major R.A.M.C.
OC 108th Field Amb.

140/321

1087 T.A.

July 1918.

COMMITTEE FOR THE
MEDICAL HISTORY OF THE WAR
Date: 6 SEP

WAR DIARY

Army Form C. 2118.

108th Field Amb. Co.

Vol 34

19

Place	Date	Hour	Summary of Events and Information	Remarks and references to Appendices
PROVEN	1/9/18		Major S.B.B. Campbell proceeded on one month leave of absence from 2nd July to 2nd August 1918.	
		9 am	36th Divisional Horse Show held on the Aerodrome Grounds at PROVEN, this Ambulance took 1st prize in the Horse Ambulance Wagon class, all credit is due to the transport officer Capt. J.C. Roth.	
		5 pm	G.H. staff conference of O's C Field Ambulances at the O.D.M.S's office. The Division is moving to a new area, this Ambulance will move tomorrow from PROVEN to ROZEN Camp on the POPERINGHE - WINTON Road a mile then come under the administration of 108 F. Brigade.	JCR
	2/9/18	9.30 am	Unit landed in full marching order with transport complete. Balliere Camp handed over to a relieving party from 99th Field Ambulance. Certificate that Camp was left in a clean + sanitary condition was obtained before leaving.	
WILKINS CAMP Sht 27 F.25.a.2.9 (Ref AWF 6 Standard Area)		12 noon	Arrived at end of first days march and put up in huts in WILKINS Camp a fairly good accommodation, 23 sick were brought along in FA.	JCR

Army Form C. 2118.

WAR DIARY
or
INTELLIGENCE SUMMARY
(Erase heading not required.)

Instructions regarding War Diaries and Intelligence Summaries are contained in F. S. Regs., Part II and the Staff Manual respectively. Title pages will be prepared in manuscript.

Place	Date	Hour	Summary of Events and Information	Remarks and references to Appendices
WILKINS CAMP.	2/7/18	9.45 a.m.	The unit complete with transport left Wilkins Camp marching via St JAN-TER-BIEZEN, RATTEKOT, STEENVOORDE to EECKE, a particularly beastly march owing to numberless stoppages caused by the transport in front of us and roads and blinding dust.	
EECKE Sheet 27 O.1 to C16 c 7.0		1.30 p.m	We arrived at EECKE 1.30 p.m. Men are exasperated & troops B.Wth. marshals & scattered, pitched tents for the sick that accompanied the unit.	
Onto CAEETRE Road Q. 20.	4-7-18		Capt E.P. Rea rejoined this unit after three months temporary duty as Medical Officer with "B" Siege Park. Unit remains at EECKY admitting & treating sick from its own Brigade Area shelled during the night, some artillery horses killed in the field next to our transport.	&ct
"	5/7/18	7 a.m.	Drill & training for the men commenced this morning in addition improvements have been carried out at the billets, more tents are being erected to accommodate sick.	&ct
		2 p.m.	Pay-out parade for the men.	&ct

WAR DIARY
or
INTELLIGENCE SUMMARY

(Erase heading not required.)

Army Form C. 2118.

Place	Date	Hour	Summary of Events and Information	Remarks and references to Appendices
E.C.K.E.	6/7/18	6 a.m.	Brigade Operation Order received, the Brigade is moving tonight to take over the ST JANS-CAPPEL Sector of the line from the French. Movements of Ambulance not yet notified.	
		4 p.m.	R.A.M.C. Operation orders received. 103rd Field Ambulance to form a Rest Station at a site to be notified later, to be ready to move at short notice.	
	7/7/18	11 a.m.	A.D.M.S. visited the unit, no definite site for Rest Stn. yet selected.	
		4 p.m.	Orders received from Q.D.M.S. to proceed at once to this office to discuss alternative sites, A.D.M.S. a O.C. visited OCHTEZEELE (nr CASSEL) - HARDIFORT a.s.o the accommodation in the former was better, he was asked to proceed there early tomorrow.	
	8.7.18	6 a.m.	Camp was struck at ECCKE, all wagons packed.	
		8 a.m.	Unit proceeded in full marching order with transport complete a proceeded by march route to OCHTEZEELE via ST. SYLVESTRE-CAPPEL - CASSEL - WALMERS-CAPPEL arriving at OCHTEZEELE at 12.45 p.m. having made a most excellent journey, transport via CASSEL omitting road made on new line.	

WAR DIARY
or
INTELLIGENCE SUMMARY.

(Erase heading not required.)

Army Form C. 2118.

Place	Date	Hour	Summary of Events and Information	Remarks and references to Appendices
OCHTEZEELE	6.7.18			
	7/H 29 d		Billets were found for the men in various barns, and a small portion of a grass field has been reserved for the erection of canvas for the accommodation of patients. There is a station just beside the Hospital at some convenient spot to unload, to get cases sent down by train. This will make an ideal Rec Station.	
(about 1½ M. N.W. of CASSEL — 1 mile S. of ARNEKE)				
	8.7.18		The majority of the men are Engineering, tightening fence as to the guide ropes. Bell tents but a heavy handcrack drove most of them back to the lines.	J.B.L.
	9.7.18		600 available canvas was heeled so as to be ready to receive sick Lotinies. Also a the day spent in general fatigue duties & Sanitary improvements. Train of the men not actually employed will commence tomorrow.	J.B.L.
	10.7.18	10am	Training of personnel started, Physical exercise drill & lectures being carried out under the supervision of the Officers.	J.B.L.
		2pm	First convoy [?] of 47 patients received from 110th Irish Ambulance.	
		3	2nd M.A.C. Car.	
	11.7.18	2pm	Visited X Corps Adj Gen & arranged about the use of their Spoken Lorry to Champittie.	J.B.L.
		7pm	A.D.M.S. visited us & gave us his warning that we will probably take over site the CASSEL – WATTEN Road.	J.B.L.

WAR DIARY
or
INTELLIGENCE SUMMARY
(Erase heading not required.)

Army Form C. 2118.

Place	Date	Hour	Summary of Events and Information	Remarks and references to Appendices
OCHTEZEELE	12/7/18	9 am	O.C. accompanied by Capt E.S. Sowerby visited the proposed new site and after considerable difficulty interviewed the farmer arranged to remove the huts & erect camp in the field. This should make a most excellent Rest Station site.	
			The day as far as possible was being observed as a holiday.	↯
"	13/7/18	9 am	Advance party proceeded to occupy the new billets near LEDERZEELE.	
		10 am	Capt S.R. Rea R.A.M.C. detailed to take over Medical & Sanitary charge of 36th Division. Reinforcement to camp at MILLAM near WATTEN.	
		2 pm	Visited Area Commandant NOORDPEENE & arranged for the transport Field.	↯
	14/7/18		Wire received from D.D.M.S. notifying that Lt. Col. M. Shepherd had been posted to this unit in relief of Capt. a. Q. M. Pertichosy. Prepared plan for new Rest Station received from D.D.M.S. I Corps. Routine. D.A. & Q.M.G. of the Division visited & inspired the Hospital site.	↯
	15/7/18		& arranged to arrange for extra canvas. A.D.M.S. visited the Ambulance, held a Medical Board & a draft from	↯
	16/7/18	10.8 am	O.C. with A.D.M.S. visited the proposed new Rest Station site near LEDERZEELE. A.D.M.S. was a bit impressed by it	↯

Army Form C. 2118.

WAR DIARY
or
INTELLIGENCE SUMMARY.
(Erase heading not required.)

Place	Date	Hour	Summary of Events and Information	Remarks and references to Appendices
OCHTEZEELE	16/7/18	Cont.	We then visited D.D.M.S. X Corps at ZUYTPEENE, & asked for permission to hire the Hangars & Huts of a disused French Aerodrome on the ZUYTPEENE–LEDERZEELE Road about 2 miles E. of LEDERZEELE, but this has not for the moment been decided to enlarge the present site & camp on the Road. Station was pushing further instructions from the Corps.	
		2 pm	Capt. or Dr. Shephard R.A.M.C. reported his arrival off leave.	
		7 pm	Lt. Col. Th. Lh. Shepard R.A.M.C. reported his arrival from 34 General Hospital on relief of Capt. Tewkesbury who has been admitted to W.I.M.L.A. for duty there.	J.G.L
		11 pm	A.D.M.S. Operation order received in the event of an enemy attack. This unit is to dispatch one Bearer Sub. Division to the Plein Dreuvy Station to proceed thence in Cars of the X Corps M.A.C. Three lorries Motor Ambulance Cars allotted & proceed forthwith to the Main Dressing Station 710 Field Ambulance. Heavy bombs dropped on the Bopm front, aeroplane & rockets	J.G.L

WAR DIARY
or
INTELLIGENCE SUMMARY

Army Form C. 2118.

Place	Date	Hour	Summary of Events and Information	Remarks and references to Appendices
OCHTEZEELE	17/7/18	11 a.m.	Corps S.p.m. Ltry arrived to carry out the disinfection of clothing & blankets	
		2 p.m.	Capt. O.M.J. Tenterden R.A.M.C. reported his departure from the unit after almost 4 years service with it, he is a first loss to us but No 74 General Hospital to which he is posted will be the gainer.	
		2.30 p.m.	A.D.M.S. Medical Arrangements for new area received orders will be carried out at 109th Field Ambulance & on attempts days will be transferred from there to the Rest Station by the Motor Cars & Wagon of 108th & 109th Field Ambulances.	J.R.L.
"	18/7/18	10 a.m.	Arranged with O.C.A. Commandant NOORDPEENE Billets the use of Hot Baths all day tomorrow. Shall be able to bath the whole unit & the patients in Hospital also. Also arranged for 50 men corrugated iron & wood for the erection of Clothing Shelters at the Hospital & some huts for Bathing the Sick Cases.	A.R.
"	19/7/18	3.00 p.m.	By wish of the men commenced a continual running for day until 3.30 p.m. Confetti was issued from Corps that our Home Line were not in a running order. Also to urge them to the other ranks of the need running otherwise	A.R.
		1.20 am	Cable W of amongst for the delivery of Medical comforts.	J.R.L.

Army Form C. 2118.

WAR DIARY
or
INTELLIGENCE SUMMARY.
(Erase heading not required.)

Instructions regarding War Diaries and Intelligence Summaries are contained in F. S. Regs., Part II. and the Staff Manual respectively. Title pages will be prepared in manuscript.

Place	Date	Hour	Summary of Events and Information	Remarks and references to Appendices
OCHTEZEELE	29/7/18		Today Convoy having completed the disinfection of all the blankets of the unit was sent back to the HQrs M.T. Unit at Inxysch.	
		12.a.m	Proceeded in Ford Car to meet the A.D.M.S. at the main Dressing Station (110th Field Ambulance) & accompanied by Lt. Col. O'Grady he visited the A.D.Stn at ROSSIGNOL (close to MONT DES CATS) a number of deserted houses was found close to this Stn. and it was decided to salve these, with the permission of Div HQ, & respect him at our present site, so as to increase the accommodation for patients. Lt. Col. O'Grady very kindly offered to do this salving & remove the material to this Headquarters viz EECKE, & our Engineer will then cart it to OCHTEZEELE. 10 men & 1 N.C.O. to be sent tomorrow to assist in the salving, they will be returned see by 110th F.A.	
		6 p.m	Returned via Dunkerque railhead & asked for permission to remove these huts & also to obtain bricks from GODEWAERSVELDE, decision will be notified tomorrow morning.	
		7 p.m	Returned to OCHTEZEELE having had a most interesting & enjoyable afternoon.	

WAR DIARY
or
INTELLIGENCE SUMMARY.

(Erase heading not required.)

Army Form C. 2118.

Place	Date	Hour	Summary of Events and Information	Remarks and references to Appendices
OCHTEZEELE	21/7/18	11 am	ADMS inspected the Hospital and Transport Lines. General elderly men who were brought in front line duties.	
		5 pm	RADMS X Corps inspected our transport lines and was to inform them one new consignment horse-drawn from the Ambulance Stores.	JJ
	22/7/18	9 am	Received telephone message from ADMS X Corps that marquees were being sent to site for new Rest Station. Today is working for building huts to erect them. 30 men = 3 N.C.Os have been sent under Capt Smale.	
		5 pm	Message from ADMS of the Division to say that Troops from ADMS & Staff this will be most useful at our Guard Station.	JJ
	23/7/18	10 am	Visited the new Rest Station site via LEDERZEELE with RAOMS X Corps. The marquees, latrines etc. are all in process of erection.	JJ
	24/7/18	11 am	G.O.C. 36th Division visited and inspected the Rest Station	
		12 noon	The first loads of sakeel huts arrived. The work of reconstruction will be commenced at once.	
		9 pm	Rode over to LEDERZEELE to inspect the work at the new Rest Station. The 20 Marquees have been erected, huts in bottom of property.	JJ

WAR DIARY
or
INTELLIGENCE SUMMARY.
(Erase heading not required.)

Army Form C. 2118.

Place	Date	Hour	Summary of Events and Information	Remarks and references to Appendices
OCHTEZEELE	25/7/18		Corps Motor Lorry arrived to carry out the disinfection of clothing of the patients to Hartuts.	
		10 am	Capt. J.S. Clark R.A.M.C. turned out for temporary duty with 36th M.G. Batt in relief of Lieut Stewart M.O.R.C. who required a rest.	
		4 pm	A.D.M.S. 36th Div. arrived and inspected some cases in the Hospital.	
		6 pm	On Return home gave an opinion on cases to the patients to D.D.M.S. removing to entrain the men persons - most of the comments were very favourable.	ft
"	26/7/18	10 am	Received an urgent telephone message from the D.D.M.S. X Corps to meet him at the LEDERZEELE Sig which was inspected by Brig Gen Lipp.	A.P.C.
			A scheme for building was discussed, & the work to progress.	
"	27/7/18	10 am	Message received from D.D.M.S. X Corps that 30 Convalescents were being sent today to LEDERZEELE to do light work at the Corps Rest Station.	ft.
		3 pm	Lieut W.Q. Wood R.A.M.C. reported his arrival for duty.	
"	28/7/18		A.D.M.S. visited the unit and reviewed some men in Hospital who are unfit for trench duty	ft
			Two Officers suffering from Scabies admitted the Line B a recommend in a skilled Ambulance Hospital for lack of skills	ft

WAR DIARY
or
INTELLIGENCE SUMMARY.
(Erase heading not required.)

Army Form C. 2118.

Place	Date	Hour	Summary of Events and Information	Remarks and references to Appendices
OCHTEZEELE	29/7/18	12 noon	Attended a Conference of O's C. Field Ambulances at the A.D.M.S. Office. Final arrangements were made for reinforcing the forward positions in the event of any attack. This unit to send two Bearer Sub. Divisions complete and two additional Officers to the M.D.S.	
"	30/7/18		Major E.S. Sowerby M.C. proceeded on 8 days leave in France, on a visit to his Brothers. Arranged with Major Jay O.C. 20th Div. M.T. Company to carry out the reinoculation of his men.	
"	31/7/18	2 p.m.	Rode over to LEDERZEELE to inspect the attachment in Km on the Corps Rest Station owing to the frequent changing of plans, this is being considerably delayed.	
		4 p.m.	The Consultant Physician II Army visited the Camp of inspected the Camp Disinfecting Section - later these are the three divisions against which he recommends all possible precautions are taken off	

J. J. Johnston D. Col.
O.C. 108th Field Amb'ce.

140/3200.

COMMITTEE FOR THE
MEDICAL HISTORY OF THE WAR
Date 5 OCT 1918

108 y. T. O.

August 18

WAR DIARY or INTELLIGENCE SUMMARY

Army Form C. 2118.

108 3rd Army noted Vol 35

Place	Date	Hour	Summary of Events and Information	Remarks and references to Appendices
OCHTEZEELE 27/H.29.d. (H.M.S. M/C6521)	1/8/18		Colonel A. Fullerton C.M.G. Consulting Surgeon to the Army visited and inspected the Rest Station. He gave us quite an interesting discourse on Surgery at the Base & in forward Medical Units	Sgd
OCHTEZEELE 1.0.2.5.0/47.28.	2.8.18	2pm	Motored to the site for X Corps Rest Station with Dr D.M.S. Corps. to meet the D.M.S. and the Consulting Physician to the Army (Colonel Soltan) The position of huts was discussed, but work is being delayed owing to lack of material.	
		3 pm	The 136th Divisional Band arrived to play selections to the patients but owing to the fact that it is simply pouring rain & to have no piano available for an indoor performance, he have with regret to allow them to return to Divl. Headquarters.	
		6 pm	The Australian (109th Fld Ambce Pierrot troupe) gave a concert to the patients. This too has been an open air show but the inclemency of the weather was that impossible to thanks to the Mann the patients will not be disappointed by having given no performance to use the school room. The concert was a great success.	Sgd

Army Form C. 2118.

WAR DIARY
or
INTELLIGENCE SUMMARY.
(Erase heading not required.)

Instructions regarding War Diaries and Intelligence Summaries are contained in F. S. Regs., Part II and the Staff Manual respectively. Title pages will be prepared in manuscript.

Place	Date	Hour	Summary of Events and Information	Remarks and references to Appendices
OCHTEZEELE	3/8/18	10 a.m.	The D.D.M.S. arrived & inspected the Hospital, as the place has covered with mud & not looking its best. I'm afraid he was not at all pleased.	
			The Cook is being posted on Tomorrow & pronted decent weather, we should soon have a creditable show.	
		5 p.m.	Major M.R. Campbell reported his arrival from one months leave of absence.	
	4/8/18	5.30 p.m.	Visited LEDERZEELE about the men on Attachment there.	
		11 a.m.	Attended Thanksgiving service was held in the Local Church to celebrate the recent victories & to mark the beginning of the 5th (and final) year of the War. An invitation was extended to the Officers & men of this unit to attend and all the Officers & almost 100 men paraded. One of our men preached at the Organ & the Church was tastefully decorated with the British, French & American flags.	
		2 p.	Visited LEDERZEELE with Major Campbell & pointed out the plan of the Camp & the work to be done.	
		3.30 p.	Rev Tyrwhitt D.A.C.G. & Capt. held the Service at The Div. Rest Stn.	

WAR DIARY
INTELLIGENCE SUMMARY

Place	Date	Hour	Summary of Events and Information	Remarks and references to Appendices
OCHTEZEELE	5/8/18		Commenced work on the perforated dining-room and arranged with the farmer to extend our Hospital on the Wheat field opposite as soon as the crop has been reaped. He is starting on this at once.	
		3 pm	The Merry Mauve Melody Makers the Concert Party of the 36th Division arrived to give the patients a treat; it was impossible to get the School room, so the show will be held in the School yard.	
		6 pm	The Concert was a howling success & we hope to have them soon again.	SP
	6/8/18	10 am	Major S.R. Campbell attended a Conference at EBBINGHEM the New Dyshase Centre for the Army; members of Cases of Dysentery to us agains but so far all Rectal Swabs sent from patients in this Rest Station have been negative.	
		3 pm	Rode over to BOLLEZEELE to see an American Dentist attached to 133 Field Amb. at present administering II Corps Rest Station no luck of again tomorrow unless & leave Warrant arrives in the meantime.	
		6 pm	Received authority from the A.D.M.S. to draw out 12 Spray Le BLANC But. for trial in the Rest Stn, this will be a great boon.	SP

Army Form C. 2118.

WAR DIARY
or
INTELLIGENCE SUMMARY.
(Erase heading not required.)

Instructions regarding War Diaries and Intelligence Summaries are contained in F. S. Regs., Part II. and the Staff Manual respectively. Title pages will be prepared in manuscript.

Place	Date	Hour	Summary of Events and Information	Remarks and references to Appendices
OCHTEZEELE	7/8/18	10 a.m.	Visited LEDERZEELE and inspected the work on the Corps Rest Stn. The Pierrot troupe of this Unit gave a free Concert in the Y.M.C.A. CASSEL. The hall was packed & the performance much appreciated.	RJ
		6 p.m.		
"	8/8/18	11 a.m.	D.D.M.S. X Corps visited & inspected the Rest Station, and seemed satisfied with the work that was being carried on.	
		3 p.m.	The Band of 36th Division arrived & gave selections until 5 p.m.	
		4 p.m.	A.D.M.S. 36th Div. arrived & inspected the work, & made a number of "cranks" suggestions for the Chambres. He was just before him a total def.	
			Word was just heard a will be acted on without delay.	SJ
"	9/8/18	2 p.m.	Message received from D.D.M.S. X Corps to proceed in a Car & meet him up at Corps H.Q. to inspect the Corps Rest Station at LEDERZEELE. It is desired to remove the entire row of tents, the management of the place was discussed & he I suggested that it could be run by a Field Ambulance of the Division in reserve; the suggestion seemed to find favor with the D.A.M.S. & the splitting up of my unit will be avoided.	
		2 to 4 p.m.	Visited 2 patients using the NOORDPEENE bath, possibly in the vicinity of 9th M.A.	SJ

Army Form C. 2118.

WAR DIARY
or
INTELLIGENCE SUMMARY.
(Erase heading not required.)

Instructions regarding War Diaries and Intelligence Summaries are contained in F. S. Regs., Part II. and the Staff Manual respectively. Title pages will be prepared in manuscript.

Place	Date	Hour	Summary of Events and Information	Remarks and references to Appendices
OCHTEZEELE	10/8/18		Routine. the Construction work in the Camp is progressing satisfactorily.	
		6 p.m.	Our Priest tonight gave a Concert at II Corps Rest Station BOLLEZEELE (133rd Field Ambulance) They have been asked by us again as we improving	JJ
"	11/8/18	3.30 p.m.	The D.A.C.G. X Corps (Rev Tipnhitt M.V.O) held the Service at the Divisional Rest Station.	
			Capt J.C. Ross R.A.M.C. went to LEDERZEELE & inspected the work there	JJ
"	12/8/18	10 a.m.	To-day there has been a succession of Inspections & visitors	
			Lt Col Green = Major Thomm (A.A. & Q.M.G. = D.A&Q.M.S 36th Division) arrived & had a look round, they seemed pleased with the reconstruction work that has been carried out.	
		12 a.m.	A.D.M.S. 36th Division arrived. Some cases of Dysentery have occurred & he is anxious there all Drainsa Cess Pits etc carefully as far as possible & hoped us to inspect a large increase in the numbers.	
		3 p.m.	The 36th Divisional Band played selection to the patients until 5 p.m.	
		5 p.m.	Lt Col HEMPHILL D.S.O. Cmdy 107 Field Ambce arrived. He is taking over the Corps Rest Stn at LEDERZEELE, He was shown the Plans etc of the place & arrangement for taking over.	JJ

Army Form C. 2118.

WAR DIARY
or
~~INTELLIGENCE SUMMARY~~
(Erase heading not required.)

Instructions regarding War Diaries and Intelligence Summaries are contained in F. S. Regs., Part II. and the Staff Manual respectively. Title pages will be prepared in manuscript.

Place	Date	Hour	Summary of Events and Information	Remarks and references to Appendices
OCHTEZEELE	13/8/18	11 a.m.	Visited Corps Rest Station LEDERZEELE with the O.C. 107 Field Ambulance who is taking it over tomorrow. The plan of the place was explained & the proposals for work got to be carried out. The personnel will be withdrawn tomorrow when the handing over is completed.	JSJ.
"	14/8/18		The inter-Ambulance Competition to select the two competitors for the I Corps show in the combined Ambulance - Water Cart Claws was held at Div HQ. The players were most punctilious & a thorough kit-inspection than of an examination which became part of a kit-inspection. First place was easily won by 149 Field Ambulance, with 110 FA a fairly good second.	
		6 p.m.	The "OPTIMISTS" the Concert party of 30th Division gave a show at the Div Reception Camp which is quite close to our Hospital. An invitation was extended to this unit of to the patients & the show was much appreciated. Going on leave tomorrow. Handed over command of the unit to Major S.B. 13 Campbell R.A.M.C.	JSJ

J.E. Johnston Lt. Col.
O.C. 108 Field Ambulance

Army Form C. 2118.

WAR DIARY
or
INTELLIGENCE SUMMARY.
(Erase heading not required.)

Instructions regarding War Diaries and Intelligence Summaries are contained in F. S. Regs., Part II. and the Staff Manual respectively. Title pages will be prepared in manuscript.

Place	Date	Hour	Summary of Events and Information	Remarks and references to Appendices
OCHTEZEELE	15/9/18		Lieut Colonel J.G Johnston MC RAMC proceeded on leave. His evening dress. On number of marching cases had increased two into average one post up for them. Breakfast cases average 2-3 daily.	AMC
	16/9/18		Visit from ADMS 36th Div. & DADMS 36th Div. Hospital was inspected and several items were brought to our Boss known of cases have no messing equipment.	MR
	17.9.18.		All the skin cases were transferred to a special camp on field on other side of noon main hospital separate ablution bench & latrines have been provided. Major Smith has arranged a circuit to an hospital. The NYD N's but only to the rain it had to be postponed. Dress was also them. The Red Cross depot at WATTEN.	AMC

WAR DIARY
or
INTELLIGENCE SUMMARY.
(Erase heading not required.)

Army Form C. 2118.

Place	Date	Hour	Summary of Events and Information	Remarks and references to Appendices
OCTIEZZILE			Visit from A.D.M.S. at 2-4.5 p.m. He inspected the Camps & Hos.	
	18.8.18		attended the C.of E. Church service at 3.30 pm. Three men taken	
			by the D.A.C.G. & hops. (Rev Tyrrell W.V.O.). Drainage area has	
			increasing with supply. Capt Pilsworth of Drainage Contr.	MDC
	A.8.18		Difficult found places at from 3-5 pm and no Recept	
			appreciation by the patient. I sent to Divisional Headquarters	
			to see A.d.L.M R.E. about July walking on the Camps. He sent	
			me his consent	MDC
	20.8.18		got 200 double disinfector Bg. Division taken Eng. A Runner has	
			his Lectr. is reported at a rest Station and B Runner has	
			no is trips tout up. This the Latrine to chiefs have	
			been completed. All lacrets is new being Burnt.	MDC

WAR DIARY
or
INTELLIGENCE SUMMARY.

Army Form C. 2118.

Place	Date	Hour	Summary of Events and Information	Remarks and references to Appendices
OCHTSZEELE				
	21	11	The G.O.C. Major General Coffin VC DSO visited the Camp at 11 a.m. and inspected it. He seemed to be pleased. Drove round & cement Lines & Cpls R.E. during visit was to all to PT the new COR horse Jumped	
	22	18	The Ambulance Circuit Sports. The R.9'ths Jam a Circuit Rifle at 6 p.m. to the battn. The latter seemed to enjoy it very much has not known to have taken out was	MSR
	23	18	To day 20 stables were shown down to Divisional Burily Company. These with the numbers already made by our Goo. enabled pro to start issuing the during hay at 6 p.m. to there harmay Divisional Circuit Paul Jan a very excellent Circuit to the bakery. Capt BRENNAN GSo in charge of Same	MR

WAR DIARY or INTELLIGENCE SUMMARY

Army Form C. 2118.

Place	Date	Hour	Summary of Events and Information	Remarks and references to Appendices
12 CCS BEF	24.8.18		Major Cooke M.C. DADMS & Major Howes DADMS visited the Camp in the afternoon and inspected the work. Our advance party went over to 2nd Corps Rest Station and gave & erected tents & a patients mess.	MSC
	25.8.18		Padre Hall Presbyterian Chaplain held a service at 2.30pm & Padre Tippett on the C.of.E at 3.30 "	RSR
	26.8.18		An incident occurred when an ambulance went over to Warnins Carpel to pick up Pte M.T. Gann but was lost by a few minutes.	JMR
	27.8.18		A.D.M.S arrived about 11 am. He inspected the Camp and then saw a number of cases recommended for medical board. At 2.30 pm the Divisional Band arrived & played several selections to the patients	JMR

Army Form C. 2118.

WAR DIARY
or
INTELLIGENCE SUMMARY.
(Erase heading not required.)

Instructions regarding War Diaries and Intelligence Summaries are contained in F. S. Regs., Part II. and the Staff Manual respectively. Title pages will be prepared in manuscript.

Place	Date	Hour	Summary of Events and Information	Remarks and references to Appendices
OCHTEZEELE			The Spray Bath has been put up a few days before but is to be taken down as Division wants it. This entailed taking down part of the bath tent.	
	27.8.18		Lieut Stephend went to Watten to draw Red X Stores chiefly plates, spoons etc	
	28.8.18		A wet day.	ntk
	29.8.18			
	30.8.18		11 am Lieut Col O'Reilly OC 107th arrived with unit marching thro' R. Resting Staff in their way to X Corps Rest Staff.	
		3.30 pm	A.D.M.S. arrived and inspected the Camp. He seemed to be satisfied with the purpose	
		10 am	Conference at A.D.M.S. Office of O.C. F.A's. O.T was arranged that 109th St moves S to SCRE and also that from time, hut. 110 to moved relieving by which he could go to site occupied by 109T at D.26.c.5.3.	QBK

Army Form C. 2118.

WAR DIARY
or
INTELLIGENCE SUMMARY.
(Erase heading not required.)

Place	Date	Hour	Summary of Events and Information	Remarks and references to Appendices
OCATEZSKE	31.8.18	7.30 a.m	Major Joseph M.C. T/o O.R. proceeded as advance party	
		1 p.m	to take over from 109th F.A.	
		2 p.m	110th F.A. arrived & took over Dutroul RxS Station with IT 370 Patrol	
		3 p.m	Unit marched S/b and proceeding via CASSEL & St MARIE CAPELLE we arrived at our destination at 6.7½ p.m. One & Four were billeted to in the farm and out houses Convent.	
		10 p.m	Lient Colonel Johnston M.C. arrived and resumed Command of Unit.	Sd J. Louifort M.C. Major Comdg

149/332y

Sept 1915

10 x 6 - 0

WAR DIARY
or
INTELLIGENCE SUMMARY.
(Erase heading not required.)

Army Form C. 2118.

108 Fld Amb

Place	Date	Hour	Summary of Events and Information	Remarks and references to Appendices
Near ST MARIE CAPPEL	1/9/18		Returned from leave last night took over command from Major Magill DSO	
ShurF WOOD P26.a.5.4		11 am	Lt Col Magill D.S.O. who is a/A.D.M.S. called to see us. the question of keeping in touch with our Corps moving forward was discussed. It was decided that we remain here for the present & take over the line when it settles somewhat.	
Divn Sch (CASSEL)		3 pm	Proceeded to ZWYPEENE (Corps H.Q.) to draw imprest money for pay	JRJ
		4 pm	Reported to Walter Corps to Div. H.Q. for temporary duty	JRJ
	2/9/18	10 am	Major E.S. Somerby M.C. detailed to proceed for temporary duty to Hq Field Amb Base	
			Capt J.C. Roff proceeded on 14 days leave of continent leave to the United Kingdom	
		4 pm	Lt Col. Magill D.S.O. a/A.D.M.S. paid us a visit & it is arranged that we take command by the D.G. of the 4th Maw Dressing Station to the become in connection with a Brimson Rest Station	JRJ
GODWAERSVELDE	3/9/18	9 am	Read advance party left to transfer & marched off at 9.45 am	JRJ
E. E. C.K.L Sanqk 10.F. J28 c.1.3			Main Body Cleaning at 11.30 am by FMP car are awaiting for about 200 patients	

Army Form C. 2118.

WAR DIARY
~~INTELLIGENCE SUMMARY~~
(Erase heading not required.)

Instructions regarding War Diaries and Intelligence Summaries are contained in F. S. Regs., Part II. and the Staff Manual respectively. Title pages will be prepared in manuscript.

Place	Date	Hour	Summary of Events and Information	Remarks and references to Appendices
EECKE	4/9/18		Receiving patients in our new Rest Station our 70 admitted today only dientots cases now being transferred to the old station at OCHTEZEELE. Orders received from A.D.M.S. to hold the 9ao Centre in readiness as a large number of such cases might be expected. Work of conversion of the Camp from a Main Dressing Station to a Divisional Rest Station being vigorously pushed forward.	JS
"	5/9/18		About 20 slightly gassed cases (Mustard) have been admitted now of them show serious symptoms a only a few are that bad. Major Somerby M.C. sent to help the 10/9 D/Mont at their M.D.S. Numbers rapidly increasing our 160 remaining today; about half of them gassed today's cases have been much more serious and a number have been badly blistered.	JS
"	6/9/18		Lieut Ward R.A.M.C. came down from a Cas. J.S. Clark R.A.M.C. had to go up to take his place as temporary M.O./c 15th Batt Royal Irish Rifles. The accommodation is being increased by the addition of the green from the Division or the Corp.	JS

(89475) Wt W25587/p60 600,000 12/17 D. D. & L. Sch. 53a. Forms/C2118/15.

Army Form C. 2118.

WAR DIARY
or ~~INTELLIGENCE SUMMARY~~
(Erase heading not required.)

Instructions regarding War Diaries and Intelligence Summaries are contained in F. S. Regs., Part II and the Staff Manual respectively. Title pages will be prepared in manuscript.

Place	Date	Hour	Summary of Events and Information	Remarks and references to Appendices
EECKE	4/9/18		Owing to the numerous Cases coming in, 3 Marquees received from Corps have been erected — two from 110th Field Ambulance. This evening we have over 300 Cases remaining including 150 Cases of Gas (Mustard.) B. Col Nofell A/A.D.M.S. called. He is to reconnoitre the Asylum at BAILLEUL tomorrow as it is likely this Unit will move up there from a Main Dressing Station as the line is now stabilising.	JJ
	8/9/18		We treat of 'Gassed' Cases is mainly dry, only a few being admitted today & these are mostly cases with late manifestations. Weather today very Windy. A Canvas Camp not at all comfortable. One of our Brigades coming back to rest moved up past us for the moment. Church Service held at 2.30 pm.	JJ
	9/9/18		One N.C.O. & 4 men detailed as holding party for the Officers in Asylum BAILLEUL. These N.C.O.C & 20 men detailed to take over the A.D.R. of the evacuation from this line. Brig Gen Brook CMG DSO A/G.O.C 36th Division inspected the Rest Station & Gas Centre & expressed approval of the	JJ

WAR DIARY
or
INTELLIGENCE SUMMARY

Army Form C. 2118.

Place	Date	Hour	Summary of Events and Information	Remarks and references to Appendices
BAILLEUL	10/9/18		Visited & inspected the cellars in BAILLEUL ASYLUM. There are quite capacious & should make a good Dressing Station when cleaned out. Called with O.C. 109 Field Ambulance and arranged to take over ROCHE FARM & the evacuation of the line from him at 12 noon tomorrow. He will take over from us the working of the Divisional Rest Station.	SF
ROCHE FARM	11/9/18		Moved from FLÊTRE after handing over the Div Rest Station to 129th Field Ambulance, & took over the evacuation from the line from 109 Fd Amb. Major Sowerby with 53 other ranks relieving the 109 D personnel in the ADS and Dressing Station (NEUVE EGLISE)	
BERTHEN			Advance Base H.Q. established at Roche Farm (BERTHEN). Lieut W.O. Word RAMC, having just arrived & reported for duty with a B.W. draft, was detailed to a C.C.S.	
			Relief was completed during the night.	SF

WAR DIARY
or
INTELLIGENCE SUMMARY.
(Erase heading not required.)

Army Form C. 2118.

Place	Date	Hour	Summary of Events and Information	Remarks and references to Appendices
Rocl.Farm	27/9/18		Visited the Advanced Dressing Station & made a tour of the forward posts with Major Sowerby R.A.M.C. there is a fairly good carry from the Regimental Aid Post of the B. attalion in the line. We are now using Bearer relay posts instead of carrying posts as at first. Very good yesterday. Class and Walsh Stretcher are one for drive up to the Regt. Aid Post.	
			Other Battalions in Support - Reserve.	
			With Adv Dressing Station in [?] but the Engineer are [?] some [?]	SS
			Commences to put in cabins shelters that will [?] sound [?]	
			Inspected the cellar in BAILLEUL ASYLUM with Lt Col Greene	
	28/9/18		A.A. & Q.M.G. - Major Gorti Brits of the Division into the Division. They have decided to put a Battalion of Infantry into this Divn area - only one the thing in the forward portion of the Artillery that will give us trouble with a column to get up to the Brig Hdqrs, & CO's. Dugouts. The cellar would be a good Brigade Hdqrs. The work of clearing the cellar & school of the wards is being pushed forward.	JP

WAR DIARY
or
INTELLIGENCE SUMMARY.

(Erase heading not required.)

Army Form C. 2118.

Instructions regarding War Diaries and Intelligence Summaries are contained in F. S. Regs., Part II. and the Staff Manual respectively. Title pages will be prepared in manuscript.

Place	Date	Hour	Summary of Events and Information	Remarks and references to Appendices
ROCH FARM	14/4/16		Capt E Sharp R.A.M.C. a reinforcement received from the Base and is taken on the strength.	
			Visited the Advanced Dressing Station now on the Shelling road by 9/k	
BAILLEUL ASYLUM	15/4/16		Had grater warm Rest from to Asylum Ballium. Took over the Mobile billets, the present Dressing Station on the	
28/6/16 S.III/24-8			Road opposite Asylum Main entrance, will be maintained for the present.	
			Enemy requested a direct hit with a Gas Shell on the Adv. Dressing Station on it at the Ambulance Dressing was killed, a about 12 other ranks Gassed. Major Sanders & Major Purnell was also Gassed and had to be retired.	
			Major Bough Campbell, Capt Denne detailed for duty at the A.D.S. Dressing Station	
			The present position at A.D.S. at NEUVE EGLISE is being continually shelled, also really not enough as a Dressing Station, New Campbell, a Building rooms from war Souland City of	

WAR DIARY
or
INTELLIGENCE SUMMARY.
(Erase heading not required.)

Army Form C. 2118.

Place	Date	Hour	Summary of Events and Information	Remarks and references to Appendices
ASYLUM BAILLEUL	16/9/18	9 am	Accompanied by Major CROSSIE D.A.D.M.S. I visited the new A.D.S. selected by Major Campbell this is located in a farm standing about 1 mile East of NEUVE EGLISE on the WULVERGHEM ROAD. The site was approved & arrangements were made with the Royal Engineers to start fortwith on the work of making it more to less shell proof	
			Major Shuety M.C. has evacuated (Grippe) to No 17 C.C.S. Capt W.M. Brenny M.C. & Capt E.A. Lundry M.C. reported this arrival for duty & was taken on the strength.	
	17/9/18		A working party of 30 O.R. one drummer 36 O.R. Divers then went round the M.D.S. & pointed out improvements to be carried out to the cellar	
		10am	Visited A.D.M.S.	
		2pm	A.D.M.S. visited the A.D.S. & addressed both to be Quartermaster of the hand carriage system & arranged that Can be sent right up to the R.A.Ps at night.	
			The question of Refry transfers has been discussed and it's so decided to send all surplus down to the D.R.S. 104th Fd Amb'ce	

WAR DIARY
or
INTELLIGENCE SUMMARY.
(Erase heading not required.)

Army Form C. 2118.

Place	Date	Hour	Summary of Events and Information	Remarks and references to Appendices
ASYLUM BAILLEUL	17/4/18	Noon	Summoned to D.A.M.S. Office & received orders for the relief of the Division now here by the 34th Division. Orders to this effect to be issued out by first order to hand. To be A.D.S. going different to receive relief.	
		11.0 am	The main portion of the Unit will move tonight to Rouge Jean via BETHUNE 2nd Echelon with B.H.Q. with all units of 35th Division at Present from the Rear.	
		5pm	Unit transport (less 1 Horse Ambr Wagon, 1 Watr Cart, 1 Maltese Cart) with all surplus personnel preceded by Mar'l route to ROCHEBERRY Head Quarters remained at BAILLEUL in G relief was completed. Major Campbell R.A.M.C. Capt Davis R.A.M.C. + 50 OR arrived from the A.D.S. + forward posts having been relieved by the G.O. Daily Duty. Relief of all posts was complete by 12 midnight	J.S.
	21/4/18	1 am	Field Ambce H.Q. & all remaining personnel + transport moved to ROCHE FARM leaving a small Enquiry Attachment at BAILLEUL	J.S.
		9 am	Unit will be intelligence tomorrow morning	

WAR DIARY
or
INTELLIGENCE SUMMARY.
(Erase heading not required.)

Army Form C. 2118.

Place	Date	Hour	Summary of Events and Information	Remarks and references to Appendices
ROCHE FARM 1½ S. of BERTHEN	30/9/18	5 pm	Unit complete with transport paraded at ROCHE FARM & marched via BERTHEN - BOESCHEPE - GODWAERSVELDE - FECKE to a farm on the ECCKE - ST. SYLVESTRE - CAPPEL Road, 1 mile E of the latter place. The starting point in GODWAERSVELDE was reached at 7.15 pm the whole time taken by the unit in reaching point. The hope was completed & the G.O.C. 101st Bde Brigade that coffee was served to the men & Unit reached at 9 pm. Arrangements were made for them to bed in any inexpressible barn.	
Piguile C.b.5 farm on the ECCKE CAPPEL RD 1 mile E of FECKE	21/9/18	9 am	Medical Arrangements received from the A.D.M.S. Field Ambulance to take over GWATIA FARM on 22nd inst. Advanced Party to be sent today.	
		Noon	Brigade move orders received. Unit to march to WATOU tonight.	
		7 pm	Unit paraded & marched to HOSPICE WATOU route via STEENVOORDE - DROGLANDT. starting point was passed at 8.25 pm & unit arrived at 10.30 pm. The men are billeted in Nissen Huts & are very comfortable. Hot tea was served out to them on their arrival.	

WAR DIARY
or
INTELLIGENCE SUMMARY.
(Erase heading not required.)

Army Form C. 2118.

Instructions regarding War Diaries and Intelligence Summaries are contained in F. S. Regs., Part II. and the Staff Manual respectively. Title pages will be prepared in manuscript.

Place	Date	Hour	Summary of Events and Information	Remarks and references to Appendices
WATOU HOSPICE	27/9/18	10 a.m.	Under orders received from A.D.M.S. 36th Division, the unit paraded complete with transport & proceeded by march route to GWALIA FARM via the POPERINGHE — ELVERDINGHE Road, via COUTHOVE. International Corps arriving here at 1 p.m. This area is well known and now used.	
37/K.L.R.C.				
5½ m. W. of POPERINGHE				
GWALIA FARM	28/9/18	11 a.m.	Attended a Conference of O.C. Field Ambulances + 15 men Officers at the Office of A.D.M.S. 36th Division we received instructions to bear on Clearing Station at 13 am Parties in readiness to move off at two hours Notice.	
"A.D.M.S. 36th				
3 miles NE of POPERINGHE on the ELVERDINGHE			Cdr W.M. Cheong M.C. – Capt J.C. Rath are placed in Charge of the Forward Bearer Major S.L.S.Y. Campbell will co-operate with them from the Advanced Dressing Station while Capt F.A. Lundy will be at the Main Dressing Station. Visited A.D.M.S. 59th Division & found that advisers at all his A.A. Posts & also his Ambulances in the event of an advance.	
		4 p.m.	A.D.M.S. visited Hd Qu at GWALIA FARM.	

WAR DIARY or INTELLIGENCE SUMMARY.

Army Form C. 2118.

Place	Date	Hour	Summary of Events and Information	Remarks and references to Appendices
GWALIA FARM	24/9/18		The men are resting except for the necessary cleaning of weapons and equipment. Orders issued to the Brown Officers of the Companies & all non duties to have various spots.	
			2 Rhodesian Cadets before NCOs & men on Parade with the Brigadier. Major Campbell visited Brigade this afternoon & made the necessary arrangements to	ff
	24/9/15		Weather showery. Cleaning up of Cars &c continued. Runner post Brigade Divisions detailed & arranged.	ff ff
"	24/9/18		Routine.	
		2.P.M.	II Corps visited us & gave us a sketch of the Medical arrangements.	
		10 P.m.	110th Field Ambulance arrived & are accommodated with our men	ff
	25/9/18		Letter by 2nd Army Commander referring to the coming rain.	
		10 am	B.P.m. C 38th Division arrived & held a Conference given by the details of Divisional movements.	
		11 am	With A.P.M.C. & visited the Dressing Station in the Prison YPRES.	ff

WAR DIARY
or
INTELLIGENCE SUMMARY

Army Form C. 2118.

Place	Date	Hour	Summary of Events and Information	Remarks and references to Appendices
GWALIA FARM	29/9/16		C of E and RCMs arrived with ADMS. 39th Division told we take over here as soon as our Division goes into action.	
		6pm	The Ambulance less horse transport moved to PRISON YPRES & we thus accommodated in the cells for the night.	
			The Division is in front and are expecting b/s into action tomorrow. Major Campbell & O.C. Bearers is in Gas Touch with the Brigades.	※
PRISON Y.36.C.29.9.19		6AM	Major Campbell Capt J.C. Roth & Capt W.M. Chesney with the Bearer Divers of the Field Ambulance plus a Line Sub-Division of 109th Field Ambulance and Capt Whit with 50 OR Infantry attached as Stretcher bearers marched off 6pm in touch with the Brigades they were with them.	
I.2.6.3.2		12 noon	The Wheeled Stretcher Carriers & the Ambulance Cars of the Division are parked at HOOGE on the YPRES - MENIN Road	
		9am	I made a tour of the forward area & get in touch with the Bearer Officers the ground is very bad of evacuation from this front will be very heavy work. Relay p.o.s are at JARGON CROSS ROADS 28(J.7.d.9.2) GLENCORSE WOOD 28(J.14.b.7.7) & POLYGON WOOD 28(J.9.d.2.1)	※

Army Form C. 2118.

WAR DIARY
or
INTELLIGENCE SUMMARY.
(Erase heading not required.)

Instructions regarding War Diaries and Intelligence Summaries are contained in F.S. Regs., Part II. and the Staff Manual respectively. Title pages will be prepared in manuscript.

Place	Date	Hour	Summary of Events and Information	Remarks and references to Appendices
YPRES (Prison)	30/7/17		This place has now been converted into the Corps Main Dressing Station, the Majors opposite the Prison has been taken over + is being run by the personnel of this Field Ambulance, under the D.C. 87th Field Ambulance. Owing to the absence of the troops further relays have been established one in Huts at BEECHHERE 26 (J.12.d.8.5) + one just E. of TERHAND 28 (K.15.a.4.5) here the roads are quite good + wheeled stretcher carriers are used + as soon as the intermediate roads are passable the Field Ambulances will be able to operate in this portion. So heavy + rapid was the evacuation of cases the work of the bearers which facilitated the evacuation has been very heavy.	
		11 a.m.	A.D.M.S. 36th Division consulted A.D.S. Galby on Ford Car through to the front area, but unfortunately this has been closed soon of its arrival there. All Divisional Motor Cars placed with O.C. 110 Field Ambe + a Car parking at the School, YPRES S.	

JP Johnston Lt-Col RAMC
O.C. 108 Field Ambce.

116/3701

108 Fd. Ambce.

Army Form C. 2118.

Vol 3 ¶

WAR DIARY
or
INTELLIGENCE SUMMARY.
(Erase heading not required.)

Place	Date	Hour	Summary of Events and Information	Remarks and references to Appendices
YPRES PRISON.	9/10/18	6am	Accompanied by Major Campbell R.A.M.C. I left HQ to reconnoitre the road via ZONNEBEKE to BECELAERE the road is much congested with Belgian traffic, but of this were properly controlled the road is passable for light cars & should soon be made quite good. Visited the Bearer posts & relays controlled by Major Campbell.	
		2pm	Two light Ford Cars & two Vauxhall Cars succeeded in getting through to the forward area & one was taken from DADIZEELE back to the POLYGON POST, patients any then carried across a bad bit of country to the GLENCORSE POST & again put into Motor Ambce Cars & brought to the Main Dressing Station. The BECELAERE Post is being made an Advanced Dressing Station & a quantity of dumps, foods etc is being sent up by lender Wagon. The Major had hoped though today via GHELUVELT but was not able to reach its destination. Rations are sent up each morning by Pack animals and this has proved quite satisfactory	JJ

Army Form C. 2118.

WAR DIARY
or
INTELLIGENCE SUMMARY.
(Erase heading not required.)

Place	Date	Hour	Summary of Events and Information	Remarks and references to Appendices
YPRES (PRISON)	2/10/18	6am	Motored for the Advanced Dressing Station despatched in Jumbo Wagon to BECELAERE via POTIJZE & ZONNEBEKE. Thus assumed soon after mid-day. Visited all our Bearer posts & relays with Major Campbell. The Motor Ambulances are having a great time & the work of the Bearers is now greatly simplified.	
		5pm	A.D.M.S. called & discussed the methods of evacuation.	SJ
	30/10/18	10.30am	Visited the A.D. Station BECELAERE & the relay posts. Casualties are now much fewer in number & the evacuation is being carried out without any difficulty.	
		4.30pm	Summoned to the Office of A.D.M.S. 36th Division & received instructions to take over the Corps Main Dressing Station tomorrow morning from 87th Field Ambulance. Our Officer & 20 O.R. will be left from 109 Field Ambulance to help & these Officers will be left by 29th Division.	
		6pm	Arrived orders for transport to join H.Q. 6am GWALIA FARM.	SJ

WAR DIARY or INTELLIGENCE SUMMARY

Army Form C. 2118.

Place	Date	Hour	Summary of Events and Information	Remarks and references to Appendices
YPRES PRISON	4/10/18	8 am	Taking over of I Corps Main Dressing Station from 87th Field Ambulance completed. A personnel from 109 Field Ambulance arrived. Casualties very light during the day.	
		4 p	D.D.M.S. I Corps called but did not stay and enquiring as to the number of casualties.	SJ
"	5/10/18		Few casualties coming in during the day.	
		11 am	D.D.M.S. II Corps held a conference of A.D.Ms.S. in the Prison. It is decided that our Ambulance of 39th Division will again take over the Corps Main Dressing Stn., being helped by a tent subdivision of the Hull Ambulance as before.	
		3 pm	I accompanied Capt Allen O.C. No 4 M.A.C. over the route of evacuation from GLENCORSE WOOD with a view to getting M.A.C. Cars to take over this part of the evacuation.	
		5 pm	Capt Wallace arrived as a reinforcement and is taken on the strength of the Unit. A D.S. man skilled today carrying casualties amongst the staff.	SJ

Army Form C. 2118.

WAR DIARY
or
INTELLIGENCE SUMMARY.
(Erase heading not required.)

Instructions regarding War Diaries and Intelligence Summaries are contained in F. S. Regs., Part II. and the Staff Manual respectively. Title pages will be prepared in manuscript.

Place	Date	Hour	Summary of Events and Information	Remarks and references to Appendices
YPRES (PRISON)	6/10/18	10 a.m.	89th Field Ambulance took over charge of the II Corps Main Dressing Station.	
		11 a.m.	Attended a conference at the A.D.M.S. Office, arrangements for the next attack were discussed & are briefly as follows :— 110th Field Ambulance will take over the evacuation from the forward area, they will be assisted by 2 Bearer Sub-divisions from this Unit and two Officers. This Ambulance is attached to this Corps Main Dressing Station and will as far as possible look after the intents of our own Division, and will keep records of all Divisional Casualties passing through both at the Main Dressing Station & at the Walking Wounded A. Station.	JSJ.
"	7/10/18	9 a.m.	Visited the Advanced Dressing Station at BEECELAERE and the various Relay posts; a made arrangements for handing over to 110 Field Ambre. Major Campbell returned to Head Qrtrs. with me & we arranged the two Bearer Sub-divisions be attached to 110th Field Ambulance when they take over the evacuation from the forward area. YPRES should by H.V. throughout the whole afternoon.	JSJ.

Army Form C. 2118.

WAR DIARY
or
INTELLIGENCE SUMMARY.
(Erase heading not required.)

Place	Date	Hour	Summary of Events and Information	Remarks and references to Appendices
YPRES (PRISON)	8/10/18		26 Bearers from the line returned today to Headquarters. There are being fitted & charged as they come in and rested so as to be ready to go again as soon as required. The men on heavy duty in lots, so that in a few days all will have been rushed & rested.	
		12 bm	From noon today all stretcher cases have been brought the whole way in Motor Ambce Cars, coming via ZONNEBEKE & POTIJZE, the first cars took 40 minutes ROUND. Leaving all Cars tuned on this journey so as to find the actual time taken on the worst Road. Walking wounded will continue to come via the old GLENCORSE Road & will then to transport Ste on the roads. Arranged with 110th Field Ambce for the Motor Ambulances of the Division to return for the men who are actually for the lines, their has been left to mutual arrangement	JPL
"	9/10/18	11am		
		1pm	A.D.M.S. called & arranged about the Evacn for & of the sick to the Rest Station with Senior. I visited the XIX Corps M.D. Stn. to Schol YPRES & asked them to send all my sick to the PRISON.	
		5pm	G.O.C. 36th Divsn. visited the Dressing Station & expressed approval	JL

Army Form C. 2118.

WAR DIARY
or
INTELLIGENCE SUMMARY.
(Erase heading not required.)

Place	Date	Hour	Summary of Events and Information	Remarks and references to Appendices
YPRES. (PRISON)	10/6/18	10 am	Inspected the Horse Lines & transport, work of retaining stables continuing	
		12 noon	Visited 109 Field Ambulance & returned Capt Swan R.A.M.C. to them for duty, as under the new arrangements my own Medical Officers will be relieved from the line.	
		2.30pm	Evacuation from the forward area handed over to 110th Field Ambulance Major Campbell, Capt Roth & Capt Cheney with all bearers returned to Headquarters	
			Capt E.A. LUMLEY R.A.M.C. detailed to proceed to I Army Rest Camp for a fortnight	H
			Observation by Major Campbell, the Bearer Sub-divisions were organised & divided into their squads ready for the next attack, everything will be completed by this evening.	HL
,,	10/10/18	3pm	D.D.M.S. II Corps called & arranged that the dumps of 47 Infantry will be handed over to the Corps Walking Wounded Station	
,,		4pm	A.D.M.S called & discussed the move to a more forward position as soon as the Military Situation permits probably on Tues 1 day.	HL

WAR DIARY
or
INTELLIGENCE SUMMARY.

(Erase heading not required.)

Army Form C. 2118.

Place	Date	Hour	Summary of Events and Information	Remarks and references to Appendices
YPRES (PRISON)	13/10/16	9 am	Orders received from 110 to Field Ambulance to send up the two Bearer Sub-divisions as soon as possible and in addition the men from 109th Field Ambulance still attached to us.	
		2 pm	Major S.B.B. Campbell R.A.M.C. & Capt W.M. Cheomy M.C. R.A.M.C. both 72 O.R. left for the Advanced Dressing Station. The men are carrying skeleton equipment & each man has one shell dressing with him.	
			YPRES was continuously shelled throughout the evening & all night.	
	14/10/16		About 100 casualties passed through during the night	
		5.30 am	The barrage opened for renewed attack by the II Army. Casualties from the actual battlefield did not arrive until noon & then continued in a steady stream throughout the day.	
		11 am	The D.D.M.S. from Q.H.Q. (Major General Thompson C.B.) with the Officer i/c Reinforcements (Lt Col Davidson C.M.G. D.S.O.) visited the Corps M.D.S. & inspected the Dressing Station.	
		6 pm	Some liberated civilians arrived from WINKLE - ST ELOI and numerous German wounded are being brought in	

Army Form C. 2118.

WAR DIARY
or
INTELLIGENCE SUMMARY
(Erase heading not required.)

Place	Date	Hour	Summary of Events and Information	Remarks and references to Appendices
YPRES. (PRISON)	15/10/18		Lieut. A. D.M. L.A. Shepherd R.A.M.C. proceeded on leave to U. Kingdom. The number of casualties coming through are very much diminishing due to the fact that some Divisions (36th) have opened their Main Dressing Stations in front of the 2 own found. Expecting orders to move forward consequently am getting all movable packing done.	
"	16/10/18	10 a.m.	Four rumours received the Divisional advance has gone hell ? Some civilians have come in from ISEGHEM + INGLEMUNSTER. II Corps Main Dressing Station in the Prison YPRES closed down, all equipment etc being packed in anticipation of a move forward.	JF
		4 p.m.	D.D.M.S. II Corps arrived with orders for us to move forward at once to PASSCHENDAELE Station, select a suitable site there and from a Corps Entraining Station from tomorrow all casualties will be evacuated by hosp-gage train to C.C.S. BRIELEN.	
		9 p.m.	Arrived at PASSCHENDAELE, it is pitch dark + quite impossible to select any ground. So spent the night on the roadside.	JF

(A91753) Wt W3356/P360 600,000 12/17 D.D.&L. Sch. 52a. Forms/C2118/15.

Army Form C. 2118.

WAR DIARY
or
INTELLIGENCE SUMMARY
(Erase heading not required.)

Place	Date	Hour	Summary of Events and Information	Remarks and references to Appendices
PASSCHENDAELE STATION	7/11/18	6am	At daybreak the district was examined & the nearest possible site to the station selected & the erection of the Canvas commenced, by midday 25 marquees were ready for occupation and at 2pm the first patients arrived by light railway from the old entraining point at WATERDAMHOEK. Soon afterwards Motor Ambulance Cars started to arrive direct from the Main Dressing Station and for the first train at 5pm almost 100 Casualties were admitted. We have now temporary shelter for about 300 cases, as all the men are under Canvas. This is now the regular Corps route of evacuation, we have two temporary trains per day from 100 to 162 patients for each train, the work of enlarging the Camp is continuing. All surplus Corps Medical Stores are being transferred here from the Main Barracks YPRES from the old Post Station.	
"	16/11/18	11am	O.C.M.S. called & inspected the arrangements, Army Buckle Attached.	

WAR DIARY
or
INTELLIGENCE SUMMARY

Army Form C. 2118.

Place	Date	Hour	Summary of Events and Information	Remarks and references to Appendices
PASSCHENDAELE STATION.	19/10/18	11 a.m.	D.D.M.S. I Corps called & issued instructions to Corps attached to this station. The Hospital trains are very late today. Morning train due at 10 a.m. did not leave until 1 p.m. & the evening train due at 5 p.m. did not get away until after midnight. Numerous civilians wounded & unwounded are coming down. Some of them very long waits at railhead. I have sent up a Soyer stove to make them tea & coffee. I have arranged with the R.S.O. to draw the material necessary to supply this. The Division I understand fires into the line tonight again. There was a big rush of Casualties during the day, over 300 were evacuated by the morning train & one also by the evening train. Extra coaches had to be put on, but the entraining Station was cleared by 9 p.m.	JJ
"	20/10/18		D.D.M.S. II Corps called during the day, & detailed lorries to remove stores from Bowsby Camp.	JJ

Army Form C. 2118.

WAR DIARY
or
INTELLIGENCE-SUMMARY.
(Erase heading not required.)

Instructions regarding War Diaries and Intelligence Summaries are contained in F. S. Regs., Part II. and the Staff Manual respectively. Title pages will be prepared in manuscript.

Place	Date	Hour	Summary of Events and Information	Remarks and references to Appendices
PASSCHENDAELE STATION	24th	11 a.m.	D.D.M.S. II Corps called just as he was starting to entrain. 265 cases evacuated in the morning train. This station will probably move shortly to LEDEGHEM. Lieut Wallace R.A.M.C. proceeded today to take our Medical Charge of 15th R.I. Rifles from Capt J.S. Clarke RAMC of this Regt. Owing to a breakdown on the line the Temp. Ambulance train was delayed but some extra trucks were secured & 150 cases evacuated at 6 p.m.	
		7 p.m.	A.D.M.S. 36th Division called & inspected the Entraining Station. Temporary Amb. (Lines) Train promised for 8 a.m. did not arrive until 11 a.m. and so was delayed until 13.30 before getting away. Consequent on this delay, a special train was secured for the evening evacuation & over 300 cases were got away by 7 p.m.	
	22/10/18	2 p.m.	D.D.M.S. II Corps called & was informed of the delay in the trains this Station & not how likely to move to LEDEGHEM as a	

Army Form C. 2118.

WAR DIARY
or
INTELLIGENCE SUMMARY.
(Erase heading not required.)

Instructions regarding War Diaries and Intelligence Summaries are contained in F. S. Regs, Part II. and the Staff Manual respectively. Title pages will be prepared in manuscript.

Place	Date	Hour	Summary of Events and Information	Remarks and references to Appendices
PASSCHENDAELE STATION	27/10/18	7.30 p.m.	Commenced entraining before there is a rush at Raikhad = 350 cases were loaded to 09.00 Train left at 09.00 by the C.C.S.	
	28/10/18	7 am	Capt J.S. Blake R.A.M.C. reported his departure on leave of absence	appx. 290
		9 am	Only 70 cases on the morning train numbers diminishing.	
		3.30p	D.D.M.S. II Corps called & enquired into number of attention and blankets. 300 stretchers = 300 blankets just received from D.R.S. Am temporarily out of action with D.Hanger D.D.M.S. very kindly sent another officer from 29th Division to carry on.	JSB
		6 pm	Evening train — only 60 patients	
			Morning train 130 + 136	
	29/10/18	9.30 am	Capt Markham is transferred to this Unit from 110th Field Ambulance Capt Cheaney M.C. is transferred in exchange to 41st Division. Owing to a breakdown on the line it was not possible to run an evening train, all cases were made comfortable in the Magazine & kept overnight in the hope that the Railway will be cleared in morning	JSB

Army Form C. 2118.

WAR DIARY
or
INTELLIGENCE SUMMARY.
(Erase heading not required.)

Instructions regarding War Diaries and Intelligence Summaries are contained in F. S. Regs., Part II. and the Staff Manual respectively. Title pages will be prepared in manuscript.

Place	Date	Hour	Summary of Events and Information	Remarks and references to Appendices
PASSCHENDAELE STATION	24/10/18	7am	Train left this morning not about 500 cases on board, the station is now cleared.	
"	17/10/18		Nothing of importance throughout the day. Casualties now rapidly diminishing, only 8's sitting cases on morning train.	ff
		10am	D.D.M.S. called & named me that the Division is being relieved & that we would probably move at an early date. A warning order was issued & preparation made for quick packing.	
		6pm	Advance party arrived from 103 Field Ambulance 34th Division - A.D.M.S. Medical arrangements received, our relief to be complete by 18.00 tomorrow night. This Ambulance is moving to LES TRIEZ CAILLOUX S.E. of HALLUIN to form a Divisional Rest Station.	ff
	25/10/18	8am	Despatched advance party to new destination this morning, being sure the work of striking marquees is continuing.	
		4pm	103rd Field Ambulance arrived at PASSCHENDAELE	
		6pm	Entraining Station & all Stores handed over to incoming unit.	ff

Army Form C. 2118.

WAR DIARY
or
INTELLIGENCE SUMMARY.
(Erase heading not required.)

Instructions regarding War Diaries and Intelligence Summaries are contained in F. S. Regs., Part II. and the Staff Manual respectively. Title pages will be prepared in manuscript.

Place	Date	Hour	Summary of Events and Information	Remarks and references to Appendices
PASSCHENDAELE STATION.	29/10/18	8 am	Unit complete with transport paraded at Passchendaele & marched off to new destination route MOIRSLEEDE – ST PETERS CROSS ROADS – MENIN – HALLUIN.	
LES TRIEZ CAILLOUX		1 pm.	Arrived at LES TRIEZ CAILLOUX. The unit is situated in an old French Civil Hospital. This has been a magnificent place & with some work should make an ideal Rest Station. There is plenty of light & air, but the walls are very cold. The lot have had installation having been dismantled by the Boche before leaving & also the pumping system.	✓
29R.33.f.7.3 40.000			A list of these drawings it will become quite a good Rest Station & is likely to be kept well filled by the present epidemic of Influenza.	
1 mile S.E. of HALLUIN		8 pm	A.D.M.S. 36th Division visited the Hospital. Capt S.A. Lumley M.C. detailed as M.O. of 153 Bde. R.F.A. Capt S.P. Rea just rejoined from '13' Siege Park reported his departure on leave.	✓

J. Johnston Lt Col RAMC
C O mdg 19th 3rd CA Amlance

140/2401

108 T.A.

26/1/18

COMMITTEE FOR THE
MEDICAL HISTORY OF THE WAR
Date 14 JAN 1919

WAR DIARY
or
INTELLIGENCE SUMMARY.

(Erase heading not required.)

Army Form C. 2118.

Place	Date	Hour	Summary of Events and Information	Remarks and references to Appendices
La Thieu	Oct/Nov		X Corps inspected the troops in training & prepy.	
	1.11.18		schools though the Hohool to an of H Trees to approved	
			Lent Colonel J Johnston M.C. had to proceed in road convoy to	
			an area of supplya.	P.S.C.
	2.11.18		Lieut J Stevenson M.C. U.S.A. was posted to 96th A.B.de	
			R.F.A. and on arrival of the troops of the unit	
			Capt J Morham was posted to A/hair	P.S.C.
	3/11/18		Padre Liggatt held a Service at 2.30 P.m. in the	
			Cleering Room. This was well attended by patients	
			and personnel.	P.S.C.
	4/11/18		Capt J C Babb and S Moreses of Mousam to	
			Lee A.D.M.S. about a file to D.R.S. - MT from	
			finds a first Side can found it was Involunta	
			School.	P.S.C.

WAR DIARY
or
INTELLIGENCE SUMMARY.
(Erase heading not required.)

Army Form C. 2118.

Place	Date	Hour	Summary of Events and Information	Remarks and references to Appendices
Le Thiest			Col J C Rith and J proceeded again to Mouscron	
Carihow			and sent a party of 12 men under an NCO to a	
	5.11.18		tribing park to get 2 pgs D.R.S. we have to get	
			a consignment of horses etc. and met with Genl Pierru	
			the intendant. Every act he been notified.	Pt C
	6.11.18		Went received J at 5 Pm to Ecole Industrial MOUSCRON.	
			In time reported at 8.15 am and there were several new	
			cases of Sabies & equipment to we get.	
			8 Rui Cases, 3 D.C.Ts were transferred to 110 F.A	Pt 2
Mouscron	7.11.18		No D.R.S. is now in working order. A Consultation	
			General received an building with 240 120 sick	
			Reap Crohi D.A.S.D.S. with an ambulance at 3.30 am	
				ASSi

WAR DIARY
or
INTELLIGENCE SUMMARY.
(Erase heading not required.)

Army Form C. 2118.

Place	Date	Hour	Summary of Events and Information	Remarks and references to Appendices
Mousehon	8.11.18		Capt S.P. Rea was appointed Educational Officer to the unit, to relieve 110th FA in the afternoon.	ASE
	9.11.18		Conference at ADMS office at 11.00 hours. O.C 110. FA field Ambulance was present. It was decided to have a combined Church Parade at 110th FA ST at 2.30 p.m. on 10-11-18. ADMS inspected DRS in the afternoon. Three of the men were awarded the MM. namely. h/Cpl Cann Ptw Kennedy & Pte Shannan.	PSE
	10.11.18		3 Officers & 10 OR paraded at 1.30 pm for Church Parade. Padre Wright & helper conducted the Service. The men looked very smart in band. A DmS Spoke to them after the Service & advised them that as the Armistice having been signed wished on queuing proceeded to the Pany Place and made a report of it. At 11 p.m.	PSE
	11.11.18		Arrangements of Dental hi khange. Major hinhan went to Am hirican Stores at Ty and got a dental outfit. Lieutenant han had been in Paris.	PSE

WAR DIARY
or
INTELLIGENCE SUMMARY

Army Form C. 2118.

Place	Date	Hour	Summary of Events and Information	Remarks and references to Appendices
Moustron	12.11.18		Sent in a few names for DSM and certificates 3 men may have apparently between the various hers as all deserve even less than the men work throughout to our best always reached its highest standard.	MC
	13.11	18	E. Capt Gibson was awarded a bar to his M.M. and Pte H Burke and Drover Workman (MT) to M.M.	MC?
	14.11	18	A SMS visits the area and informed us that we were going to do salvage at Ditz Basket Camp. Took the men a short route march.	MC

WAR DIARY
or
INTELLIGENCE SUMMARY
(Erase heading not required.)

Army Form C. 2118.

Place	Date	Hour	Summary of Events and Information	Remarks and references to Appendices
MOUSCRON	15/11/18	2 pm	Unit paraded for a Route march. B/Keep the men fit.	
near TOURCOING		4 pm	Major S.M.S. Campbell attended a meeting of the Divisional Sports Committee, it is decided to put out a regular Sports programme	
Sheet 39 G.O. 0-0-0			with intra unit contests.	
S.23.		8 pm	1/Lt. A.R.McL.A.D. Shepherd reported his arrival from leave	J.S.
"	16/11/18		Visited 10-9 & 110th Field Ambulance's & arranged rendez-vous for this Attachments attending the Army Church Parade at ROUBAIX tomorrow. Capt. J.C. Ruth of this Unit will be in Command.	
		1 pm	Capt. S.P. Rea R.A.M.C. & Capt. J.S. Clark. R.A.M.C. reported their arrival from leave of absence. 1/Lieut. J.K. Denny. M.C. U.S.A. reported his arrival also taken on the strength.	J.S.
"	17.11.18	6.30 am	Capt. Ruth with the Attachment of 50 O.R. marched off for the embussing point to attend Church parade in ROUBAIX.	
		2.30 pm	Unit paraded in full strength & marched to 110th Field Ambulance there to attend a Combined Church Parade of the Ambulances.	J.S.

WAR DIARY
or
INTELLIGENCE SUMMARY

Army Form C. 2118.

Place	Date	Hour	Summary of Events and Information	Remarks and references to Appendices
MOUSCRON	7/11/18	3pm	A.D.M.S. 36th Division attended Church Parade, he had seen the march past at ROUBAIX and expressed his approval of the smart appearance & turn out of the R.A.M.C. detachment under Capt Roth.	
			D.D.M.S. X Corps visited & inspected the Rest Station.	S.F.
	13/11/18	2pm	A mass meeting of the Ambulance was held and a lecture delivered to Major J. Mothan R.A.M.C. on "Demobilisation & Reconstruction". This has helped to keep the men with keen attention afterwards. Committee were elected to arrange sports etc & make the necessary arrangements for celebrating the Armistice in France.	S.F.
	19/11/18	11am	Major Campbell & Major Horton attended a conference in the A.D.M.S. Office, the discussion being how best to keep the men employed & arrange for their amusements during the demobilisation period to hear the plans of Amerchishkan be an all paint?	
			The A.D.M.S. has formed a Cup for a sectional football Contest between the three Units.	
	13/11/18		Lecture on Submarines etc by Cmdr Lieut. Sampson R.N. D.Offr	S.F.

WAR DIARY
or
INTELLIGENCE SUMMARY

Army Form C. 2118.

(Erase heading not required.)

Place	Date	Hour	Summary of Events and Information	Remarks and references to Appendices
MOUSCRON	20/11/18	12.45pm	D.M.S. X Corps accompanied by A.D.M.S. X Corps arrived to say Goodbye. He left a message of appreciation for the men & especially of the work done during the recent advance.	
			Major Boyd Campbell attended Sports Committee meeting at Div HQ	SBJ
	21/11/18	11.30am	A.D.M.S. 36th Division visited and inspected the Rest Station, he expressed approval of the Hospital & Dining-room arrangements but suggested larger washing overlay. There will be erected as soon as bricks & material can be obtained.	
		1pm	Major S.B. Boyd Campbell awarded the Military Cross for gallantry & good organization during the recent advance.	
		6pm	We received that Capt J.S. Clark is to proceed Home & be discharged. We are sorry to lose a good Officer	SBJ
	22/11/18	10am	Capt J.C. Rath proceeded to B.R.C.S. Stores at Ouvering to get items etc for the Convalescents to Hospital	
		11am	Col Agnew A.D.M.S offered us a Cinematograph show for Sunday but this was accepted with thanks	SBJ

Army Form C. 2118.

WAR DIARY
or
INTELLIGENCE SUMMARY.
(Erase heading not required.)

Instructions regarding War Diaries and Intelligence Summaries are contained in F. S. Regs., Part II. and the Staff Manual respectively. Title pages will be prepared in manuscript.

Place	Date	Hour	Summary of Events and Information	Remarks and references to Appendices
MOUCRON	23/11/18		Lieut. J. S. Rea, R.A.M.C. reported his arrival for duty on transfer from the 25th Division & is taken on the strength.	
		2.30p	The Ambulance football team played 13th Batt. R.I.R. Lot for Leader 2-0	
		6 p.m.	A thiot Aire was held for the men & proved a huge success.	
			The arrangements were made by Capt J. C. Ross of this unit.	JJ
"	24/11/18	2.30p	The Unit paraded full strength & attended a Comrade Church Parade at the 110th Field Ambulance; the A.D.M.S. attended & after the Service a rehearsal of Medal presentation Parade was held. Major J. Moham R.A.M.C. Education Officer gave a lecture to the Unit on "Reconstruction after the War".	JJ
"	25/11/18	2.30p	Our Concert Party gave a performance in the theatre of 110th Field Ambulance.	JJ
			Capt J. S. Clark R.A.M.C. awarded the Military Cross for gallantry during the recent advance whilst M.O. to a Battalion of R.I. Rifles.	
	26/11/18	4 p.m.	Occupied by Major Mahan on Educational Officer I attended a lecture on AIRCRAFT at this East African Campaign, the lecture was slight & airy, and though lecturer knew, perhaps, there way he talked so little of Aircraft.	JJ

(N4175) Wt. W3333/P1395 600,000. 12/17 D. D. & L. **Sch. 52a.** Forms/C.2118/13

WAR DIARY
or
INTELLIGENCE SUMMARY

Army Form C. 2118.

Place	Date	Hour	Summary of Events and Information	Remarks and references to Appendices
MOUSCRON.	27/11/18		A.D.M.S. 36th Division visited the Rest Station and inspected the medical as we are getting somewhat over full. He arranged that a certain number of our convalescents could be sent to 110th Field Ambulance. Keeping only the acute cases here. Paid home to Major Cook. D.A.D.M.S. the sum of 1250 francs to purchase turkeys for our Xmas dinner, he hopes they arrive. Wire received to expedite departure of Capt. J.C. Clark for release from the Army.	JF
"	28/11/18	6pm	Our Regimental troops gave a concert to 15th Batt R.I.R. – had a great reception	JF
	29/11/18 11am	Visited 109 Field Ambulance & arranged to have the use of their ground for purposes of ceremonial drill.	JF
		2.30pm	Bttl. Section football match. 6th Royal Irish Rifles but ground was occupied by another unit – had Staff work by Sports Committee	JF
		5pm	Attended a short interesting lecture on demobilization by Major Bodin. I know in six months. GOOD.	JF

WAR DIARY
or
INTELLIGENCE SUMMARY.
(Erase heading not required.)

Army Form C. 2118.

Place	Date	Hour	Summary of Events and Information	Remarks and references to Appendices
TOURCOING	29/11/18	6.30 p.m.	Our Concert Party gave a show to 12th Batt. R.I.R. and had another roaring reception. They are improving. This is to be a full day.	
"	30/11/18	9.30 a.m.	Field Ambulance paraded & marched to STERHOEK. The morning was spent in Section & Company drill & practising the march past in column of Section. After dinner a football match was played between C Section 1st & A Section 1st & A Section 2nd & C Section 2nd were beaten but not disgraced. The unit marched home arriving at 4 p.m.	
		6 p.m.	A Whist drive was held opened a huge success. 230 entries were received but we were unable to seat so many, a hundred or more will be held for those who were left out. Capt J.S. Clark M.C. presided & is struck off the strength.	

J. Johnston Major RAMC
Comdg 128 Field Amb.

No. 108 F.A.

Dec 1917

COMMITTEE FOR THE
MEDICAL HISTORY OF THE WAR
6 MAR 1919
Date

108 **Army Form C. 2118.**

Army Form C. 2118.

WAR DIARY
or
INTELLIGENCE SUMMARY.
(Erase heading not required.)

Place	Date	Hour	Summary of Events and Information	Remarks and references to Appendices
MOUSCRON	1/12/18		Received warning of preliminary Ceremonial parade to be held on 3rd inst.	
		2.30pm	Church parade. Continued the attendance was good.	
		4pm	Received my leave warrant, off tomorrow 5.30 am. Major S.B.S. Campbell M.C. will take over Command in my absence. JJ	
	2.12.18		Lieut Colonel F. Johnston M.C. proceeded on leave this morning. Capt Thurston and 3 attended a conference at Avelin this morning to discuss ceremonial parade which is to take place on 3rd Dec.	
		2.30 p.m.	A Lee 108 Jn played A.S.C. 110 in competition, A.S.C's match. Yn game was easily by 5 goals to nil	
		6.15pm	Arrangements re Ceremonial Parade tomorrow are cancelled	
	3.12.18		A duel wet day. Capt Robb arranged a shoot shoot for the men at 6 p.m. 72 entries shot for prize	

Army Form C. 2118.

WAR DIARY
or
INTELLIGENCE SUMMARY.
(Erase heading not required.)

Instructions regarding War Diaries and Intelligence Summaries are contained in F. S. Regs., Part II. and the Staff Manual respectively. Title pages will be prepared in manuscript.

Place	Date	Hour	Summary of Events and Information	Remarks and references to Appendices
Morbecque			B Sec 108th FA played A.S.C. 108th FA at football	
	4.10.18		on the ADMS cup. The latter won by 3 goals to 2.	
			The ADMS & DDMS VIII Corps allowed the band music.	
	5.10.18		Capt J.R. Mitchell RAMC was evacuated to CCS with a critical eruption. He had symptoms of a Chemical A.D.M.S. visited instruction re a Chemical parade for the 6th	
				NSE
	6.10.18		Ambulance paraded at 7.45 am & marched to at 8 am to Aeroplane Pound near Hallun The Ceremonial Parade went off very well 3 Officers and 115 OR returned from the unit a Rev Keary D.A.C.G. those talks to by Corps who spoke by Capt S.P. Rea woven instruction from ADMS	AAQC AAQC

WAR DIARY
or
INTELLIGENCE SUMMARY.

Army Form C. 2118.

Place	Date	Hour	Summary of Events and Information	Remarks and references to Appendices
At M Sur			Major Nathan visited No 10 Stationary Hospital to see Capt Thatcher RAMC. He found him considerably improved	
	7.12.18	2 pm	A Sec played BYC District WDiv team	
		10 pm	Sec went to Rontain to see the King	OK
	8.12.18		Church Parade at 2. a.m.S. Sergt A.S. Beer was awarded the Silver Cross of Greece	
	9.12.18		Draft of WS with between ASC 10th & Y Base 11th to ASC — had in a car in the Column of 3-1. Train was present. Post	
	10.12.18		Rain came in about a resumed parade in the Q Sun RE Cpl Crummick much better at Dix Sur	Pk

WAR DIARY or INTELLIGENCE SUMMARY

Army Form C. 2118.

Place	Date	Hour	Summary of Events and Information	Remarks and references to Appendices
Ft Minescamp	11.12.18		Been has received that two men Burnell & Lane & Co. from a Rest Station to keep troops in hospital 16th at two Tracy Callan 2 8.5 cases. 7 high & 3 Cuartu Soto. was taken over to the Rte. 14.30 hours Ambulance reported to SMroll forward 8 109 TFA here an incident between 108 TFA & 110 TFA. The former here an incident gave by 2 Sub. to 1. 17.00 hours Capt Roper took the Ambulance Concert Party over to 109 TFA & gave them a Concert which was much enjoyed by that unit	
	12.12.18		Ceremonial Parade was carried at 7.30 am kept Nissen & Capt Roper attend at the NOWS. Attd.	
	13.12.18		Ambulance paraded at 10 am & marched to 118TFA where they were drawn up in dos clum 8 Section. Capt. Senior & Effn in notional comment them Parachute (?) attend the march Pipes Drum & the last two church the received Harvester Ride.	

WAR DIARY
or
INTELLIGENCE SUMMARY.
(Erase heading not required.)

Army Form C. 2118.

Place	Date	Hour	Summary of Events and Information	Remarks and references to Appendices
MOUSCRON	14/12/18		Three Coal miners were sent to Concentration Camp at LILLE for demobilisation. Major MORHAM took over temporary Command of Ambulance from Major S.B.BOYD CAMPBELL. M.C.	JM
MOUSCRON	15/12/18	5:30 am	Major S.B.BOYD CAMPBELL. M.C. proceeded to England, his contract with the Army having expired.	JM
		11 am	Ambulance marched to No.7 TRIEZ CAILLOUX under Captain J.C.ROBB. Move completed at 12:30 pm	
TRIEZ CAILLOUX	16/12/18	9:45 am	Unit marched past Confrere Champion Corps Commander at the Aerodrome HALLUIN. One Balmain was sent to Concentration Camps at LILLE for demobilisation	JM
"	17/12/18	am	MAJOR MORHAM rode to MOUSCRON to see DDMS Corps (XI) regarding the Hospital.	JM
	18/12/18		DADMS XV Corps visited TRIEZ CAILLOUX	JM
	19/12/18	-	Lieut Shaw proceeded to No.1 F.Am.B. to proceed to BRUGES at the following day, but this was cancelled, the men returning the same night.	JM
	20/12/18	5:30 pm	Col. R. JOHNSTON reported from General Leave	JM

WAR DIARY
or
INTELLIGENCE SUMMARY.
(Erase heading not required.)

Army Form C. 2118.

Instructions regarding War Diaries and Intelligence Summaries are contained in F. S. Regs., Part II. and the Staff Manual respectively. Title pages will be prepared in manuscript.

Place	Date	Hour	Summary of Events and Information	Remarks and references to Appendices
TRIEZ CAILLOUX	21/12/18		LT. COL. JOHNSTON resumed command of this Ambulance.	
		2:30 pm	"A" Section 108th F. Amb. & played A.S.C attached at football, the latter winning by 2 goals to 1.	
		6:30 pm	A Whist drive was held, Sgt. ROBINSON foaming the winner	
"	22.12.18	10 am	Paid the men of the Unit & arranged final details for the Xmas feast.	
		11 am	Col. E. Church Parade, no Presbyterian enjoyments.	
		3 pm	C.O. & Capt. Rae met 6 COURTRAI to Officers Cadre Depôt this Lad returned to COLOGNE.	
			Visited B.R.C. Store to draw materials for the Hospital & for the Patients	
	23.12.18	9 am	Dinners busy decorating for tomorrow our last Xmas in France as a Unit. Everyone has just completed in time and 30 Turkeys are	
			Our men over has just completed in time so that there can be no hitch in the proceedings have started today.	
		6 pm	Our Pierrot troupe gave a Grand Concert in the School Room.	
	25.12.18	10 am	A holiday for all. Church Parade.	
		1 pm	Dinner consisting of all that has has got & eat a hand down for Stout & Beer, be was in his better saying he has true the King had no better owner. R.A.M.S. allied to wish all a Merry Xmas & had a rousing reception.	
			After Xmas the day went well & everyone was pleased.	

WAR DIARY
or
INTELLIGENCE SUMMARY.
(Erase heading not required.)

Army Form C. 2118.

Place	Date	Hour	Summary of Events and Information	Remarks and references to Appendices
LES TRIEZ CHILOUX	26/11/18	8am	Major J Morham & Capt Spree proceeded to GHENT to represent the unit at a Fete given by the Faculty of Ghent at the Photo of the Poster	
		6pm	The Concert Party gave a show to No 10 Squadron R.A.F. who had a grand reception. Back to winter quarters again	JJ
	27/11/18	8.30am	Visited Capt Mitchell at a stationary Hospital. He is improving.	
		1pm	Concert Party gave a show to 110 Field Ambulance which has attended to A.D.M.S. Have not yet heard his verdict.	JJ
	28/11/18		Today we were to have played the finals for the A.D.M.S. Medals but this was postponed as in report in due to M.O. way	
		3pm	attend a meeting of XV Corps Medical Society	
		8pm	Accompanied A.D.M.S. to above mentioned meeting and had a very interesting paper on Vincent's Angina read by Major Bruce R.A.M.C. after an A.D.M.S. invitation attended the revue given by the Marines Divisional Concert Party, this is one of the best shows I have seen in France.	JJ

WAR DIARY
or
INTELLIGENCE SUMMARY.

Army Form C. 2118.

Place	Date	Hour	Summary of Events and Information	Remarks and references to Appendices
LESTRIEZ CAILLOUX	30/12/18	2 pm	D.A.D.M.S. XL Corps visited the Hospital, approved the obtained from him to draw extra fuel in order to keep the central heating apptatus going.	
	1/1/19		Lectured the men on Demobilization & explained the various Army Forms already in use.	
			Arranged with 199 Field Ambulance to march the men over Time for the March on Wednesday Jan 1st	
	2/1/19	1pm	D.A.D.M.S. visited the Rest Station	
		6pm	Dined with the A.D.M.S. and had a real jolly evening reminiscing over our days & training & work in this line.	

J. Johnston Lt Col RAMC
Comdg 109 "Irish Centre"

Jan 1919

36 DIV

Box 2298

121/3440

No 108 + a

WAR DIARY
or
INTELLIGENCE SUMMARY.
(Erase heading not required.)

Army Form C. 2118.

108th Amb

Place	Date	Hour	Summary of Events and Information	Remarks and references to Appendices
LESTREM	2/1/19	10 am	Unit paraded full strength & proceeded by Motor Route to SERQUEUX to witness the final for the Kirke medals by the A.D.M.S. of the Division between A Section 109 Field Ambulance & the R.A.M.C. attached to 108 Field Ambulance. A very keen match resulted in a win for the 109 F. Amb. but the Horseman Cup, newly instituted, to close by 1 goal to NIL. Dinner of tea were arranged for by the D.D.M. 109 Dulligence to marching back again in lorries at 6 p.m.	S.F.
CAILLOUY and South of HALLUIN				
	3/1/19		Routine. One concert party gave a show to 2 R. Irish In at RENIX which was so much appreciated that a return visit has been arranged	S.F.
	4/1/19		Routine. Ben 15 Bn 1/2 leaves from the Bulln for Units 3 yrs ser.	S.F.
	5/1/19		Pay Parade for the Bn. 2nd Ben 1/2 of w demobilisation on long service	S.F.
	6/1/19	5.30 am	One of our Horses has been stolen from the Stables this morning, this practice is becoming rather frequent in the neighbourhood.	S.F.

WAR DIARY or INTELLIGENCE SUMMARY

(Erase heading not required.)

Army Form C. 2118.

Place	Date	Hour	Summary of Events and Information	Remarks and references to Appendices
LES TRIEZ	7/1/19.		Have received at RONCQ, special orders have been issued to the Guard against any similar eventualities.	
CAILLOU	8/1/19.		Inter unit Football Match between B & C Sections, the former won by 2-0. Major J. Morton R.A.M.C. proceeded this morning on 14 days leave. Five men proceeded to day to Concentration Camp LILLE for demobilization. Miss Una Ashwell's party gave a concert in MOUSCRON, 17 seats were allotted to this Unit & the same was much appreciated.	JL
"	9/1/19		Our troupe gave a Show in MOUSCRON, there was a crowded house & everything went well for this first big attempt. Permission given for the issue of the 1914-1915 Star, almost 300 men in this Unit will be eligible.	JL
"	10/1/19		Seven men sent to Concentration Camp, LILLE for demobilization.	JL
"	11/1/19		One man. Capt J.C. Rgt. R.A.M.C. awarded the Belgian Croix de Guerre.	JL
"	12/1/19.		Football Match with 122 Field Coy R.E. in the front final of Divisional Competition — Result - Engineers 3 R.A.M.C. B 1.	JL

WAR DIARY
or
INTELLIGENCE SUMMARY

(Erase heading not required.)

Army Form C. 2118.

Place	Date	Hour	Summary of Events and Information	Remarks and references to Appendices
LESTRIEZ	12/1/19		R.A.M.C. 36th Division visited the Hospital.	
CAILLOUX		2p.m.	Sick nursing to take part in a 3 mile Cross Country run Expected to 10 C.C.S.	
"	14/1/19	1pm	A photograph of the Officers who came to France with the Division in 1915 was taken in the Square MOUSCRON. The groups was larger than generally anticipated.	☒
			Capt J.C. Roth R.A.M.C. of this unit has been granted permission to wear the badge & rank of Major pending notification in the Gazette.	
			Pte Crampied man of the unit Awarded the Decorazione Militaire Italy.	☒
	15/1/19		Capt S.P. Rea & Lt. B.M. Shepherde have gone to try to find Brussels the beautiful Belgian Capital.	
		2pm	A Football Match between 108 & 109 ZA Ambers had to be cancelled owing tournament proving too strong as a counter-attraction.	☒
	16/1/19	5.30pm	Our troupe gave a Concert to the troops of 109 Brigade at RONCQ & had a great reception.	
			Capt Rea & Lt Shepherd returned from Brussels.	☒

Army Form C. 2118.

WAR DIARY
or
INTELLIGENCE SUMMARY.
(Erase heading not required.)

Instructions regarding War Diaries and Intelligence Summaries are contained in F. S. Regs., Part II. and the Staff Manual respectively. Title pages will be prepared in manuscript.

Place	Date	Hour	Summary of Events and Information	Remarks and references to Appendices
HS MESS 2 CHILLON	17/1/19	11am	Attended a Conference at A.D.M.S. Office of O.i/C of Field Ambulance and Quartr. Masters to discuss equipment & drew up a scale for the new organisation of Field Ambulances into two Sections.	
		6pm	Visited Lille & attended the Pantomime ALADDIN playing there in the New Theatre by our 30th Division.	
	18/1/19		Three of our men took part in the Divisional Cross Country race. Meeting of representatives of the three Field Ambulances forming a R.A.M.C. Divisional team for the Corps & Army Competitions.	
	19/1/19	2.15	Attended a Rugby match at HALLUIN. R.A.F. ground between 36th Divisional Team & the M.G. Battalion Guards Division. The 36th Division won a magnificent game by 26 points to 8.	
	20/1/19	2pm	An R.A.M.C. trial match was played today to pick the R.A.M.C. Divisional team. Some good football was shown.	
			Had a meeting of the Minstrels discussed Cadre strength & to ask for Volunteers. The meeting was very successful. Many friends were aired and about the required number came forward.	

WAR DIARY
or
INTELLIGENCE SUMMARY.

(Erase heading not required.)

Army Form C. 2118.

Place	Date	Hour	Summary of Events and Information	Remarks and references to Appendices
LES TRIEZ	21.1.19		Seven men proceeded today to Army Concentration Camp LILLE for demobilization	
CHATELOAK		2 pm	A second mass meeting of the Ambulance was held to discuss Cadre & demobilization problems; it was decided that no married man irrespective of service should be included in the Cadre unless as a Volunteer.	JJ.
"	22/1/19		Visited 109 Field Ambulance at STERHOEK. Second Trial match played Probables Versus Possibles.	JJ
"	23/1/19	11:30 am	Attended a Conference at the A.D.M.S. Office. Subjects discussed Honours – Awards, Demobilization and Equipment.	JJ.
"	24/1/19	10:30	R.A.M.C. Divisional Team to play 109th M.G. Battalion in the XI Corps Competition for matches today. They are playing a team from 109th Infantry Brigade. Result R.A.M.C. team 3. 109 Brigade 1.	
		7:30	Our Concert troupe gave a performance to 109 Brigade at RONCQ. This was a great success, the artists being called upon for several encores. Brig. Gen. Hersey D.S.O. expressed his pleasure at the show.	JJ

Army Form C. 2118.

WAR DIARY
or
INTELLIGENCE SUMMARY
(Erase heading not required.)

Place	Date	Hour	Summary of Events and Information	Remarks and references to Appendices
LESTIEZ	25/1/19	11 am	Attended a Conference at Divisional Headquarters, subject for discussion, the formation of a Divisional Dinner Club, & Old Comrades Association. It was decided to form a Dinner Club and Local Associations for keeping in touch with the men. A Committee of three (Lieut-Col Allen D.S.O. 16th R.I. Rifles, Lieut-Col Simpson C.M.G. D.S.O. 173 Brigade RFA Col. Lieut-Col Johnston 109 2/CA Ambulance) were appointed to draw up rules the & submit them to a General meeting of the Officers of the Division.	
CAILLOUX		14.45	Attended a meeting of the XI Corps Medical Society at MOVERIA. A most instructive lecture on Anaesthetics was given by Major Marshall 10 C.C.S.	JJ
"	26/1/19		Church Service was held at 11 am.	
	27/1/19	11.00	Attend a Committee meeting of the 36th Div Old Comrades Association to draft rules the to which will be submitted to a General meeting of the Division on Sunday. Major Markham R.A.M.C. reported his arrival from leave.	JJ

WAR DIARY
or
INTELLIGENCE SUMMARY.

(Erase heading not required.)

Army Form C. 2118.

Place	Date	Hour	Summary of Events and Information	Remarks and references to Appendices
LESTREZ CAILLOUX	28/4/19		Attended a final meeting in the Hotel de Ville Mouscron at 3pm.	JS
"	29/4/19	11am	Meeting of Officers of Division arranged for Friday. Lecture & Discussion with the men Subject "Temperance Reform"	JS
"	30/4/19	11am	His Royal Highness the Prince of Wales is paying a visit to the Division. Lecture & Discussion with the men Subject "Total Abstinence".	JS
"	3/1/19	11am	Labour of Studies. Cadre for the Unit formed, consisting of Lieut Col Hughes Major J.C.Robb & Lieut Snyched, 6 Serjeants & 36 O.R.	JS

No. 106 Field Ambulance.

108 F.A.
Army Form C. 2118.

WAR DIARY
or
INTELLIGENCE SUMMARY
(Erase heading not required.)

31

Place	Date	Hour	Summary of Events and Information	Remarks and references to Appendices
LESTRIEZ	1.2.19	11 am	Lecture - Discussion on Sport.	
CAILLOUX (Chat Hallie)			Conf. of Engineers held on the absence of RE Nations and of one MT driver, who absented himself & amp; who has not rejoined.	H.
	2.2.19	10.30	Church of England Communion Service held.	H.
		11.30	Presbyterian Service held.	H.
"	3/2/19	10.00	Major J. Moham R.A.M.C. proceeded to 110th Field Ambulance to carry out the Dental work of the Division, the attending Dentist being indisposed.	
		11.00	Debate for the men — Des Professionalism of Sport.	H.
"	4.2.19	10.00	Bras & OR Games from Field Cashier to pay to men.	
		11.00	Attended 1st General meeting of 36th Division Old Comrades Association.	H.
		Mn.00	Pay out.	
"	5.2.19	11.30	Attended a Conference of Officers a.O.R. of the three Field Ambulances at H.Q. 110 Field Ambce to discuss the formation of an Old Comrades Association for the men of the R.A.M.C. Two Ambulances voted for separate Ambulance Associations, a one for a joint Association.	H.

WAR DIARY
or
INTELLIGENCE SUMMARY.
(Erase heading not required.)

Army Form C. 2118.

Place	Date	Hour	Summary of Events and Information	Remarks and references to Appendices
LES TRIEZ CAILLOUX	6.2.19	10.00	Dentist from 110th Field Ambulance attended to a large group of returned men, Boxer, Chicks & others.	
		12.00	Lt-Col Davidson OC 109 Battre visited the Ambulance.	
		18.00	A very successful Boxing Competition was held in which the Officers participated & was allowed to escape alive.	SJ
	7.2.19	11.30	Conference at ADMS Office. Various matters were discussed. The principal being the formation of a R.A.M.C. Old Comrades Association within the Division & the ADMS Wishnie pointed out that this matter is most important as now if the war was completed he would come to such heights.	SJ
"	8.2.19	09.30	Major J. Norham R.A.M.C. attached for depot work with 110 2/A Ambler.	
		11.00	At G.H.Q a Committee meeting of the White Division Old Comrades Association. An Executive Committee was elected & amongst other Matters discussed. It was unanimously decided to ask His Royal Highness the Prince of Wales to become Patron of the Association.	SJ

WAR DIARY
or
INTELLIGENCE SUMMARY

Army Form C. 2118.

Place	Date	Hour	Summary of Events and Information	Remarks and references to Appendices
LES TRIEZ	9/2/19	11.30	Presbyterian Service was held in the Recreation room.	
CAILLOUX		15.00	Addressed a mass meeting of 109 Field Ambulance on the question of the Ex-Service Comrades Association, giving them the outlines of what has already been done by this Unit.	St.
"	10/2/19	11.00	Addressed the men putting forward the claims of the Post billum Army. There were no volunteers. Must be a poor outlook.	
"		15.00	Attended a "Pioneer" meeting in Hotel de Ville, MOUSCRON.	St.
"	11/2/19	09.00	Major J. Horton R.A.M.C. attd M.A. at 110th Field Ambulance for Dental duties.	St.
"	12.2.19		Proceeded on duty to BOUCOGNE for Red Cross Stores & returned same day, having successfully accomplished my mission & obtained some Red Cross visitors, and the troops gave a	St.
"	13.2.19		special show in their Honour.	St.
	14.2.19		Routine	St.
	15.2.19		Routine	St.
	16.2.19		Routine	St.

WAR DIARY
or
INTELLIGENCE SUMMARY

Army Form C. 2118.

(Erase heading not required.)

Place	Date	Hour	Summary of Events and Information	Remarks and references to Appendices
LES TRIEZ	17.2.19		Permission received for Major J.C. Ryott R.A.M.C. & Capt S.P. Rea R.A.M.C. to proceed for 3 weeks to the Mickleham Convalescent Home MENTONE. 8.)	8.)
CAILLOUX	18.2.19		Routine	
"	19.2.19		D.D.M.S. XV Corps. accompanied by the D.A.D.M.S. visited the Hospital. They seemed concerned at the large number of German Prisoners admitted and from S.C.T. Just received a number of the Patients	8.)
"	20.2.19		Demobilization proceeding apace. 6 more men off today.	8.)
	21.2.19		Three Divisional H.T. amplices to now establishment transfers to No 1 Coy.	8.)
			36th Divisional Train.	8.)
	22.2.19		Routine.	8.)
	23.2.19		Routine.	8.)
	24.2.19		Visited 109 Field Ambulance & discussed demob. problem with Lt Col. Davidson.	8.)
	25.2.19		Had tea with the A.D.M.S. He looks very fit after his month's holiday - very happy in his role of Bridegroom. (See check for ADMS)	8.)
	26.2.19		Routine	8.)

Army Form C. 2118.

WAR DIARY
or
~~INTELLIGENCE SUMMARY.~~
(Erase heading not required.)

Place	Date	Hour	Summary of Events and Information	Remarks and references to Appendices
LES TRIES CAILLOUX	27.2.19		Orders received to move to MOUSCRON. Patients are to be transferred to 110th Field Ambulance & this Unit will form into Billets; in case to receive patients from 1st March & the move to be completed by March 3rd.	
—	28.2.19		20 Z Forms sent today to collecting Camp LINSELLES. Lieut Shepherd proceeded to MOUSCRON to arrange Billets etc for our move.	

J Johnston Lieut Col RAMC
Comdg 108 Field Amb.

160/3 551

17 JUL 1919

1092 7.a.

Mai 1919

Army Form C. 2118.

WAR DIARY
or
INTELLIGENCE SUMMARY
(Erase heading not required.)

108 Field Ambulance
Col Field Ambulance
"C" Cadre

Vol 4 2

Place	Date	Hour	Summary of Events and Information	Remarks and references to Appendices
Rue de la Gare des Mallines	1.3.19		We cease to function as a Hospital here today, surplus hospital stores are being moved to 110th Field Ambulance today.	JRS
		14.00	League Football Match played with 36th Bde R.G.A. The RAMC team won by 2 – 1	JRS
"	2.3.19		There seems to be some misunderstanding over our Billets in Tournai. OC "B" is investigating. So all will be well !! All Patients transferred to 110th Field Ambulance.	JRS
"	3.3.19		Arranged with the Medical Officer i/c 23 Labour Group stationed in MENIN to take on the work of scattered small Units there up to the present this had been done by us.	JRS
	4.3.19		Pouring wet day. We get orders to move, but still we manage to reach MOUSCRON and get mostly well settled in. A rear-guard has been left with some stores.	JRS
MOUSCRON (Boys' School)	5.3.19		Lieut Shepherd joins a French unit to Les Trois Cailloux to see remainder of stores removed & withdraw remainder of men. Certificate to now obtained to fM Shepherd.	JRS

(A9175) Wt W335/P560 60,000 12/17 D.D.&L. Sch. 83a— Forms/C2118/11.

WAR DIARY
INTELLIGENCE SUMMARY
(Erase heading not required.)

Army Form C. 2118.

Place	Date	Hour	Summary of Events and Information	Remarks and references to Appendices
ASCHEN Just Schot	6.3.19		Adm. S. visited us & had a look round. Men all engaged in cleaning up the place, themselves and the vehicles.	
	7.3.19		Routine.	
	8.3.19		Men & men sent to Concentration Camps. We will soon be Cadre & shall HOPE!	
	9.3.19	11.30	Combined Church Parade with 110 Field Ambulance in the Theatre.	
		16.00	A.D.M.S. came to tea & cheered us up wonderfully. ~~Which was but in~~	
"	10.3.19	14.30	A.D.M.S. called a meeting of R.A.M.C. Officers in the Division to discuss the formation of a R.A.M.C. 36th Division Officers Dinner Club & it was unanimously decided to form a Dinner Club. 1st Dinner to be held in Belfast on the day or night preceding the 36th Divisional Old Comrades Association Dinner. Various points were discussed but in the end it was decided to leave all the work to the Secretary & to the Meeting Committee which has been chosen. I will do this. A success.	

WAR DIARY
or
INTELLIGENCE SUMMARY.
(Erase heading not required.)

Army Form C. 2118.

Place	Date	Hour	Summary of Events and Information	Remarks and references to Appendices
Maus CROM	11.3.19		Great excitement today. Major J Markham has an unexpected a sudden telegram to proceed home to Canada on He is moving so had some prior claims — to go but he decided to ask the advice of the a.b.m.s. before making up his mind	
"	12.3.19		The usual call for a number of Medical Officers for the Army of Occupation and a number from this Division rejected H.Q. Major Markham has decided to face the risks of army life.	
"	13.3.19		Shewna Ismaelia inn was very near to H.Q. and I was from the Unit sent to Concentration Camp billets for Smith.	
"	14.3.19		Visited 109th Field Ambulance to say good-bye to Major Pabrill who is for the army of occupation, many old & valued friendships are about to be broken.	
"	15.3.19		Farewell dinner to Major Markham who departs tomorrow to England on demobilisation. Arrangements for "Old Comrades dinner" completed. He expect a merry thing.	

WAR DIARY
or
INTELLIGENCE SUMMARY.

Army Form C. 2118.

Place	Date	Hour	Summary of Events and Information	Remarks and references to Appendices
SCR ON	16.3.19	9.30	Major J. Moiham R.A.M.C.T. reported his departure on demobilisation	JJ
		10.30	Conformed Church Service held with 110 Field Ambulance.	
	17.3.19		St Patrick's Day in the Morning. Shamrock sported first thing, later by the Irish troops. A holiday for the men	JJ
		19.30	O.C. Officers Dinner held in the Chat ROUBAIX. 23 were able to attend & he had a very jolly dinner, a jolly evening & a happy reunion	JJ
	18.3.19		2nd "1916" men for the Rhine Armies sent to report to Capt St Picton	JJ
			who is taking a draft up to BONN.	
			Football match played with 14 M.A.C. at TOURCOING resulted in a Win for	
	19.3.19	14.00	the R.A.M.C. by 5 Goals to Nil. There is a Kit in the 101 Boys yet.	JJ
			Capt. J.O. Raft R.A.M.C. – Capt S.P. Ree R.A.M.C. reported their arrival from	
	20.3.19		the Teechelam dépôt. MENTONE. Both are my hands & much improved	JJ
			from their stay in the South of France.	
	21.3.19	11.00	Major General C. Coffin V.C. D.S.O. G.O.C. of the Division called to say Goodbye. He is off tomorrow to command a Brigade of the 1st Division on the Rhine	JJ

WAR DIARY
or
INTELLIGENCE SUMMARY.
(Erase heading not required.)

Army Form C. 2118.

Place	Date	Hour	Summary of Events and Information	Remarks and references to Appendices
MOASCAR	22.3.19		The new Army form G. 1098 has received today giving the detailed equipment of a Field Ambulance of two Sections. the work of sorting out will be commenced immediately & all surplus stores returned.	
"			We received that owing to the staying strike at home, all leave & demobilisation is held up for the present.	SJ
"	23.3.19	9.30	Continued Church Service with 36th Machine Gun Battalion.	SJ
		15.00	G.O.C. XV Corps visited the Division & bid farewell to Comdg Officers	SJ
"	24.3.19		Capt J.C. Roth transferred to 110th Field Ambulance.	
		20.00	R.A.M.C. Officers W.O's N.C.O's & men held in the Scout College.	SJ
"	25.3.19		Capt S.P Rea & J.C Roth proceeded to Ypres district with an Official photographer to secure photographs of places specially interesting to this Division.	SJ
"	26.3.19		Col Ruck C.M.G. D.S.O. A.D.M.S. of this Division since December 1917 leaves today for England, his work he finished on the breaking up of the Division.	
			Capt S.P. Rea will command the Unit during his absence on Leave.	SJ

WAR DIARY
or
INTELLIGENCE SUMMARY.
(Erase heading not required.)

Army Form C. 2118.

Place	Date	Hour	Summary of Events and Information	Remarks and references to Appendices
MOUSCRON	27/3/19	9.30	Snow, cold and windy in morning. Marie Carter Lt 2 D. L.C. Shepherd returned 25 hr leave 25.3.19	SPR
Do	28/3/19	6- 11	A snowy rain morning. Capt J.C. Ruth ans Queens Lt J morning. To get copies of fares and billet area of where opened photographs for .... Amb phoned at 25/3/19. See was very .... SPR	SPR
Do	29/3/19	6- 10	See any snow falling a .... in our lot. Snowy afternoon. Snow ...... a ...... of the .... are as	SPR
Do	3/3/119	9- 10	Frosty Rain and Snowy in the morning. O.c is remaining. Mule were sent off this morning by ...... of ...... C of L Sunny 9.30 a there of this Camera. Lin Capt H	SPR
Do	31/3/19	9.30	A snowy morning with a trace of frost. Lin Pts men were sent to DADOS for fatigue duty. The men of h have had a draw to keep SPR	

SPR Capt Ram
a .... 108 Field Ambulance

140/3550

17 JUL 1919

108A F.A.

Apr. 1919

109 Fd Amb
Army Form C. 2118
Nov 41

WAR DIARY
INTELLIGENCE SUMMARY
(Erase heading not required.)

Place	Date	Hour	Summary of Events and Information	Remarks and references to Appendices
MOUSCRON	1/6/19	a.a. 10	Church parade wise Sn and a Reverence the Quin 30 new to one 4 mm Q. try the new.	
Do	02/6/19	a.a. 10	Raining. Rev Survey morning. One Crotend and 40 Rate Sue via Frances 23 36" Hotel Reservine Irini viving. weer dine of Cauve & End of 36" Reservine Irini Rase. 3PR	
			I hand the 4.a. on eleven am. Rev Hrwrighton extent 23 fer the Evening a evening his men or Butts reported contain from to extent with his retreat owing to the main of sent from collection to dance in the Hotel de Ville MOUSCRON gurin the 36th DIVL (ULSTER) Officers inc CAPN J.C. ROBB RAMC & LT W PARNELL RAMC 110 F.a. we left at 2.a.m. 3/6/19. We examined the Opera Jeuy. See	
Do	3/6/19	a.a. 10	Survey pleasant and Rain is the mornin. One motor own depart 23 36" were Div. M.T. Coy. came Ruary.	3PR
Do	4/6/19	a.a. 10	The day is fine and Rain not See. A morris variing in Evenig Sun 23 36 DEN M.T Coy Andrew 369 Div. M.T Coy	
Do	5/6/19	a.a. 10	Survey pleasant morning. 9 men Er 15 Solomons drawn to sea	See

WAR DIARY
or
INTELLIGENCE SUMMARY.

(Erase heading not required.)

Army Form C. 2118.

Place	Date	Hour	Summary of Events and Information	Remarks and references to Appendices
MOUSCRON	5/11/18 cont		tox shun from enemy between Esq at End Shapene. km of were shapnel of several chants. One shell in native surround to Spennely, west the D.A.P.M.Q the Groomers	SPOL
Do	6.11.19	9	that Cpl. E Sermin 9.30 a 2 Pm Cpl. F 11.30 a.m. the Evening shi common that wire from a R.A.P. 10 A.R.C.S. & Sey Ormes NATHAN unavailed lep. in Sin km of watch the same burning with Com to wrath tri chemin Byrde & Seney stemmey.	SPOL
Do	7/11	10.70	Sunny pleasant Morning Sergt. A S BELL PTES W.J M'COY and S MACKEY were detailed 2 Lt ll 2 etor 2 A P M PARTS on enemy library DRIVER NATHAN ASC MITCHELL the wint keeps busy Great the new are busy in a clean out of the L. The flashing this common 110 F.A. offerers munition and a movery men I make a town of of hearing So an Getting in So the offerers commies, interiors.	SFL

Army Form C. 2118.

WAR DIARY
INTELLIGENCE SUMMARY.
(Erase heading not required.)

Instructions regarding War Diaries and Intelligence Summaries are contained in F. S. Regs., Part II. and the Staff Manual respectively. Title pages will be prepared in manuscript.

Place	Date	Hour	Summary of Events and Information	Remarks and references to Appendices
MOUSCRON	8/4/19	10am	This morning opened fully but the Germans after the guerre to Div & the morning was on the...	
	9/4/19		At A.S.C. my dear mummy, Rain fell heavily the afternoon. 110° Again a drive to Carnoi theatre, 8 men of the 7A have invited D. NATHAN A.S.C. M.T. and skills have amused yesterday alone 87 being 13 km into camp for PARIS.	$100 SPO
	10/4/19		My army Rain gunning. Rain fell the afternoon. The day was a trying one.	SPe
	11/4/19		Very wet this morning. Pte S. IRVINE and J.C. BUSHELL & this man eye freed to PARIS from 11.4.19 - 17. 4-19. De not to return again this turn. We are not D.SE LOSIE civilian to Casa hospital. Op 6. Cartlin Lieutenant suffered several wounds at 1.30 p.m. There was some rain in the afternoon.	SOR

WAR DIARY
or
INTELLIGENCE SUMMARY.
(Erase heading not required.)

Army Form C. 2118.

Place	Date	Hour	Summary of Events and Information	Remarks and references to Appendices
MOUSCRON	12/4/19	a.2. 10.30 a.m.	A wet dull morning. Went at 10.30 a.m. to Dr Selosse 5 Rue de Luxembourg and examined 5 men recommended for 5 weeks leave on independent grounds. Practice agreed, recommended. Papers to Div. D.A.P.M. & there the usual procedure. Saw men 9.	SPR
"	13/4/19		Easter & Brussels. Sun morning for 3 days. Returned from leave yesterday & assumed Command of the Unit from Capt. SP Rea. Some changes have taken place during last fortnight. Equipment etc has been reorganised & we are now equipped on a two section basis. No Church Service we held today.	SP
"	14/4/19		Routine — Drew 5,000 francs from Base Cashier to pay the Unit. The men are holding a dance tonight. The question of keeping them amused is a serious one, as Camp life is very monotonous. Lieut Col Marriott O.C. 62 C.C.S. called to inspect the Hospital. He is S.M.O. Courtrai Area and we come under his jurisdiction.	SP SP

(A9473) Wt W.2355/P360 600,000 12/17 D.D.&L. Sch. 52a. Forms/C.2118/43.

WAR DIARY
or
INTELLIGENCE SUMMARY.
(Erase heading not required.)

Army Form C. 2118.

Place	Date	Hour	Summary of Events and Information	Remarks and references to Appendices
MOSSON	15.4.19	10.00	Went to LILLE to get definite instructions from the A.D.M.S. I. Div. and knew M.O.'s will be left to each Division, all others will be sent to some other appointment.	
			Capt S.P. Rea R.A.M.C. appointed to take over charge of the Cadre of 107th Field Ambulance at STERHOEK.	
"	16.4.19		Routine	
"	17.4.19		Our football team played a challenge match with 2nd R. Inniskilling Inf. but beaten 1-0. the score represented the play.	
			Orders received from A.D.M.S. I Div. to send Capt. O.W. Bannon to 75 Liston Group at WERVICQ & Capt A Anthram to No 23 Liston Group at VLAMERTINGHE. to relieve two men for the "Rhine	
"	18.4.19		Good Friday. Weather still remains miserably cold & dull	
		13.30	Attended the local Hospital with Doctor Selarse to examine a number of women suspected of having spread Venereal disease amongst the troops.	
"	19.4.19	10.30	Examined the Shells from the homes seen yesterday for Groceries. No positive cases were found in this Lot, though most of them looked one.	

Army Form C. 2118.

WAR DIARY
or
INTELLIGENCE SUMMARY.
(Erase heading not required.)

Place	Date	Hour	Summary of Events and Information	Remarks and references to Appendices
MEUPORT	20.4.19		Easter Sunday. A cold, wet, miserable day.	
		9.30	C of E Service held in the Theatre combined with 110 Fld Amb.	H
"	21.4.19		Easter Monday observed as a holiday throughout the Fifth Area, by order of the G.O.C.	
		20.00	Any cheerful Revue was given by this Unit in the Theatre.	H
"	22.4.19		Visited 109 Field Ambulance at SLEEHOEK, & found everything in order.	H
	23.4.19		Capt. S.P. Rea R.A.M.C. & Lieut Parnell R.A.M.C. reported departure for leave to the United Kingdom.	H
	24.4.19		Routine. Weather still very wintry.	H
	25.4.19	13.30	Attended at the Civil Hospital & assisted the local Doctor to examine suspected source of Venereal disease amongst the troops.	H
	26.4.19	08.00	A party of 25 from the 3 Field Ambulances, left via Bus for a tour, visiting BRUGES, OSTEND & ZEEBRUGGE. This outing is arranged by Corps & should be most enjoyable & instructive.	H
		14.00	Divisional Sports held, but owing to the inclemency of the weather there was a very low turnout of competitors.	H

Army Form C. 2118.

WAR DIARY
or
INTELLIGENCE SUMMARY.
(Erase heading not required.)

Place	Date	Hour	Summary of Events and Information	Remarks and references to Appendices
MASCRON	27.4.19		Routine	JJ.
	28.4.19		Routine	JJ
	29.4.19		One of our Ambulance tried by GGCM for absence without leave for 7 days. He was arrested in Paris under a Civilian name	JJ.
	30.4.19		Heavy storm during the night a continuing today with little Coll. We are not going to see the end of April others than a most howling March	JJ.

J S Johnston Maj RAMC
Commdg 108" Field Ambce.

Major Field Ambulance

WAR DIARY
or
INTELLIGENCE SUMMARY.
(Erase heading not required.)

Army Form C. 2118

Place	Date	Hour	Summary of Events and Information	Remarks and references to Appendices
MOUSCRON	1.5.19		Great Socialist demonstration & procession of Civilians in the Town All troops	
			having to keep away from these meetings. It poured heavy rain	
			all day, otherwise were no disturbances.	JJ
	2.5.19		Routine. Pay out	JJ
	3.5.19		Weather still dreadful poured heavy rain & storm	JJ
			Proceeded to Bombyn to collect Red Cross Stores	JJ
	4.5.19		Visited 169 Field Ambulance STERVOEK.	JJ
	5.5.19		Summer has come at last, today was very glorious. Hot. Routine	JJ
	6.5.19		Routine	JJ
	7.5.19	15:00	Football Match played between our R.A.M.C. Team & 2nd R. Innis Fus.	JJ
			Result a draw 1 Goal each. Replay to take place on Sat.	JJ
	8.5.19		Routine	JJ
	9.5.19		Inspection by the Deputy Quarter Master General. British Troops in France	JJ
			after standing to all day this inspection did not come off.	JJ
	10.5.19		Capt. S.P. Rea R.A.M.C. - Lieut Powell R.A.M.C. reported their	JJ
			arrival from leave & absence to U.K.	JJ

108

WAR DIARY
INTELLIGENCE SUMMARY

Army Form C. 2118

Place	Date	Hour	Summary of Events and Information	Remarks and references to Appendices
MOUSERON	11/5/19		Triumph Motor Cycle stolen last night from the Orderly Room. The circumstances point to civilians with civilian on impression Court of Inquiry will be held.	
"	12/5/19		Routine	
"	13/5/19		Court of Inquiry held into the loss of a Triumph Motor Cycle consisting of Capt White 16. K.R.Rifles, Lieut Wilye 36th M.G. Batt. + a Lieut of the 36th Div R.P.A.	
"	14.5.19		Routine.	
"	15.5.19		Capt J.C Roth reported departure for 8 days leave to the S. of France. Circular received that all units of this Div will be broken up in this Country + will not go Home as Cadre	
"	16.5.19			
"	17.5.19		Routine	
"	18.5.19		10 O.R.s Amenity's sent to Concentration Camp St ANDRE. Lieut	
"	19.5.19	13.30	A very enjoyable dance was given by the men of the Unit.	
"	20.5.19		Posters being supplied from the civilian population. Routine	

WAR DIARY
or
INTELLIGENCE SUMMARY.
(Erase heading not required.)

Army Form C. 2118.

Place	Date	Hour	Summary of Events and Information	Remarks and references to Appendices
MOUSCRON	22.5.19		R.A.S.C. personnel attached to Field Ambulances to be relieved from 15 to 40 o.r. 1 W.O. 1 Sgt. + two Drivers the remainder be sent to the Reserve Park Coy LILLE.	
"	23.5.19		Routine.	
"	24.5.19		Routine.	
"	25.5.19		Proceeded to COURTRAI to visit 62 C.C.S.	
"	26.5.19	20.00	Capt. J.C. Roth. R.A.M.C. reports his arrival from leave to S. of France. The usual weekly dance was given by the Amusements Committee of the Ambulance + was most enjoyable.	
"	27.5.19		Routine	
"	28.5.19		Routine	
"	29.5.19		Routine	
"	30.5.19		Routine	
"	31.5.19		Routine	

L. Johnston Lt.Col RAMC
Commdg 107 Field Ambce.

149/3585

23 AUG 1919

10811 F.A.

June 1919

WAR DIARY
or
INTELLIGENCE SUMMARY.

Army Form **C** 2118.

108

Place	Date	Hour	Summary of Events and Information	Remarks and references to Appendices
Mousc R.D.W.	1/6/19		Wire received from A.D.M.S. II Corps that all 1914 R.A.M.C. men are to stand	Cancel
"	2/6/19		Concentration Camp LILLE on June 14th, this will reduce the unit to 16 O.R.	
			Routine	
"	3/6/19		Routine	
"	4/6/19		All 1914 men (21 O.R.) proceeded today to Concert Camp LILLE	
			for demobilization	
"	5/6/19		Routine	
	6.6.19		Handed over Command of the Unit to Lieut A.B.R. L.A. Shepherd R.A.M.C	
			in accordance with instructions received from A.D.M.S. II Corps H/s.	
				L. Johnston Lt Col R.A.M.C
			6 . 6 . 19.	O/C 1st M.A.C. British Army.

WAR DIARY
or
INTELLIGENCE SUMMARY.
(Erase heading not required.)

Army Form C. 2118.

Place	Date	Hour	Summary of Events and Information	Remarks and references to Appendices
Moascar	1/7/19	noon	Took over command of Unit from Major S.H. Johnston M.C.	Appendices
"			R.A.M.C. this day. Will accept subsequent	roster name
"				
"	2/7/19		Routine	Sgd
"	3/7/19 5.6.0		Routine	Sgd
"	4/7/19		Lt. Col. S.H. Johnston M.C. R.A.M.C. proceeded to Kantara	Sgd
"	5/7/19		en route for Demobilisation. Whole routine	Sgd
"	10/7/19 6/7/19			
"	7/7/19		Thirty horse handed in to E & L.L. Corps all horse	Sgd
"			Transport vehicles	
"			Handed in all Medical Equipment [?] 5-31" Ambulances etc	Sgd
"	3/7/19		Routine	Sgd
"	21/7/19		Routine Vauxhall car covered to M.T. Corps	Sgd
"	22/7/19		Handed in all Ordnance Equipment of Unit to B.C.E & D.O.	Sgd
"	23/7/19		Horse	Sgd
"			Seven men have gone to Demobilization Camp Kantara for demob. Sent	
"	4/7/19		Remedy M.T. O.F.C Sent 1 to M.T. Corps for duty	

WAR DIARY
or
INTELLIGENCE SUMMARY.
(Erase heading not required.)

Army Form C. 2118.

Place	Date	Hour	Summary of Events and Information	Remarks and references to Appendices
Mazagon	25/2/19	—	Routine	J.a.d.
"	26/2/19	—	Routine	J.a.d.
"	27/2/19	—	Routine	J.a.d.
"	28/2/19	—	All storage collected and sent to S.C.O. Tourane. Nom. R. of No. 110 Field Ambulance N.C.O.'s & Shepherd and Parnell p.E. 110 Field Ambulance prepared proceed this day to 6th B.G.H. in accordance with A.M.D. 5's Area instructions. Two N.C.O.'s and one man proceed today to Tourane. Camp of No. 1 Annexe for distribution. (This Unit no nearer to went till Equipment has been handed in, accordance sent to Base. Inspect record closed and forwarded to Base for necessary clearance certificate.	J.a.d.

F. R. Shepherd Capt. R.A.M.C.
O.C. 110 Field Ambulance